G000140319

Robert Knight

PLUTO PRESS
London • Concord, Mass

First published in 1991 by Pluto Press
345 Archway Road, London, N6 5AA
and 141 Old Bedford Road,
Concord, MA 01742, USA

British Library Cataloguing-in-Publication Data
Knight, Robert
    Stalinism in crisis.
    1. Communist countries. Politico-economic systems
    I. Title
    330.91717

    ISBN 0–7453–0464–8

Library of Congress Cataloging-in-Publication Data
Knight, Robert, 1950–
        Stalinism in crisis / Robert Knight.
        p. cm.
    Includes bibliographical references and index.
    ISBN 0–7453–0464–8
        1. Communist countries—Politics and government. 2. World
politics—1985–1995. I. Title.
    D850.K58 1991
    909'.097170828—dc20   90–45316
                                                                CIP

Typeset in 9.5/11.25 Stone by Stanford DTP, Milton Keynes
Printed and bound in the UK by Billing and Sons Ltd, Worcester

Contents

Map	overleaf
Introduction	1
1. The Failure of Perestroika	9
2. The Stirrings of the Soviet Working Class	29
3. The Upsurge in the National Republics	53
4. Eastern Europe in Ferment	71
5. China: the Road to Tiananmen Square (by Mark Wu)	93
6. Revolutions Betrayed: the Soviet Union in the Third World	125
7. Farewell to Eurocommunism	145
8. Marxism Before and After Stalinism	171
Suggested Reading	194
Index	199

CHINA: provinces and autonomous regions (*)

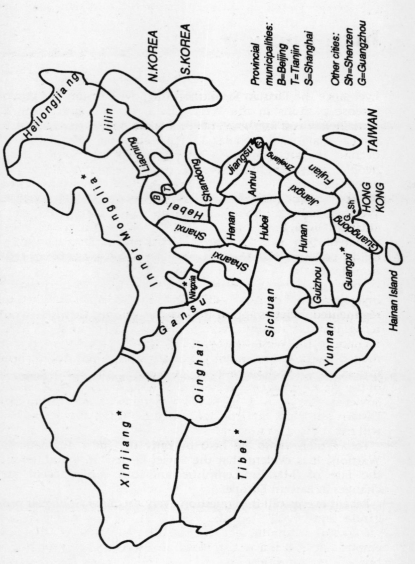

Introduction

Ever since the Russian Revolution the Soviet Union has provoked intense passions in the West. Lenin, Trotsky and Stalin, even Khrushchev and Brezhnev, have all taken their turn as the focus of media attack and popular indignation. The Soviet Union has become the archetype of a totalitarian society, keeping its own people under the heel of an austere tyranny and bent on extending its 'evil empire' around the world. The Cold War myth of 'Soviet expansionism', the threat of an Eastern invasion of Western Europe, provided the focus for cohering the Western alliance throughout the post-war period. According to conventional wisdom in the West, the Soviet bloc had been for so long rigidly controlled from the centre that it was incapable of change from within.

Today many Western experts should be eating their words. The image of totalitarianism is difficult to sustain at a time when these regimented societies appear to have transformed themselves out of recognition, virtually overnight. That once mighty military menace to the Western way of life, the Warsaw Pact, has simply melted away. Yet as recently as November 1988, Harold Brown, former American defence secretary, expressed the mainstream view of the Washington establishment: 'Next to the maintenance of the Soviet system in the USSR itself, preserving Marxism-Leninism in Eastern Europe is the icon for whose retention the Soviet Union will risk (indeed go to) war.'

Today such views are held by only the most dogmatic Cold Warriors. It is evident that the Soviet leadership is indifferent to the fate of 'Marxism-Leninism' and can easily accept major changes in Eastern Europe.

Recent events call into question every theme of Cold War propaganda and reveal that the Soviet Union has no deep-seated ideological commitments. As the disintegration of the Soviet empire shows, it is a system based on a series of compromises, not one of total authoritarian control. The Warsaw Pact was never much of a threat to Western security and now the collapse of military morale in Eastern Europe exposes the fragile foundations on which it has always rested.

The dramatic developments of the late 1980s have exposed only what was always evident about the Soviet Union to anybody who looked under the surface. When it suited Western observers to reveal the true state of affairs in the Soviet Union they had little difficulty unearthing the facts. During the Second World War, for example, the British Ministry for Information was busily engaged in working out arguments in defence of the Stalinist system. One of its reports noted:

> While the Trotskyist policy was to bolster up the security of a weak USSR by means of subversive movements in other countries controlled by the Comintern, Stalin's policy has been and continues to be one of monitoring a strong Russia maintaining friendly diplomatic relations with other governments ... The ideologues and doctrinaire international revolutionary types have increasingly been replaced by people of the managerial and technical type, both military and civil, who are interested in getting practical results.

How reassuring for British civil servants to find the Kremlin being run by 'people like us'! This accurate description of the essential characteristics of the Soviet bureaucracy confirms that the Western establishment was well aware that the Stalinist regime was much more concerned with day-to-day administration than with conspiring to achieve world domination.

Unfortunately the Western left was often taken in by official propaganda about the Soviet Union. For many decades left-wing commentators responded to establishment hostility to the Soviet Union by proclaiming that the Stalinist system was a positive model. When even critical observers could find something progressive about Soviet society the Kremlin had no difficulty in finding apologists for its rule in the West. In Britain, the Fabian reformers Beatrice and Sidney Webb, despite their prejudices against Marxism, became ardent supporters of the Soviet system after their visit in 1932. They argued that the Soviet bureaucracy was 'the unavoidable apparatus of any highly developed industrial community'.

Like the Webbs, many on the far left believed that the Soviet Union was progressive because, in the 1930s, the capitalist system appeared to be in a state of terminal decay. At a time when the capitalist world was afflicted by slump and mass unemployment, the Soviet Union appeared to be moving forward and rapidly building a planned modern industrial economy. In fact Stalin's industrialisation was not the result of the higher efficiency of a socialist planned economy. It was achieved through sacrificing the lives of millions of workers and peasants and the destruction of Soviet agriculture. The defeat inflicted by the Soviet Union on Hitler's armies during the Second World War also helped to legitimise claims for the progressive character of the Soviet system. But it was the heroism of the Soviet people, not the Stalinist system, that defeated Nazi Germany.

However, the contrast between Soviet industrialisation and capitalist depression, and the contribution of the Soviet Union to the defeat of fascism, helped to endow the Stalinist model with a progressive image. In reality the fact that the Soviet Union could be seriously considered as a viable model was a testimony to the weakness of the capitalist system. It was the crisis of the world capitalist order in the 1930s and 1940s that gave Stalinism its international prestige.

The inability of the capitalist order to establish a stable international balance of forces is the key factor in explaining the longevity of the Stalinist system. After the Stalinist takeover in the mid-1920s, the Soviet Union survived because world capitalism was too weak to force it out of existence. Imperialist rivalries in the 1930s and during the Second World War gave the Kremlin more room to manoeuvre. The collapse of capitalism in Eastern and Central Europe allowed the Soviet Union to establish a new bloc of satellite states. The disintegration of capitalism in many parts of the Third World allowed the Soviet Union to extend its global influence in the post-war period. The victory of revolutionary movements strongly influenced by Stalinism in China, Vietnam and Cuba confirmed the inability of the imperialist powers to keep a grip on events in the Third World. The success of the Stalinist model was a by-product of the fragmentation of Western imperialism, rather than the result of any dynamic within the Stalinist system itself.

The Western powers had every reason to perpetuate the myth of the Soviet threat to the Western way of life. As long as the Soviet Union served as a model for progress, Western imperialism had little to worry about. The Soviet bloc provided the ideal counterpoint to the West. Through the Cold War the genuine conflict between classes and ideas in Western societies was transformed into an external geopolitical struggle between two systems. Any attempt to change capitalist society could be easily discredited by pointing to the failures of the Stalinist bureaucracy. Inadvertently the Soviet bloc became an important force for preserving the status quo: by its very existence it acted as an argument against real social change. It was the most effective advertisement for the virtues of the capitalist system.

It is now universally apparent that Soviet society is the product, not of the Russian Revolution, but of its defeat. The Soviet bureaucracy emerged through destroying the remains of working-class power and by capturing the machinery of state. That a society without any internal dynamic of its own should have survived so long is little short of a miracle. This historical accident can be explained only by the conjunction of an isolated state, in which a working-class revolution was overturned by its own inheritors, and a world capitalist order that was too weak and divided to take advantage.

Today, however, the Soviet Union has finally reached an impasse. It is obvious that a society that enjoys neither the advantages of the market nor those of a workers' system of planning cannot continue for much longer. Ironically, the Soviet bureaucracy, the main beneficiary of the existing order, has also come to the conclusion that it can no longer carry on in the old way. The bureaucracy is a social stratum in search of a new identity and a new role in society. Gorbachev and his colleagues are happy to throw 'Marxism-Leninism', the official jargon that has become a universal embarrassment, out of the window. They are also prepared to introduce the market, believing that they can transform themselves into a new ruling class running a restored capitalism. However, there is no historical precedent of an established industrial society making the transition back to capitalism. The difficulties thrown up by Gorbachev's drive to reform the Soviet system by extending the role of market forces, both internally and internationally, are what constitute the crisis of Stalinism which is the focus of this book.

The Soviet bureaucracy has signalled its intention to go all the way in restoring capitalist relations. It is prepared to make major political changes, including abandoning the 'leading role' of the Soviet communist party and encouraging private enterprise in all spheres of economic life. Our first three chapters are devoted to the internal crisis of the Soviet Union itself: the problems facing Gorbachev's campaign of perestroika, the role of the Soviet working class and the growing volatility of the national republics.

The lack of commitment of the Soviet leadership to the system over which it has presided for more than half a century is truly astonishing. A leading West German bank report has noted the sense of desperation that currently drives the Soviet establishment to embrace the capitalist system: 'Especially at the highest decision-making levels in Moscow, one can sense a distinct fear of being, economically at least, decoupled from the bandwagon of history for good.'

The determination of the Soviet leadership to abandon the past means that in all the Stalinist regimes nothing can any longer be taken for granted.

It is easy to declare the intention of returning to capitalism, but it is much more difficult to achieve this transition in practice. Chapters 4 and 5, on Eastern Europe and China, focus on these difficulties in areas where the Stalinist system was never as firmly implanted as it was in the Soviet Union in the 1930s. As the June 1989 massacres in Tiananmen Square in Beijing confirmed most forcefully, the conversion of Stalinist leaders to the principles of the market and political pluralism has yet to be carried through into the creation of a viable liberal democracy. Though events in Eastern Europe have been less repressive, democratic trends remain fragile. The euphoria surrounding the emergence of opposition movements and candidates in elections throughout the Eastern bloc in the early months of 1990 soon subsided. As unemployment grew and food queues lengthened, many of the new 'democratic' political figures turned out to bear a close resemblance to old Stalinist bureaucrats. The economic prospects for the Soviet Union, China and Eastern Europe are grim in both the short and medium terms and it is evident that the transition to the market is more likely to bring inflation and hardship than prosperity. As a result there is a lot of talk about the market, but much less action.

It is clear that the transition process has been initiated from the top downwards. The masses are active, but remain excluded from real power. It is also evident that it is easier for the top bureaucrats to agree to change than it is for them to win popular backing for the transition project. In these circumstances it would appear that it is only a matter of time before force becomes the main lever for bringing in the new order. How far the new order in the East is likely to approximate the goal of Scandinavian-style liberal capitalism is a matter for conjecture. It appears likely that these regimes can only be transformed in a limited and uneven sense and only as semi-colonies of the West. Polish workers in Berlin and Estonian labourers in Helsinki are already emerging as the new cheap migrants of the Western world.

It is now virtually certain that the West will recapture the East. Gorbachev has raised the white flag as Stalinism prepares for unconditional surrender. Does this mean a major victory for Western imperialism? The answer must be yes and no, but the closer we look, and the more time moves on, the more the balance moves towards the negative. By capturing the Soviet bloc, the West is importing a source of growing tension and instability within its own ranks. The re-incorporation of the Soviet Union and Eastern Europe into the capitalist world will mean the end of the post-war order and the delicate international balance of power that was established only after decades of intense rivalry and war. The diplomatic tensions already unleashed by the moves towards the reunification of Germany indicate the likely direction of future conflict in Europe and the wider Western alliance. In the long term the demise of Stalinism is likely to intensify forces of fragmentation in the capitalist world.

At the same time it would be foolish to ignore the negative impact that the destruction of the Stalinist model has already had on world politics – in Nicaragua and South Africa as well as in the Eastern bloc. Chapter 6 is devoted to the consequences of the Soviet Union's rapprochement with the imperialist world order for the radical regimes and liberation movements it has traditionally sponsored in the Third World. In Chapter 7 we examine the evolution of Eurocommunism, in response both to developments in the Soviet Union and to domestic pressures in Western Europe. Communist parties that 15 years ago dominated the left are now divided and demoralised and desperately searching for a new identity.

In the process of supervising the transition to capitalism, the Soviet bureaucracy has rigorously criticised not merely its own tradition, but the whole legacy of Marxism. Our final chapter traces the current crisis of Stalinism, not to Marxism, but to the Stalinist theory of 'socialism in one country' and its destructive influence over 60 years. Gorbachev's 'new thinking' is not so much a critique of Stalinism as an attack on Marxism itself. This is necessary because the project of capitalist restoration demands that Marxism and its devastating critique of a society based on the market and exploitation, and its insistence on the necessity for world revolution, must be discredited. In this sense Gorbachev is the authentic inheritor of the Stalinist tradition. Just as Stalin attacked Marxism through the campaign against Trotskyism, Gorbachev carries on the onslaught on Marxism through the medium of a critique of Stalinism. The only difference is that Gorbachev is prepared to go the whole way and accept capitalist ideology without even retaining Stalin's socialist rhetoric. Having done so much to discredit communism over the past 60 years, the final contribution of Stalinism is to do all it can to destroy the basic principles of Marxism.

For the time being left-wing ideas are marginalised as right-wing triumphalism prevails and progressive ideas are treated with derision. Marxists face a monumental challenge of reclaiming and rebuilding a new tradition of social emancipation. The death of Stalinism makes this a real possibility, but it does so in circumstances in which the left is weaker than at any time since 1848. This survey of the demise of Stalinism seeks to provide an understanding of the phenomenon with a view to contributing to the development of a Marxist alternative in the years ahead.

While few books are the creation of one individual working in isolation, this one is more of a collaborative project than most. It was inspired by Frank Furedi's *The Soviet Union Demystified* which marked a major breakthrough in the Marxist analysis of the problems of transition from capitalism to a higher form of society, and rigorously exposed the lack of any dynamic in the Soviet system. This book arose out of a process of discussion and debate of the issues raised by Furedi's work in relation to the accelerating pace of events in the Eastern bloc in the late 1980s. Dave Lamb contributed much useful material on the Soviet working class and Andy Clarkson helped on the national republics. On Eastern Europe Russell Osborne and Joan Phillips provided useful comments and criticisms arising from their visits to Poland, Hungary, Czechoslovakia and the GDR. The chapter on China is separately credited to Mark Wu, who has travelled extensively in China and has studied its political development over many years. Daniel Nassim and Kirsten Cale contributed to the chapters on the Third World and Eurocommunism, respectively. Acknowledgements are also due to Mike Freeman and James Heartfield.

Rob Knight
London, March 1991

1 The Failure of Perestroika

Five years after the launch of perestroika the Soviet leadership was even further away from solving the problems of the national economy than when newly appointed premier Mikhail Gorbachev launched the reform process in 1985. Instead of the increased prosperity promised by the Soviet leadership, most people experienced a decline in living standards in the late 1980s. The widening gap between the aspirations raised by the rhetoric of reform and the reality of food queues and empty shelves created a strong current of popular opposition to the Gorbachev leadership. Opposition to the leadership took an increasingly political form, particularly in the 14 national republics which make up the Soviet Union outside Russia. By 1989 burgeoning nationalist movements and militant strikes in the mines and on the railways had begun seriously to destabilise Soviet society.

Perestroika may be defined as the attempt to introduce market relations into the Soviet economy through a process of gradual economic reform. In late 1989 deputy prime minister Leonid Abalkin acknowledged the failure of these reforms:

> The economic situation has continued to deteriorate over the past 18–24 months or so. So far we have not succeeded in halting the growth of negative processes. This applies particularly to the consumer market, the budget deficit and money circulation. There is growing dissatisfaction with the progress of the reform and social tension is rising ... In the majority of industries and enterprises production is not growing, or if it is increasing, this often comes about through the pushing up of prices. No improvement is to be observed in the quality of output and technical progress is at a standstill. How under these conditions can we count on improving matters in the economy?[1]

Though the failures of the Soviet economy have been widely discussed, both in the West and in the Soviet Union, there have been surprisingly few attempts to analyse *why* perestroika has failed. Broadly speaking there are two different explanations of the regime's lack of success in introducing the market into the Soviet Union.

The first blames a supposed deeply inbred hostility to the market in Soviet society. This point of view is well summed up by two Soviet economists quoted approvingly in a Western collection:

> A significant part of the population of the economically leading regions of the country where there predominated less than a century ago patriarchal structures and an orthodox culture orientating the individual to the saving of souls through various forms of social philanthropy and charity, censuring any form of social struggle and competition, regards economic entrepreneurship just as before with distrust and hostility.[2]

The second explanation attributes the failure of the market to the resistance of the bureaucracy to change and its obstruction of the reform process. This view has been advanced by the left-wing economist Ernest Mandel who argues that if the 'blockage' of the bureaucracy could be removed, the problems of Soviet society could be easily resolved.[3]

Some commentators merge both arguments into the general proposition that bureaucratic inertia is the result of the inherent proclivity of Russian society to reproduce authoritarian methods. For example, Marshall Goldman, in his comprehensive survey of the Soviet economy, concludes that Gorbachev's difficulty is not new:

> The czars had the same problem. John Stuart Mill noted back in 1859, 'The Czar himself is powerless against the bureaucratic body; he can send any one of them to Siberia, but he cannot govern without them, or against their will. On every decree of his they have a tacit veto, by merely refraining from carrying it into effect.' In just this way, Soviet bureaucrats blocked Khrushchev, and before long he had to back off and return more and more of the decision making power and organization to Moscow.[4]

Although there can be no doubt that the bureaucracy plays a negative role in Soviet society, such explanations fail to grasp the specific problems facing the reform process. It is absurd to attribute the failure of the market in the 1980s to the persistence of the prejudices of the 1850s. The Revolution in one way and

Stalinism in another transformed the way of life of the people in what is now the Soviet Union, giving post-war generations an entirely different experience of existence. Describing the influence of state bureaucrats in the Soviet Union does not explain why they have greater power than bureaucrats anywhere else in the world. Nor does it help explain why, even when the bureaucracy does try to reform itself, with the backing of the leadership, that it still cannot significantly improve economic conditions.

By the close of the 1980s there was no escaping the fact that Gorbachev's ambitious reform programme had exposed only the unreformability of the Soviet system. The resulting plight of the Soviet Union was acutely summed up by the pseudonymous 'Z', an observer close to the US state department, at the beginning of 1990: 'Gorbachev is left with the worst of two possible worlds: an old one that refused to die and a new one without the strength to be born.'[5]

The problems that arise from attempting to make the transition from the Stalinist system to a modern market economy are at the heart of the current crisis of the Soviet Union.

The Soviet Economy

The key to understanding the resistance of the Soviet economy to reform lies in understanding the kind of society that was created after the 1917 Revolution, not what existed beforehand. In the 1920s and 1930s the Soviet government under Stalin abolished private ownership of the means of production and thus eliminated the capitalist market. It replaced the market with a centralised command system with complete power residing at the top levels of the communist party. Power was to be exercised through a system of state and party officials appointed by and responsible to the top party leadership, the *nomenklatura* or bureaucracy.

It is important to note in passing that the Stalinist system has nothing in common with the Marxist conception of a workers' state. From a Marxist perspective the only justification for abolishing the capitalist market is that it can be replaced by a more efficient form of production. The Stalinist system has proved itself in practice to be even less efficient than capitalism. The reason for this lies in the lack of working-class control over society, which is immediately evident to any observer of the Soviet system.

A market system has a dynamic for development because it can, through the operation of competition, constantly eliminate inefficient firms and institute new points of growth. The labour time of society is allocated to efficient areas and eliminated from inefficient areas through the operation of the market itself. The fact that this happens spontaneously, outside the control of individual capitalists, means that the market is outside the control of society itself. The domination of society by the drive to make profit condemns a system based on the private wealth of a minority to advance in fits and starts interspersed by periods of stagnation and crisis.

The capitalist system can generate enormous wealth and draw the whole world into its orbit, but it can only make a few countries prosperous by impoverishing and terrorising a great many more. Even in the prosperous countries sustained expansion can only be achieved between episodes of recession, with mass unemployment, homelessness and poverty in the heartlands of capitalism. Capitalism continues to make technological advances, but only at the same time as it multiplies social and ecological disasters.

For Marxists, the alternative to the market is a system in which the labour time and resources of society are consciously allocated by society as a whole, through a system of workers' management. Such a system could eliminate the chaos and waste of capitalism because the whole of society would become involved in deciding how and where resources should be allocated. Waste would be avoided because it is in the interests of the whole of society to raise the general standard of living. It would be possible to promote efficiency through a democratic framework that would enable the working class to influence decision-making at every level and thus correct mistakes in planning or production. In the Soviet Union, by contrast, Stalin presided over the elimination of the embryonic elements of workers' control established after the Revolution and installed a system of bureaucratic terror. The Soviet Union cannot be characterised as a 'workers' state': the working class has played no active role in society as a class since the 1920s.

The absence of either the market mechanism or workers' management has meant that for the last 50 years there has been no mechanism for the efficient allocation of labour time in the Soviet Union. Though all decisions are taken by and through the centre, the central bureaucracy has no control over most areas of production and distribution and is incapable of regulating all elements in the economy. The result is that the economy as a whole operates spontaneously, but without the discipline of the market, leading to the large-scale waste and inefficiency that have dogged the Soviet economy since the Stalin era. The Soviet system is closer to anarchy than to a planned economy.

In recent years Soviet economists have openly acknowledged the chaotic state of their system and have concluded that the only way forward lies through the reintroduction of the market. This is how leading economic reformer Nikolai Shmelyev summed up the record: 'Attempts to establish 100 per cent control over everything lead to such spontaneity, to such an uncontrollable situation that all anarchy becomes a paragon of order by comparison.'[6]

In the absence of effective national planning individual enterprises are obliged to try to make everything they need rather than rely on official supplies of essential raw materials and components. Whenever supplies are available, every enterprise tries to hoard them, leading to waste in one plant, shortages in another. Such autarchic practices make nonsense of any idea of a coherent national division of labour, or a national plan.

In his recent assessment of perestroika, Gorbachev's economic advisor Abel Aganbegyan described the extent of economic activity outside the national plan:

In just one district the collective and state farms erected buildings to a value of 400 million roubles, while their allocation of metal, cement, building equipment, bricks and wood was sufficient for only 60 million roubles worth of building. We are talking here about resources which are legally supposed to be planned and allocated only by centralized agencies. What this means in effect is that five-sixths of this region's agricultural building was achieved through illegal methods of direct exchange and barter with industrial, construction, transport and other enterprises. It also means that the local party and soviet were directly involved in this activity.[7]

The only way the Soviet bureaucracy can compensate for its inability to implement proper planning is through the direct exercise of its power in society. The Soviet Union has always been rich in reserves of both labour and raw materials and the abolition of private property has given the bureaucracy direct control over these resources. Although the bureaucracy has never been able to allocate resources efficiently, it has been able to use its power to concentrate the energies of society in targeted areas. In the 1930s, Stalin's machine enforced the industrialisation of the Soviet Union by terrorising millions of workers into the factories and mobilising plant and raw materials on a massive scale. The bureaucrats gave top priority to heavy industry and defence, ensuring by their constant personal intervention that at least these key spheres of the Soviet economy worked with a modicum of efficiency.

By the 1950s the process of industrialisation had largely been completed, at the cost of millions of lives and a vast waste of resources. Over the past 40 years the Soviet bureaucracy has grappled with the problems of producing higher quality goods, rather than simply enormous quantities, with trying to achieve intensive rather than extensive growth. Because of the absence of either a market or workers' democracy there is no pressure on enterprises to improve the quality of their products, as long as they fulfil their quota set by the plan. The result is that much of the produce of Soviet factories is literally useless.

The problem of quality is particularly acute in the area of consumer goods. It is impossible to mass-produce modern cars, fridges or televisions by the same methods that achieved record-breaking outputs of pig iron. Industrial processes involved in producing modern consumer goods require a degree of sophistication in both technology and labour which cannot be achieved by Stalin-style economic management. In a highly urbanised society, an efficient storage and transport system is required to make agricultural products available to the consumers. The Soviet system has never been able to overcome these problems.

Ever since the 1950s the Soviet bureaucracy has been struggling to overcome the inherent defects of the Stalinist system. Identifying the basic problem as one of over-centralisation, it has periodically attempted to introduce measures to decentralise economic management. This was the central theme of the wave of reforms promoted by Khrushchev in the late 1950s which aimed to limit the power of the central ministries and to encourage local initiative. These reforms foundered on two obstacles. First, instead of promoting efficiency, decentralisation enhanced autarchy as local enterprises were forced to pursue their own survival strategies ever more aggressively in an economic climate rendered ever more hostile by the absence of central direction. The result was a loss of impetus, falls in production and higher prices. Second, attempts to introduce incentives to work harder were opposed by workers who could not see the advantage of higher wages when there was still nothing to buy in the shops.

Khrushchev's reforms failed to stimulate the economy and his attempts to take power away from the bureaucracy created a backlash which ended with his own removal from power in 1964. Under his successor Brezhnev, attempts at reform came to a virtual standstill. However, economic reform could not be postponed indefinitely: the emergence of clear signs of economic decay by the end of the 1970s generated new pressures to tackle the chronic stagnation of the Soviet system. The result, after much typical Soviet delay and procrastination, was the emergence of Gorbachev and his campaign of perestroika.

Gorbachev's reform

Gorbachev has returned to the policy of decentralisation, though he has pursued it much further and much more rigorously than Khrushchev. From the experience of the 1960s the Soviet leadership drew the lesson that the only way to stimulate the economy was by the extensive introduction of market mechanisms. This is how one Soviet economist summed up the new consensus among the Soviet elite:

> Nowhere is the need for the market disputed today. It is everywhere acknowledged that the market is indifferent to the social order, that its main function is to force commodity producers to reduce costs to improve quality of output, and to accelerate scientific-technological progress.[8]

For as long as the Soviet state remains nominally socialist the leadership has to be careful to avoid extolling the virtues of capitalism. Hence Soviet spokesmen prefer to talk about extending the market and to emphasise that they are not proposing that the Soviet Union should become a 'free market' economy along the lines of Adam Smith's or even Margaret Thatcher's Britain. Their model is Sweden, with its mixture of private and public companies and extensive social welfare system. The desire of the bureaucracy to transform itself into a class administering a controlled market system remains implicit in its public statements. Thus Dementev describes the process by which the bureaucrats can become capitalists, without making the political conclusion – the abandonment of the ideological foundations of the Soviet state – explicit: 'The development of economic independence and of commodity–monetary relations represents a progressive current of restructuring that will lead to increasing the role of indirect, value oriented pressures from the centre on economic activity.'[9]

Why are Soviet bureaucrats so circumspect about calling openly for the restoration of capitalism, given that this is clearly their objective? Because, despite their intellectual commitment to the market, they remain ambivalent about its restoration. There are two reasons for this. First, the bureaucracy as it currently exists is a product of the Stalinist system within which it plays a key commanding role: under a market system it would have no comparable role to play. Thus the destruction of the command economy would also put an end to the power of the bureaucracy as it is presently constituted. Second, the bureaucracy is fearful of the impact of the market on the working class. It is unsure of its ability to convince Soviet workers that a major change in the system is justified, particularly one which would create even greater social differentiation than exists today. Any major extension of market forces would mean higher prices, including food prices, harsher working conditions and mass unemployment.

The progress of reform in the late 1980s reveals another major problem for the bureaucracy: the fact that it is impossible to introduce the capitalist market piecemeal, step by step or sector by sector. For the market to work properly the laws of supply and demand must be able to operate throughout the national economy. As long as substantial sectors of the Soviet economy remain outside the market, it cannot operate with any degree of efficiency. On the other hand, to introduce the market at a stroke, or even over a short period, would undermine the existing social relations and could provoke great upheavals. Without any guarantee of its successful emergence as a fully fledged capitalist class, the bureaucracy has been afraid to move too fast in case its grip on society is broken and it loses everything.

The Gorbachev reforms fall into three main categories – the encouragement of self-financing enterprises, the conversion of defence industries to produce consumer goods and attempts to attract foreign investment. Let's look at these in turn.

Self-financing enterprises

Various measures have been introduced in the drive to restructure the economy and give greater incentives to managers, workers and peasants. These include provisions for the self-financing of enterprises, the legalisation of private businesses or cooperatives and the leasing of land to peasants.

Self-financing is an extension of the principle of decentralisation. At the beginning of 1989 enterprises were made responsible for their own administration and for producing a surplus for new investment. The main purpose of self-financing is to encourage greater labour discipline, both through more efficiency and the shedding of labour. Towards the end of 1989 it was estimated that some 16 million jobs would have to go to make Soviet manufacturing profitable.[10]

Unfortunately for the Soviet bureaucracy its plans to discipline labour coincided with a renewed famine of consumer goods which provoked unprecedented resistance from workers even before any changes were begun at enterprise level. This has made local managers very wary of taking on their workers in an attempt to improve productivity.

Local managers are still forced to grapple with the consequences of the overall dislocation of the national economy. Instead of taking risks with investment, they have taken advantage of shortages to raise prices and thus make greater profits, causing both inflation and falling output. The Soviet oil minister blamed decentralisation directly for a drastic fall in oil production in 1989 declaring that 'this once-flourishing industry is falling into ruin at full speed.'[11]

A fall in oil production is especially serious because the Soviet Union depends on its oil exports for the foreign currency needed to buy in scarce consumer goods.

Statistics for the economy as a whole showed that in the first three quarters of 1989 production of food, consumer goods and new housing all fell well behind target. The official growth rate was put at 3.6 per cent, but taking into account the facts that output is measured in money terms, and that inflation is between 8 and 12 per cent, it seems that output is not just stagnating but falling.[12]

By the end of the 1980s it appeared that the Khrushchev experience of decentralisation was being repeated.

The self-financing of the factories also indirectly exacerbated the problems of Soviet agriculture. Under the old system the government could step in to reallocate resources from the centre to overcome particular local or sectoral blockages. Thus it was commonplace for factories to be shut in the cities during harvest time so that workers could be sent to the country to ensure that crops were saved. However, once the factories were freed from central control, this ceased to happen, with the result that part of the harvest was lost and food shortages became more acute.[13]

The experience of the cooperatives reveals some of the problems facing the reintroduction of the market in the Soviet Union. Cooperatives grew rapidly in the late 1980s in the backward Soviet service sector. Yet within a short period of time co-ops became deeply unpopular with the Soviet people. This was partly because of their high prices by comparison with the state sector and partly because of widespread recognition of the fact that state-produced goods disappeared on a large scale only to turn up on co-op shelves at inflated prices. Gorbachev himself, though a strong supporter of co-ops, hinted at his recognition of this problem in the course of a debate in the Supreme Soviet.[14]

It was not surprising that the co-ops operated in this way because in many areas they were simply the continuation of former black market enterprises. In a way the co-ops made things worse in that when the black market was illegal it was understood that it existed to provide scarce goods for those with the money to pay for them. But the co-ops were supposed to provide goods for everybody; having raised expectations, they were more vulnerable to interference from the bureaucracy and opposition from the public. The strength of feeling against co-ops was such that three separate measures were taken in 1989 alone to curb their activities. It is nonsense however to blame the cooperatives for the supply problems of the Soviet economy. They have merely taken advantage of the shortages in the true spirit of free enterprise.

In agriculture Soviet reformers have attempted to copy the apparently successful Chinese initiative of restoring private farming. The government has offered 50-year leases to Soviet farmers; if these were taken up widely it would effectively mean the reprivatisation of the land. Private farming has obvious attractions for the Soviet leadership: it requires minimal state investment and it has an almost immediate pay-off in easing the food shortages. However, there was no great rush to go private, which is perhaps not surprising when the obstacles to operating outside the collective farms are considered. These include a lack of capital to invest in farm machinery and a shortage of serviceable tractors. Most aspiring private farmers would be forced to lease machinery from the collective farms where hostile bureaucrats whose own positions are threatened have ample opportunity to put obstacles in the way of private enterprise.

If a private farmer succeeds in acquiring land and machinery the next problem is that of getting produce to the market through the Soviet Union's antiquated storage and transport system. There is no national wholesale system through which private farmers can sell their produce, so they have to make their own arrangements to get their produce to the consumer. There is a chronic shortage of both storage facilities and refrigerated transport which means that up to 50 per cent of all fruit and vegetables rot before they get to the market.[15] Storage problems are exacerbated by inefficient transport. In 1989 the railway system came close to collapse through a combination of inadequate trains and rolling stock, industrial action by rail workers and blockades by nationalists in the republics.

This is how Moscow radio summed up the state of Soviet agriculture in 1989:

> There is a shortage of manpower in rural areas and most harvesting is done manually. The shortage of storage facilities exacerbates the situation with the requirements of some oblasts and rayons [regional and local districts] being met by less than 10 per cent. The lack of railway wagons is adding to the problem. In Moldavia there is a daily need for 300 covered wagons and 300 cold storage wagons, but only a third of these are made available; this means that every day up to 20,000 tons of produce remain in the republic instead of being delivered to outside customers. The state of affairs in road haulage is just as bleak, with rayons able to deliver just half of the scheduled amounts of fresh produce to the capital. This was the case with peaches, which were bought up by private car owners, who resold the fruit at twice and three times what was paid for it. In fact negligence in the transport sector has given rise to a wave of profiteering in fresh fruit and vegetables.[16]

Because of the continued failure of Soviet grain supply to meet demand, arrangements were now made to pay farmers in foreign currency to encourage them to produce more. It was estimated that in 1988/89 the Soviet Union had to buy 22 million tonnes of grain from the US.[17]

Swords into ploughshares

At the end of 1988 Gorbachev announced a 14 per cent cut in defence spending with a view to transferring resources to the production of consumer goods. The transformation of armaments factories into plants processing household goods reflects the leadership's commitment to transferring priority allocation from defence to consumer goods. Prime Minister Ryzhkov promised that by 1991 half the existing defence capacity would be turned over to consumer goods. However, this reform has not yet had a discernible effect on consumer goods production.

The Gorbachev leadership has also encouraged joint ventures between Western firms and the Soviet government with a view to gaining greater access to Western technology. However, overseas investment failed to take off. Despite the fact that 800 joint ventures had been formally agreed, by the autumn of 1989 only one-third of these were in operation. The main deterrent to foreign investors was the inability of the Soviet regime to guarantee returns and supplies: 'the repatriation of profits in hard currency and ensuring reliability of supplies from Soviet sources are not answered by the latest measures.'[18]

For the rouble to be convertible into foreign currencies, a precondition for the repatriation of profits, it would have to be devalued. In 1989 it was estimated that the rouble was worth less than 7 per cent of its paper value.[19]

However such a devaluation would lead to rampant inflation which would in turn risk provoking public disorder on a scale that would jeopardise the whole system. A hard tourist rouble has been introduced, but this is more an effort to prevent Soviet tourists from taking foreign currency overseas than a step along the path to full convertibility. Full convertibility is constantly put off into the future.

The only way the Soviet government can guarantee supplies is by overcoming the fundamental problems of the Stalinist system. Yet, by the end of 1989 all the signs were that the deficiencies of production and transport were getting worse rather than better. There were also signs of a growing conflict of interest over joint ventures with Western firms. Whereas the Soviet Union is primarily interested in producing goods that it can export and thus earn hard currency, Western investors are out to sell goods to tens of millions of potential Soviet consumers, rather than produce commodities to compete with their own on the world market.

Economic crisis

As a result of the failure of Gorbachev's reform programme production has continued to stagnate and living standards have fallen. There is now such a chronic shortage of consumer goods, including many different kinds of food, that in practice a rationing system exists. Some economists have warned that a national system of rationing may well be required in the early 1990s. In October 1989 the minister responsible for food reported that 243 out of 276 basic consumer goods were either irregularly available or not on sale at all.[20] Despite the fact that in 1989 the government spent 5 billion roubles, approximately one-third of its total foreign currency income, on grain and other food products the Soviet Union was still short of food.[21] To alleviate the consumer goods crisis, particularly after the 1989 miners' strikes, the government was forced to import more goods, using precious foreign currency.

Shortages of consumer goods have made it politically impossible for the Soviet government to raise prices and to end subsidies on basic foodstuffs. In conditions of general shortage such a measure, though it would give a tremendous boost to agriculture, would provoke mass discontent, and possibly famine. Soviet authorities estimate that there are already 43 million people, many of them pensioners, living below the official subsistence level.[22] Abolishing food subsidies would push many such people into starvation. Hence Gorbachev promised in 1989 that prices of bread, flour, cereals, meat, fish, eggs, milk, sugar, butter, vegetable oil and baby food, all heavily subsidised by the state, would not be raised for at least two years.[23] At the same time attempts to raise prices of some consumer goods were thrown out by the Supreme Soviet, indicating the pressures in society against raising prices. Yet despite subsidies, inflation has continued, fuelled by the overall scarcity of goods. In October 1989 Prime Minister Ryzhkov reported that in the third quarter of the year incomes rose by 15 per cent while production only went up by one per cent.

The Soviet economy is now in a vicious circle. Attempts to reform production have not worked because they only enhance the fragmented nature of the economy itself. Hence they have been more likely to depress output than raise it. Falling efficiency at every level of the economy further adds to the overall dislocation. Less goods in the shops means there is even less incentive for workers to accept changes, which in turn means even more resistance to reform.

The bureaucracy

The Soviet bureaucracy is torn by the contradictory pressures unleashed by the reform process. Many officials understand that the problems of the economy are such that the reforms can only work if they are all implemented simultaneously. Yet they have proved unable to pursue reforms systematically in any area of the Soviet economy. The bureaucrats recognise that the system forged by Stalin over which they preside is incapable of providing for the needs of a complex modern society. Yet they also recognise that their own survival is tied to the maintenance of the Stalinist system. They understand the need for change, but fear the instability that it inevitably creates. Hence they are both in favour of reform and terrified of its consequences, they provide both the impetus for change and the obstacle to change taking place. In practice the result is that the bureaucracy as a whole supports the policy of reform, but individual bureaucrats resist any measure which threatens their own position.

The contradictory outlook of the bureaucracy explains the growing conflict within the Soviet ruling élite. It is not the case that the bureaucracy is divided between reformers and conservatives as it is often presented by Western commentators. Every Soviet bureaucrat is both a reformer and a conservative. Every section of the bureaucracy can see some advantage in extending market forces, while every section is also capable of defending its own stake in the existing system if it appears to be threatened.

Take, for example, the area of foreign trade. The government introduced a new law allowing enterprises to trade directly with overseas countries. However, this law stopped short of giving complete freedom to trade and permission still had to be given by the foreign trade ministry. Ministry officials threatened by the diminution of their role in supervising trade used their remaining powers to block transactions: they created delays in getting export licenses, insisted that all imported goods were individually recorded at the border, and, in certain instances, limited and suspended trade. The fact that one section of the bureaucracy retained its grip on transactions enabled it to frustrate the ambitions of the bureaucracy as a whole to build up foreign trade.

The intense pressures on the bureaucracy have resulted in a degree of fragmentation which has taken a variety of forms. In many of the national republics, the Communist Party has moved further and further away from central control as nationalist movements have gathered momentum. At national level, radical reformers have created what amounts to a faction within the party, the 'inter-regional group'. Local party leaders have taken an increasingly independent line: when the miners went on strike in 1989 most local leaders sided with the miners against Moscow. The fragmentation of the bureaucracy introduced a new element into Soviet political life, as politburo member Yegor Ligachev clearly identified:

> Things have gone so far here that individual communists are beginning to take part in clashes between nationalities, in gatherings of all sorts of nationalist and anti-Soviet nature, in strikes. They are organising all sorts of factions ... and even in places are thinking of leaving not only the structure of the federation – that is already significant in itself – but the structure of the CPSU itself.[24]

Western commentators on perestroika have generally misunderstood the Gorbachev reforms as a campaign to remove the power and privileges of the Soviet bureaucracy. But the bureaucracy is in the lead of the reform process: it was never its intention to give up its power and privileges. On the contrary, its aim is to transform itself into a different kind of ruling group, closer to a capitalist class. The objective of perestroika was to reform the system under bureaucratic control. Gorbachev's policy has been essentially pragmatic in pushing reform as far as it can go without destroying the power of the party. Hence perestroika has achieved no real democratisation of Soviet society in the sense of a transfer of power towards the people. It has merely liberalised the existing system.

How far can the reform process go? Most Western observers fear that Gorbachev will go too far and provoke a conservative reaction that will lead to his own downfall, in the manner of Khrushchev. But this is too simplistic an interpretation of the complexities of the situation in the Soviet Union. The fragmentation of the bureaucracy itself under Gorbachev, which never happened in the 1960s, raises the question of the survival of the system in any recognisable form.

Political reform

Glasnost, the political side of perestroika, began as an attempt by the national leadership to stimulate pressure on the bureaucracy at a local level and give people a political stake in the system. The object was to create suitable conditions for a stable transition to market relations. Gorbachev put it bluntly: 'One of the prime political tasks of the restructuring effort, if not the main one, is to revive and consolidate in the Soviet people a sense of responsibility for the country's destiny.'[25]

For the bureaucracy, greater freedom of expression was a useful mechanism for finding out what was happening in Soviet society and at the same time giving people the opportunity to let off steam. Official newspapers opened their letters columns to the complaints of readers and journalists were encouraged to expose instances of corruption and waste. Gorbachev began a process of selective scapegoating of bureaucrats who were blamed for the failures of perestroika.

The leadership introduced limited electoral reforms to encourage greater identification with the system by ordinary people. Given the economic crisis the results were predictable. Once Soviet people were given the opportunity and the means to express discontent, they immediately registered their disapproval of the system. Not content with merely voting, people took to the streets in large numbers demanding numerous changes in different aspects of Soviet society. Elections brought many critics and opponents of the regime into the public eye and further legitimised dissent.

Glasnost was, however, successful in one important respect: it rallied the support of the intelligentsia around Gorbachev and the reform process. Encouraged by being given greater freedom of expression, Soviet intellectuals became the most enthusiatic supporters of perestroika. The intelligentsia has long favoured the reform of Soviet society and is little concerned about the negative impact of economic restructuring on the working class. Indeed, when Gorbachev made concessions to striking miners he was criticised by leading intellectual reformers, while there was little opposition from the same quarter to his subsequent ban on strikes. Yet, by the close of the 1980s, there were signs that the intelligentsia was beginning to lose its enthusiasm for liberalisation as the problems facing perestroika increased.

There were also signs that general public support for perestroika, never overwhelming, had also further declined. After experiencing a boom in 1987 and 1988 pro-reform magazines and papers began to lose circulation in 1989. A Moscow party official summed up the growing apathy towards reform:

> The people are tired – and not only of the tension. There are some who bluntly say today: it doesn't matter what system we have and what party, if only there were calm, if only there were enough food to eat. This is the most horrible thing. There is such political fatigue.[26]

Opening up the Soviet system to public discussion revealed a single unavoidable fact: people did not like it. The elections for the Congress of Deputies in early 1989 exposed the unpopularity of party bosses. As a result of these setbacks local elections planned for the autumn of 1989 were postponed.

Matters came to a head with the ban on strikes in essential industries in October 1989. Gorbachev turned on critical editors of pro-reform journals for implying 'that we are up to our waists in petrol and one spark could cause a conflagration'.[27] The Soviet premier tried, unsuccessfully, to sack the editor of the magazine *Arguments and Facts* because he revealed in a poll that Gorbachev himself had little popularity amongst the people. There seems little doubt that any further liberalisation of the regime will, in conditions of economic decline, only further expose the unpopularity of the bureaucracy and destabilise society.

Over the past decade the Soviet bureaucracy has so far lost its sense of identity and purpose that it is now scarcely possible to speak of it as a coherent force. It has embarked on a programme of reform because of its recognition of the inescapable bankruptcy of the system that gives the bureaucracy its role in Soviet society. Its moral crisis consists in the fact that it has totally lost confidence in the system that has sustained it as a social force, without having gained any clear idea of how it can achieve the stability apparently enjoyed by the ruling classes of the capitalist West. Its desperate survival strategies, such as promoting nationalist prejudices and cultivating regional power bases, only exacerbate the tendencies towards disintegration. Gorbachev's February 1990 abandonment of the 'leading role of the Communist Party' reveals how far the bureaucracy is prepared to go to cling on to its power. In this struggle, there are neither radicals nor hardliners, left-wingers nor right-wingers, only different degrees of desperation.

Conclusion

The fundamental problem facing Soviet society is that of making the transition between Stalinism and capitalism. The Gorbachev leadership has a fairly clear understanding of the inadequacies of the Stalinist command economy. It has also a clear vision of the Scandinavian-style capitalist utopia it would like to establish in the Soviet Union. The difficulty and the danger lies in transforming a social order cast in Stalinist rigidity for more than half a century into a radically different form of society. This process involves recasting every section of Soviet society and destroying and replacing old mechanisms of social control with new ones, all at the same time as the changes in the Soviet Union produce reverberations in the international order around the world. The prospects of effecting such a complex process of change and readjustment harmoniously – at a time of impending recession throughout the capitalist world – appear dim indeed.

The long-term decline of the Soviet economy is the single most important factor in deciding the fate of the Soviet Union. There is a consensus among the Soviet leaders that there must be some return to a market system. Though the Soviet working class has no particular ideological hostility to the market, it is strongly opposed to the further deterioration of living standards that would inevitably accompany the restoration of capitalist relations. The bureaucrats, aspiring towards capitalism but fearful of losing their positions in the Stalinist machine, constantly put off decisions about fundamental reforms affecting prices and the labour market. But continuing economic decay means that these decisions cannot be indefinitely delayed.

The problem is that for the Soviet bureaucracy to become a class it has to transform its relations to the working class by decisively defeating workers' resistance to change. This is not merely a matter of ideological debate within the Communist Party, but a political struggle that must be carried down to workplace level. The bureaucracy recognises the scale of the challenge:

> Under conditions of a chaotic market and growing scarcities, the energy of the enterprises, irrespective of what they are called, inevitably turns to speculative operations. And this, coupled with a rapid growth in the cash incomes of entrepreneurs, gives rise to a powerful wave of protest with immediate demands to stop all economic innovations. The crux of the matter is not in the ideological formalisation of these demands, but in the real interests which stand behind them.[28]

The 'real interests' of the Soviet working class will have to be crushed before capitalism can be fully restored in the Soviet Union. These are the terms of the class struggle in Soviet society in the early 1990s. If capitalism is restored in the Soviet Union it will not be as the culmination of a process of peaceful reform, but as the result of a successful offensive against the workers.

Many Western supporters of perestroika, particularly left-wingers, have failed to appreciate the importance of the conflict between the bureaucracy and the working class that has been unleashed by Gorbachev's reforms. Ernest Mandel, for example, takes at face value the reformers' claims that they are trying to make socialism work. His only criticism of perestroika is that the bureaucracy cannot carry it through. Rather than warning Soviet workers of the austere and repressive consequences of the reforms, Mandel is anxious to reassure them that the Stalinist machine can be overturned without armed resistance:

> Because the bureaucracy is not a new ruling class but a parasitic cancer on the working class and society as a whole, its removal does not require the type of armed conflict which until now has accompanied revolutions in class societies.[29]

towards the initiative of a thinking worker, highly organised, disciplined, educated and possessing a principally new technological culture.[11]

The persistent failure of the Soviet system to produce and distribute goods worth buying has meant that workers have had no incentive to work harder and earn higher wages.

For decades the Soviet bureaucracy bought stability by allowing the working class a substantial degree of 'negative control' over the system.[12] The severe shortage of labour which has always characterised the Soviet economy forced managers to hold on to workers at all costs.[13] Factory bosses often simply ignored central directives to enforce stricter discipline as fear of losing their workers to other enterprises over-rode all other considerations in the drive to fulfil the plan. Living standards rose steadily from the 1950s onwards as collusion between workers and local bureaucrats became part of everyday life.[14]

The distinctive feature of the Gorbachev reforms was the leadership's recognition that, given the scale of the crisis now facing the Soviet system, the regime had no choice but to restructure fundamentally the relationship between the working class and the Soviet system, even though this risked the stability of the whole Stalinist order. Perestroika aimed to overcome the barrier that the working class had come to represent to the survival of the bureaucratic system.

What are the reforms?

The two central themes of perestroika were the promotion of self-financing enterprises and extension of industrial democracy in the workplace. These themes were codified in the 1987 'law on the state enterprise' which built on the experience of the Andropov reforms of the early 1980s as well as earlier experiments in factory reform.[15]

The key aim in encouraging enterprises to become self-financing was to press managers to take responsibility for disciplining their own workforces. As well as being pushed into competing with one another for supplies and sales, factory bosses were given an incentive to save on wages. Any bonus payments now had to be deducted from profits made on the market rather than simply being paid for by the centre. Given that bonuses made up 55 per cent of wages this measure immediately threatened drastic cuts in workers' living standards.[16] By late 1988 some 51 million workers were employed in enterprises covered by the scheme, including the entire communications industry, 88 per cent of transport, 97 per cent of retail outlets and 50 per cent of consumer services.[17] Self-financing also introduced the threat of bankruptcy which now looms over the heads of managers and workers alike as a constant reminder of the price to be paid for failure in the market place.

The speed-ups and bonus cuts which followed the introduction of self-financing did little to invigorate the economy, but much to antagonise the workforce. Millions of job 'reviews' were launched in which managers and brigade leaders reclassified workers, virtually universally into a lower wage bracket. The reform in effect gave managers both the right and the incentive to make arbitrary decisions, resulting in an average cut in bonus payments of 20 per cent in some industries. Much of the wave of walkouts and strikes in 1988 and 1989 was organised in response to the apparently arbitrary character of regrading decisions.[18] Workers also objected to losing bonuses and suffering penalties because of production bottlenecks resulting from the general disorganisation of the Soviet economy. This is how a foreman at a Soviet diesel factory described the problem:

> A regular pace of production determines everything else. But it does not exist. You work Saturday and Sunday and then there is no work on Monday. In such circumstances it makes no sense to punish workers for lateness or absences, since idle time can last days.[19]

Such 'reforms' only make sense to a bureaucrat attempting to shift the burden of an irrational system onto the working class.

The object of promoting industrial democracy was to secure greater commitment from workers by involving them in workplace discussions. Though these reforms, modelled on experiments in Yugoslavia, were hailed by Western radicals as one of Gorbachev's innovative democratising measures, there had been several earlier attempts to extend workplace participation in Soviet factories.[20] Even Brezhnev, the arch-conservative, in 1980 called for the involvement of workers at factory level as a way of putting pressure on local managers and of finding out what the people thought about events in Poland.[21] In 1983 Andropov introduced measures designed to engage workers 'constructively' in workplace councils.[22] Gorbachev's new legislation encouraged the formation of 'workers' collective councils' which were to hold general meetings not less than twice a year to elect a committee made up of workers, managers and technicians. The committees were to run the enterprise throughout the period between general meetings and workers were even given the right to elect officials and managers (subject to ratification by a 'higher body').[23]

Gorbachev's industrial democracy measures soon turned out to be some of the least successful aspects of perestroika.[24] By 1989 workers' councils and the election of enterprise heads were scarcely mentioned in the Soviet Union. They had patently failed to give workers a stake in the system. Many former advocates of industrial democracy now began to have second thoughts. Prominent reformers now dismissed the working class, arguing that workers had been given the chance to become involved in a 'responsible democracy' but had subverted the process by demanding a 'democracy of desire'. Much to the irritation of the radical intelligentsia, workers had succumbed to such base instincts as the 'desire' for food and clothing.[25]

Scepticism about workers' councils was reinforced by the experience of participation. This is how one worker reported on a row with a manager at a council meeting: 'The upshot was that he told me that when I'm the director I can give the orders. Until then, he's the one who gets the reprimand from the *Gorkom* (City Party Committee) not the Council and not me.'[26]

As early as November 1988, the reformers recognised the failure of 'democratisation' as a real setback. Boris Kurasvilli, a legal reformer close to Gorbachev, claimed that 'perestroika has lost its first decisive battle.'[27]

The end of egalitarianism

The failure of attempts to engage workers in discussing the terms of their own exploitation in the workplace has reinforced prejudices among intellectuals in both East and West about the irredeemably conservative character of the Soviet working class. In response, Gorbachev has launched a resolutely anti-working class debate, emphasising the need to combat the traditional 'levelling mentality' of Soviet society in favour of an acceptance of wider differentials in income and social status as an incentive to enterprise and efficiency.[28] In the past, Soviet leaders bemoaned the 'egalitarianism' of Soviet society as a deterrent to the spirit of 'socialist competition' required to achieve Stalinist targets and hence as a deviation from the true principles of Soviet communism. But Gorbachev went further in identifying the basic problem in the system itself rather than in some deviation from it. Now it was the system itself that had to be changed.

A central element in the Gorbachev offensive against the working class was the 'contract brigade' system. This offensive was conducted by a new breed of economic advisors imbued with a Thatcherite distaste for the working class. Take this typical illustration of the prevailing outlook:

> Apathy and indifference became mass phenomena, theft, disrespect for honest work and a simultaneous aggressive jealousy for those who earn a lot even if they earn honestly; signs appeared of almost physical degradation of a sizeable part of the population on the ground of drinking and idleness.[29]

The 'contract brigade' system involves drawing up a contract between an enterprise and a labour brigade for the completion of a given task. Both sides agree on the specifics of the job – including the time-scale, amount of materials required and size of wages fund, including penalties and incentives. This allows the brigade leadership (usually appointed by management) to decide the number of workers required and to allocate bonuses and penalties.

The contract brigade system was first introduced in the early 1970s in the construction industry, but floundered due to working class indifference and bureaucratic hostility.[30] In the uncertain world of the Soviet economy where supplies can rarely be guaranteed, the system could never be expected to be popular. In the late 1980s, however, it was implemented in a wide variety of industries. Take, for example, the pioneering scheme introduced in transport in 1984.[31]

Transportation has long been a major problem for Soviet society. As a result of the irrationality of the system, lorry drivers have always had an interest in maximising the distances they travelled. The falsification of documents, the choice of the longest possible route and the sale of excess fuel on the black market have long been commonplace. For the experiment, brigades in 24 enterprises were contracted for certain routes and periods, ensuring that earnings were directly related to task fulfilment and efficiency. Results were impressive. There were savings in all departments – an 18 per cent fall in fuel consumption, 14 per cent fewer kilometres travelled, even a 20 per cent drop in the amount of deliveries claimed. The system revealed advantages beyond quantitative improvements in performance. By putting the responsibility on the individual worker, it encouraged higher productivity, lower absenteeism and alcoholism and less time-wasting on breaks.

By the end of 1988, more than 60 per cent of manual workers

were employed in contract brigades. However, the historic problem of the Soviet system remained to be resolved: how to generalise from a successful experiment in one sector to implement a successful reform across the whole economy. The repeated experience of the Soviet bureaucracy is that the chaotic character of the system as a whole defeats any such attempt at general reform.[32]

In addition to the difficulties of forcing workers to take responsibility for their enterprises, Gorbachev's reforms have failed to overcome the problem of shortages of consumer goods. Indeed, queues for food and other basics have become even longer while quality remains poor. The regime's response – the development of the co-ops and the conversion of parts of the military sector to consumer goods production – has not only failed to resolve the problem, but has fuelled inflation and provoked widespread popular resentment.

Workers and the 'free market'

The popular response to co-ops reveals the ambivalence of working-class attitudes towards Gorbachev and his reforms. Though workers have no objection to the market in principle, and may even regard capitalism in the abstract as preferable to Stalinism, the practical consequences of market reforms have provoked intense hostility. Though the co-ops account for only around one per cent of Soviet output and involve less than two million people, they rapidly became the targets of workers' anger. At first public opinion was favourable: a July 1987 opinion poll suggested that 87 per cent of people under 45 thought that co-ops would be a useful way of fulfilling consumer demand.[33] Within months reports of anti-co-op riots began to appear in the press.

In Volgograd, gangs of youths were enlisted by a local anti-co-op bureaucrat in what the press dramatised as a pogrom against co-op workers who were supplying tomatoes to local co-op restaurants. Their greenhouses were smashed up and all their tomatoes stolen. A large cooperative farm near Moscow was burnt to the ground by local people complaining at the high prices charged by people they condemned as 'kulaks, NEPmen and new bourgeoisie'.[34] In Kazakhstan, a three-day riot followed the announcement of rationing for basic items at the same time as co-ops were having no difficulty obtaining goods to sell at inflated prices.[35] What lay at the root of these protests was not the existence of co-ops as such – workers have long relied on the black market to obtain food and clothing – but the fact that across the Soviet Union high-priced foodstuffs were heaping up on private shelves at the very moment when public shortages were worse than ever, wages were being squeezed and unemployment was rising.

Gorbachev's close public association with co-ops contributed to his growing unpopularity in the Soviet Union. His advice to a newlywed couple he encountered on a public walkabout in Siberia, that they should buy co-op built housing, was widely regarded as revealing both insensitivity and aloofness. Millions of young people in the Soviet Union are forced to stay with their families because of gross housing shortages in the public sector and because they could never afford to buy a co-op house.[36] By early 1989 public animosity against co-ops had reached such a pitch that Gorbachev was forced to introduce measures to curb their activities.[37]

In addition to their high prices, the high wages paid by co-ops excited fury among other workers: 'What do you think I, a Sovkhoz tractor driver earning 2–3 roubles a day doing repairs feels like, when I read that somewhere an operator who makes bra fasteners makes 100 roubles a day?'[38]

The co-ops have contributed to the growing social stratification of Soviet society which has provoked widespread anger and bitterness. Popular animosity is directed not only against those who make their living in co-ops but also against the reformers who are seen as the champions of their cause. *Izvestia* reported in 1988 that 'letters are full of indignation, anger and insulting remarks about "private operators" and serious accusations against those "who allowed this to happen".'[39]

'Under-provisioning' – the return of poverty

The decisive factor in conditioning working-class attitudes to reform was that in the first five years of Gorbachev, things became much worse for most people in the Soviet Union. Poverty – officially, 'under-provisioning', a term little heard before the days of glasnost – has reached desperate levels.[40] The Soviet superpower is 56th in the world league table according to consumption per head; its infant mortality rate places it 50th.[41] Men who survive the first 12 months of life can expect to live until they are 63, placing Moscow on a par with São Paulo and Mexico City.[42]

The state of the Soviet health service makes a mockery of the claim that the Soviet Union is the world's largest 'nanny state'. In the southern republic of Kazakhstan 60,000 cases of tuberculosis were reported in 1988.[43] More than 1.7 million Soviet citizens suffer 'severe' gastro-intestinal infections each year, indicating the Third World standards of sanitation that prevail in large areas of the country.[44] Half of all Soviet hospitals have no hot, running water.[45] Some 105 million people, 37 per cent of the population, live below the official poverty level.[46] The average old age pension is so low that three-quarters of the over-sixties live below the poverty level.[47] Charities have taken over welfare functions previously provided by the state: soup kitchens have become commonplace in major cities.[48]

A profession previously unknown in the Soviet Union – social worker – was created in 1987 to cope with the increasing scale of poverty.[49] By the end of the 1980s many people were complaining that after five years of reform things were in a worse state than they had been under Brezhnev. Though it was clear that perestroika has made things worse for the Soviet working class, it was also clear that there was no going back to the old system.

'Where do we go from here?'

In its increasingly desperate struggle for survival the Soviet bureaucracy has come to recognise that the only way forward lies through the restoration of the capitalist system. However the failure of the first five years of Gorbachev's programme of pro-market reforms has led to an increasingly critical concentration on the foundations of the Stalinist system itself. The stability of Soviet social relations, which the Brezhnev era represented, is now seen as the source of the system's problems.[50] In particular, many prominent reformers now identify the stubborn refusal of the working class to shoulder the burden of the restructuring of the Soviet economy as not only a threat to perestroika, but as a threat to the survival of the bureaucracy itself. They regard the drive to extend the market as the only way to shake up the working class and force it into a more subservient relationship to the Soviet bureaucracy.

A market economy necessitates, above all, a market in the commodity labour power. For both bureaucrat and worker the move towards this sort of society is more than a *technical* matter of setting up job centres, it involves a major transformation of the *social* relationship between both groups. It means forcing managers to recognise that their survival depends on their enterprise making a profit rather than on their personal and political influence with the local party hierarchy. It means ensuring that workers have no way of surviving other than by selling their capacity to work to an employer who is free to exploit this capacity in the workplace. It means confronting both managers and workers with the harsh discipline of market forces: if the enterprise fails to make a profit, bankruptcy and collapse; if the worker cannot be profitably exploited, unemployment and poverty.

For half a century the stability of the Soviet system has been ensured by guaranteeing every worker a job and a reasonable standard of living through price subsidies. The advance of perestroika means that such constraints on the free labour market must be abandoned. Though the reforms introduced in the 1980s left the foundations of the Stalinist system intact, they still produced widespread social unrest. Going beyond these limited measures means destroying the old methods of social control; it also means that the era of the 'silent class struggle' has come to an abrupt end.

Welcome to sunny Siberia

In 1988 the Soviet leadership made clear its intention to push ahead with a drastic shakeout of jobs from industry. According to the official Gosplan estimate, the planned 130–150 per cent increase in labour productivity by the year 2000 will necessitate the shedding of between 13 and 19 million jobs.[51] One of Gorbachev's top advisors called for an immediate reduction in the state sector of 4 million workers, who could then act as a 'fund' for the developing service sector.[52] Deputy Prime Minister Leonid Abalkin claimed that more than 24,000 enterprises (one in seven) are operating with too many workers producing too few goods. He suggested that between 9 and 12 per cent of the working population would have to be laid off to 'normalise' the Soviet economy.[53]

Stanislav Shatalin, an influential social scientist, explained the consequences of 'normalisation' for the working class:

> The principles of socialism are not principles of charity which automatically guarantee a job for everyone regardless of his ability to work at it. A person ought to have to wage a daily economic struggle to hold on to a job that suits his abilities.[54]

Tatyana Zaslavskaya, Gorbachev's chief economic advisor, endorsed the new consensus that the regime could not baulk from taking harsh measures to deal with the working class:

There is no doubt that the necessity of transferring to branches of production where labour is scarce, and of moving to other areas and cities, will be faced primarily by workers who are least valuable from the point of view of the work collective; who are indifferent to work and output quality, and who take an inactive part in social life, to say nothing of idlers, drunkards, rolling stones and so on. Such a situation will lead to ... stronger labour discipline and an increase in the quality of work.[55]

The guarantee of work for all in Stalin's 1936 constitution remains a barrier to Gorbachev's project of creating a free labour market.[56] Some reformers have called for drastic measures to increase the number of workers available to the regime, by lowering the school-leaving age or raising the retirement age. Others have dismissed this approach as a return to Stalin-style 'extensive' development. Others still have pointed out that more than 28 per cent of pensioners already have jobs.[57]

Though the Soviet leaders are united in agreement that a pool of unemployed is desirable, they have experienced great difficulty in implementing this policy. For example, the shakeout of jobs in the southern non-Slav republics has created a pool of young people, who lack experience or skills for other work, but who could be a serious potential threat to law and order. The local official for youth affairs warned Soviet television viewers of the dangers:

While we have been discussing whether we can be threatened by unemployment, it has become a sad reality. In the republics of Central Asia alone, 6 million young men and women are not working or studying anywhere. Indeed, the new economic relations, which in themselves are a blessing, sometimes engender a kind of discrimination against young people in industry. Financial autonomy, or rather its current interpretation, somehow throws overboard the young – that is, unsuitable – workers.[58]

While the figure of 6 million appeared to include many people who were in between jobs, there were estimated to be around 3 million long-term unemployed in the southern USSR. Regions dominated by single industries such as cotton and oil felt the effects of perestroika in lay-offs and closures much more sharply than others.[59]

By 1989 more than 800 'employment centres' had been set up, seeking work for more than 200,000 mainly young people. Young people made up 40 per cent of those 'citizens given an official warning by the militia' to find a job.[60] Riots in Uzbekistan and Kazakhstan involved unemployed youth on several occasions. Many ethnic disturbances in the southern republics begin from resentments over skilled migrants getting work while local youth are unemployed. Such targets provide the local bureaucrats with the perfect scapegoats for a declining system.

The Soviet bureaucracy is preoccupied with the problems of social instability that will inevitably accompany rising unemployment in a country where even workers with jobs have to struggle to survive.[61] By the end of 1989 the shake-out had yet to bite among the skilled sectors of the working class in the core regions of the Soviet Union. The leadership carefully set about preparing the way for unemployment with commonsensical arguments:

> The need to look for a job – a necessity that many now working in manufacturing and services will certainly face – may also be new and unaccustomed for us ... We are used to the exact opposite – work seeking the person ... Obviously, considerable psychological reorientation will be required. We consider it natural and necessary that if, through objective causes, a job slot becomes unnecessary, the worker must inevitably be given another job ... Now we shall have to get used to the idea that finding employment is ... the worker's own responsibility.[62]

The Gosplan chief failed to clarify the 'objective causes' of unemployment, but we can agree that 'some considerable psychological reorientation' may well be required before the bureaucracy manages to persuade workers that they should go and look for work in some distant part of Siberia, the Far East or the Far North, which is the only real option for many workers in the Central Asian republics.

Someone has to pay

The Soviet bureaucracy has recognised that subsidised food and housing are an obstacle that must be overcome in the drive to allow free rein to market forces:

> Where have we ever seen prices remaining stable while things were going badly in the economy? This does not happen. Somebody must pay for the economic failures, for the crisis in

which we are living ... The time has also passed when it was possible to compensate for price increases.[63]

Not only do state subsidies 'distort' real prices, they also interfere with the role of the market in disciplining the workers. As Zaslavskaya put it, 'they reduce the motivation for strenuous and effective labour.'[64]

Subsidies have long played a key role in the Soviet economy. In 1986, subsidies accounted for 11 per cent of the state budget. In the early 1980s, consumers paid directly for only 5 per cent of education costs, 6 per cent of health care costs, 37 per cent of housing and 58 per cent of cinema, theatre and entertainment costs. Meat and dairy prices remained constant for two decades after 1962 and official rents were fixed in 1928. Subsidies underpinned the tolerable living standards that prevailed in the Soviet Union in the post-war period and helped to maintain social peace.[65] Bureaucrats identified as 'conservatives' – such as Ligachev – have openly expressed their fears about price rises, emphasising that subsidised prices in the Soviet Union have been 'the essence of social policy'.[66] The official report of the Goskomsten research institute reported that subsidies were vital in 'safeguarding the political stability in our society'.[67]

Price reform remains the most 'political' aspect of Gorbachev's economic programme. The date for the implementation of retail price rises has been put back several times since 1985 when it was first discussed as a serious possibility.[68] The option is fast becoming a necessity as the dire state of the economy forces the bureaucracy to consider the desperate measure of removing even the promise of compensation in the form of wage rises.

Gorbachev's advisors have come up with diverse justifications for price reforms in an attempt to persuade the Soviet public that such measures are useful, indeed essential for the Soviet economy. Zaslavskaya, for example, tried to present cuts in subsidies as a radical redistributionist measure: 'Anyone who benefits from subsidised prices is getting unearned income; unearned income is a violation of social justice and should be eliminated; each rouble ought to have the same purchasing power.'[69]

Others argued that price rises by their very nature would lead to a shortening of queues, thus freeing millions of workers to be employed productively throughout the economy. It has been estimated that 275 billion work hours per year are wasted in queues and the daily search for necessities; in fact the vast majority of those engaged in this activity are women.[70] The argument goes that if prices were higher, fewer workers would be able to afford the goods on sale thus reducing the queues.

Aganbegyan called for the establishment of a 'deluxe trade' sector in which better quality goods could be bought and sold at higher than average prices in order to increase the 'incentive to earn a lot of money'. He believes that prices of meat, bread and dairy products 'may have to double'.[71] Retail prices are now not due for reform until 1992, two years after wholesale prices.[72]

Fear of working-class protest is the underlying theme in all bureaucratic resistance to price reform. The Soviet leaders fear that hostility to price rises could trigger a revolt that would jeopardise national stability. The ability of the working class to go beyond the predominantly defensive actions it has undertaken so far and begin to fight positively for its own interests will be the most decisive influence on the future course of events, and it is to this question that we now turn.

How strong is the Soviet working class?

One irony of perestroika is that the bureaucracy's attempt to transform itself into a coherent, exploiting class has also begun to recreate the Soviet working class as a collective, oppositional and potentially revolutionary force. The July 1989 miners' strike revealed the potential threat of the working class to the bureaucracy, but it also exposed workers' lack of a coherent alternative to the current direction of Soviet society.

Gorbachev openly admitted that the miners' strike was the most dangerous challenge his regime had so far encountered: 'This was the most difficult trial for us in the entire four years of perestroika. We had Chernobyl. We had other difficult trials. Nevertheless, I would single out present events as the most serious, the most difficult.'[73]

Even after the state had made major concessions and got the miners back to work, lightning strikes continued to disrupt production in the mines. Gorbachev's response was to bring glasnost to an abrupt end by introducing a law to ban strikes indefinitely in key industries – coal, gas, chemical, power and transport.[74] Gorbachev himself declared the measures vital to 'protect the economy from anarchy'.[75] The atmosphere of panic was reflected in the proposal for a blanket strike ban which was dropped only after a heated debate in the Supreme Soviet.[76] It was in these controversies about how far and how fast the offensive against the working class should proceed that conflicts between so-called 'conservatives' and 'radicals' in the bureaucracy emerged.

The strike wave exposed the fragility of the bureaucracy's newly created framework for containing social discontent. At the very time when the leadership imposed its emergency anti-strike laws, the Supreme Soviet was due to debate new trade union legislation upholding the right to strike for the first time, while curtailing it in essential industries. The bureaucracy aimed to dampen militancy by setting up a network of arbitration boards and tribunals in which workers and managers would be forced to negotiate before considering strike action. The legislation also included provisions for secret ballots, a ban on picketing and a 'cooling-off' period before strike action could start.[77] The fact that even more coercive measures were imposed before this new framework for industrial relations could be discussed revealed the pressures that the working-class militancy is exerting on an insecure bureaucracy.

While the miners' strike created a mood of despondency among reformers in the Soviet Union, it encouraged a new confidence among workers. Rumours of further strikes and other 'extraordinary occurrences' became rife in the second half of 1989. Railworkers from every corner of the Soviet Union, coal miners from the far north of Siberia, the Ukraine and Kazakhstan, Metro workers in Moscow, assembly-line workers at the giant Volga Automobile Works (VAZ) car plant in Togliatti all either threatened or took industrial action in August and September.[78] Workers refused to be intimidated by the strike ban, as Yuri Boldyrev, a member of the miners' strike committee set up in Donetsk indicated: 'They have made a mistake. There will be strikes. The reaction will be negative. It shows that when they signed the agreement with us in summer, they were hypocrites.'[79]

Leonid Abalkin, a leading 'radical' and ally of Gorbachev, gave the view from the other side. Commenting on the refusal of the Supreme Soviet to support a total ban on strikes, he complained that 'everyone wants to be sympathetic and popular with their electors.'[80] The Soviet bureaucracy is clearly aware that the further development of perestroika demands measures which will be 'unpopular, tough and even painful'.[81] The end of glasnost for Soviet workers showed the direction which the bureaucracy will have to take if it is to succeed in 'liberalising' the economy. However, as Abalkin indicated, taking this step meant major problems for the bureaucracy itself. The fragmentation of the bureaucracy is being speeded up by its own fear of the working class.

The legacy of Stalinism

'I'm a Komsomol member, but I don't believe in communism. In my opinion, it's a utopia.'[82] A 26-year-old student from Kiev, quoted in the Young Communist League newspaper, expresses an opinion that is widely held in the Soviet Union. An official survey has revealed that nearly one in three 'young communists' do not believe in communism even as a distant ideal, never mind as an actually existing social system.[83]

In reality it would be difficult to find a single person in the Soviet Union today who believes that communism is either achievable or even desirable. This how a 29-year-old railway worker from Donetsk put it: 'Do I believe in communism? No, no and no. I think it's all a bluff, a fairy tale.'[84]

For most people in the Soviet Union (and indeed elsewhere) the concepts of 'communism' and 'socialism' are inseparable from Stalinism, from their experience of a stagnant and repressive society. Opposition to the effects of 60 years of bureaucratic rule inevitably takes an anti-communist form. For Soviet workers, 'actually existing socialism' means a particularly incompetent and vicious form of exploitation. Thus it is not surprising that reactions against the Soviet system are often expressed in terms that appear sympathetic to the restoration of market forces.

For example, striking miners in the Ukraine demanded the right to sell the coal they produce on the market. This was their response to a situation in which the state sets the targets and takes away the coal, giving back as little as possible in return. A report by a local party official revealed that 20 per cent of miners' homes had no water supply, 26 per cent no sewage system, 28 per cent no central heating, 63 per cent no hot water and 49 per cent no gas for heating or cooking.[85] In these circumstances it is not surprising that there is little support for socialism or communism among Soviet miners or that the market appears to offer workers more control over their own fate than the communist system.

However, though there is little ideological opposition to the market, most workers are opposed to the practical consequences of the extension of market forces, as we have seen in popular responses to the co-ops. When a group of miners from the Ukraine were asked what steps they would like to see taken to alleviate their situation there was little enthusiasm for self-financing or the market. Most expressed their desire to see the existing system overturned: 73 per cent wanted the regional coal ministry to be dismantled and 75 per cent wanted cuts in the bureaucracy. Others were in favour of some of the potential benefits of the capitalist system: 41 per cent wanted the introduction of new technology and 38 per cent wanted the right to sell their coal on the international markets to get foreign currency and buy consumer goods. However only 16 per cent thought self-financing would help them.[86]

There is little evidence for Western claims that there is great popular enthusiasm for the restoration of capitalism and widespread public support for the pro-market reformers within the bureaucracy. When Gorbachev visited Siberia in September 1988 he was heckled and jostled by crowds and he later admitted that 'everywhere I went, the people were constantly at your throat.'[87] Boris Yeltsin, the prominent Moscow reformer and hero of the Western media, is popular in the Soviet Union because of his highly publicised attacks on the party elite and the *nomenklatura*, not for his economic programme. He reserves his pro-capitalist outbursts for trips to the West. On a visit to New York City in 1989 he observed that the slums of Harlem 'we would consider acceptable living quarters.'[88] Indeed the slums and shanty towns of the capitalist world are what the pro-market reformers want to introduce on a wider scale into the Soviet Union. It is little wonder then that workers have so far shown little enthusiasm for a return to capitalism. The negative experience of the Stalinist system remains the only argument the pro-marketeers can use in favour of capitalist restoration in the Soviet Union.

The end for the elite?

The Soviet bureaucracy can no longer be regarded as a monolithic block with an iron grip on society. The events of the late 1980s have intensified conflicts within the bureaucracy, particularly between reformers who favour accelerating the pace of capitalist restoration and more conservative elements who fear the destabilising consequences for the élite as a whole. While Gorbachev has the support of much of the radical intelligentsia, some sections of the bureaucracy are attempting to articulate the fears of ordinary people as a way of slowing down the reform process. The emergence in 1989 of the 'Russian United Workers Front' reflected the efforts of a conservative section of the bureaucracy to mobilise working class support on an anti-perestroika platform.

The front's platform is a combination of populist 'anti-reform' rhetoric, Great Russian chauvinism and virulent anti-Semitism.

This reactionary mixture appears to be the last hope of that section of the bureaucracy which fears losing its privileges if capitalism is restored in the Soviet Union. The movement's first conference in Sverdlovsk in September 1989 was attended by 110 delegates from 29 towns in the Russian republics and representatives of the similar 'Inter' movements in Moldavia, Tajikistan, Latvia and Estonia. It agreed a programme calling for the end of the private sector and the co-op movement and for resistance against any attempt to break up the Soviet Union.[89] V.M.Yakushev, one of the front's leaders and a prominent academic, regards the Russian working class as the force that can 'save' Russia. Perestroika, he says, 'gives advantages to all sorts of artful dodgers, rogues and cheats and this arouses the greatest indignation in people.' Yakushev claimed to speak for the majority of workers who have 'understood and perceived intuitively something that our leading economists just cannot grasp; profit is the expression of that part of the product that maintains the non-productive sections of the economy.'[90]

Unfortunately for Yakushev, the majority of workers have also 'understood and perceived intuitively' something else, that the privileged position of the élite is also 'the expression of that part of the product that maintains the non-productive sections of the economy'. It was the crisis of bureaucratic rule and the fear of unrest which this unleashed that forced the bureaucracy to attempt reform in the early eighties. A return to the old days and the 'era of stagnation' may appeal to some of the bureaucrats who prospered while workers stood in queues, but it holds even less attraction for ordinary people than capitalist restoration.

A closer look at the groups who attended the Sverdlovsk congress gives an indication of the direction which the struggle within the bureaucracy for influence over the masses is likely to take. Representatives of more than 20 Russian 'patriotic' movements attended, including the Union for the Spiritual Rebirth of the Fatherland, the Russian Artists Fellowship, and the Union of Patriotic Organisations from the Urals to Siberia. The leadership of the National Sobriety Campaign also participated, to make sure things didn't get out of hand.[91] The 'Inter' movements are the only groups with any real support among workers and this remains restricted to the Baltic republics and Moldavia where nationalist movements have proposed excluding them from various aspects of social life.[92]

The award-winning British journalist Martin Walker covered events in the Soviet Union from the beginning of Gorbachev's term of office until he left for the US at the end of 1988. Returning to Moscow at the end of 1989 after a year in Washington, he noted two major changes. The first was the much greater social differentiation between a newly-rich minority and a not-so-newly-poor majority. The second was the increased influence of Russian nationalism and anti-Semitism. He identified 'a coherent group of politically conservative and highly nationalist newspapers' such as *Sovetskaya Rossiya, Literaturnaya Rossiya* and the armed forces daily *Krasnaya Zvezda*.[93] These papers constantly blame the Jews for the much-hated co-ops and the national minorities for the fragmentary tendencies within the Soviet Union.

It is doubtful whether the conservative sections of the Russian bureaucracy who hope to take advantage of popular hostility to the system have any real influence among the mass of people. They have nothing positive to offer ordinary Russians; the collapse of the economy precludes the possibility of 'buying-off' any section of the working class. For all the talk of a split between radicals and conservatives, between 'left' and 'right' there is no real ideological dispute over economic strategy. The differences are merely pragmatic. The 'left' understands that the market is the only hope for a bureaucracy that must transform itself into a capitalist class or die. The 'right' also favours the market, but is more fearful of the destabilising consequences of social change; hence it seeks to fall back on prejudices which the bureaucracy have long fostered as weapons of social control. The revival of anti-Semitism and Russian chauvinism is the last hope of a decadent élite which is prepared to go to any lengths to survive.

The strength of the Soviet working class lies in its enormous social weight and its increasing determination not to choose sides as the bureaucracy tears itself to pieces. The most important consequence of perestroika for Soviet workers is the way in which Gorbachev's reforms have curtailed the scope of the myriad ways of getting around the system and 'making do' that have always enabled workers to survive. Deprived of individual ways of coping with the Stalinist system, Soviet workers will be increasingly forced towards collective responses to the system's failures. The strike wave of 1989 confirmed this trend and the potential threat it poses to the regime. However, decades of Stalinism have destroyed any sense of a collective alternative among Soviet workers. The weakness of the Soviet working class lies in its ideological confusion and political disorientation. Whatever the immediate future holds, it is clear that the Soviet working class, the first proletariat in history to make a successful revolution, is now in a position to break out of the stranglehold of Stalinism and carry forward the project from which it was so catastrophically diverted in the early 1920s.

Notes

1. M. Holubenko, 'Soviet working class: discontent and opposition' in *Critique* No 4, 1975. This article provides a useful survey of the lack of an organised, working class movement in the Soviet Union, even at the most basic, trade union organisation. Until the miners' strike in July 1989, there was no tradition of even basic trade union organisation.
2. D. Mandel, '"Revolutionary reform" in Soviet factories: restructuring relations between workers and management' in *Socialist Register 1989*, Merlin Press, 1989.
3. E. Teague, 'Embryos of people's power?', *Report on the USSR*, Vol 1, No 32, 1989.
4. M. Taylor, 'Perestroika: greatest test yet' in *International Labour Reports*, No 34/35, July–October 1989.
5. Taylor, 'Perestroika: greatest test yet'.
6. F. Furedi, *The Soviet Union Demystified: a materialist analysis*, London: Junius, 1986.
7. See K.S. Karol, 'Gorbachev and the dynamics of change' in *Socialist Register 1988*, Merlin Press, 1988.
8. F. Furedi, *The Soviet Union Demystified*.
9. M. Reiman, *The Birth of Stalinism – the USSR on the eve of the 'second revolution'*, London: IB Taurus, 1987. This book covers the period during which the Soviet social formation was created and provides an excellent description of how the bureaucracy had no choice but to resort to the use of force as the primary method of overcoming economic inefficiency.
10. B. Arnot, *Controlling Soviet Labour – Experimental Change from Brezhnev to Gorbachev*, London: Macmillan Press, 1988.
11. *Izbrannye rechi i stati*, Vol 2 (Moscow: Polizdat, 1987).
12. B. Arnot, *Controlling Soviet Labour: Experimental Change from Brezhnev to Gorbachev*.
13. D. Lane, *Soviet Labour and the Ethics of Communism – Full Employment and the Labour Process in the Soviet Union*, Wheatsheaf Books, 1987.
14. B. Arnot, *Controlling Soviet Labour: Experimental Change from Brezhnev to Gorbachev*.
15. A. Aslund, *Gorbachev's Struggle for Economic Reform – the Soviet reform process 1985–1988*, London: Frances Pinter, 1989.
16. D. Mandel '"Revolutionary reform" in Soviet Factories'.

17. A. Aslund, *Gorbachev's Struggle for Economic Reform*.
18. D. Mandel *"'Revolutionary reform" in Soviet Factories'*.
19. D. Mandel *"'Revolutionary reform" in Soviet Factories'*.
20. See E. Mandel, *Beyond Perestroika – the Future of Gorbachev's USSR*, Verso, 1989 and T. Ali, *Revolution from Above – Where is the Soviet Union Going?*, Hutchinson, 1988. Both authors come from a radical tradition which habitually attempts to discover positive trends emerging from within the Stalinist movement. For a review of Mandel, see J. Gibson, 'Gorbachev and the western left' in *Confrontation*, 5, Summer 1989, Junius, 1989.
21. E. Teague, *Solidarity and the Soviet Worker*, Croom Helm, 1988. According to Teague the bureaucracy didn't know how Soviet workers would react to the emergence of Solidarity in Poland. They began by over-reacting and convening factory meetings across the country denouncing the revolt as anti-communist and anti-Soviet. In fact, there was little sympathy for the Poles, who were seen as better off and privileged by many Soviet workers. This experience indicated just how far removed the bureaucracy was from the rest of society and how dangerous this could become in the near future.
22. A. Aslund, *Gorbachev's Struggle for Economic Reform*.
23. E. Teague, *Radio Liberty Research Bulletin*, RL 486/88.
24. Teague, *Radio Liberty Research Bulletin*.
25. See the round table discussion in *Literaturnaya Gazeta*, 3, June 1987 for an example of anti-working class prejudices of the radical intelligentsia.
26. *Izvestia*, 22 March 1988.
27. B. Kurashvilli, *Moscow News*, No 23, 1988.
28. See V. Selyunin, *Literaturnaya Gazeta*, July 1989.
29. N. Shmelev, *Novy Mir*, No 63, June 1987.
30. B. Arnot, *Controlling Soviet Labour*.
31. A. Aslund, *Gorbachev's Struggle for Economic Reform*.
32. F. Furedi, *The Soviet Union Demystified*.
33. *Sovetskaya Rossiya*, 24 July 1987.
34. *Literaturnaya Gazeta*, August 1987.
35. *Morning Star*, 18 August 1989.
36. A. Trehub, 'Tough talking on Soviet living standards', *Radio Liberty Research Bulletin*, RL 438/88.
37. *Morning Star*, 18 August 1989.
38. *Izvestia*, 27 February 1988.
39. *Izvestia*, 27 February 1988.
40. See Goskomstat figures in *Ekonomicheskaya Gazeta*, No 25, 1989.

41. A. Zaichenko, *Izvestia*, 11 January 1989.
42. E. Chazov, *Komsomolskaya pravda*, 18 June 1988.
43. E. Chazov, *Pravda*, 30 June 1988.
44. E. Chazov, *Pravda*, 30 June 1988.
45. E. Chazov, *Komsomolskaya pravda*, 18 June 1988.
46. *Sovetskaya torgovla*, June 1989.
47. *Ekonomicheskaya gazeta*, No 25, 1989.
48. W. Moskoff, 'The aged in the USSR', *Report on the USSR*, Vol 1, No 37, 15 September 1989. A typical attender at a newly opened Leningrad soup kitchen indicates the depths to which the collapse of the system has reduced a sizeable section of the population. An 85-year-old woman (the vast majority of the new poor are women) who has worked all her life as a hospital attendant now receives 52 rubles per month. This figure is less than 50per cent of the official poverty level. Out of her 52 rubles, she pays 6.78 rubles rent, 4.17 rubles in heating, 3 rubles for lighting, 1.7 rubles in telephone bills, leaving 36.35 rubles for food, clothing, medicine and entertainment.
49. W. Moskoff, 'The Aged in the USSR'.
50. See T. Zaslavskaya, 'The Novosibirsk Report', *Survey*, Vol 28, No 1, 1984.
51. V. Kostakov cited in Bergson and Hough, *Soviet Economy*, Vol 4, January–March 1988.
52. See report of Draft Law on Co-operatives in *Radio Liberty Research Bulletin*, RL 111/88, 3 March 1988.
53. *Pravda*, 29 July 1989.
54. S. Shatalin, *Kommunist* (theoretical journal of the CPSU), No 14, 1986.
55. T. Zaslavskaya, *Kommunist*, No 13, 1986.
56. See D. Filtzer, *Soviet Workers and Stalinist Industrialisation – the Formation of Modern Soviet Production Relations*, Pluto Press 1986.
57. J. L. Porket, 'Unemployment in the midst of waste', *Survey*, Vol 29, No 1, Spring 1985.
58. V. Tsybukh speaking on Central Television, 1 August 1989. Cited in *Report on the USSR*, No 34, 25 August 1989.
59. *Financial Times – East European Markets*, Vol 9, 16/11, August 1989.
60. *Financial Times – East European Markets*.
61. See interview with leading Soviet 'democrat', Anotoly Vaksburg in *The Observer*, 12 February, 1989. He says, 'We are afraid of certain words, there are cases of unemployment already, but it's not a word that can be used. So we resort to euphemisms such as "redistribution of labour". Competition

for jobs is necessary for raising one's living standards. The problem is how to motivate workers who know that "if they push me too hard, there's always a job next door".' He also complains that 'the economy needs objective laws, but it's governed by theoretical ones.'

62. V. Kostakov, *Sovetskaya kultura*, 4 January 1986.
63. See first quarter economic report in *Financial Times – East European Markets*, Vol 9, 16/11, August 1989.
64. T. Zaslavskaya, *Kommunist*, No 13, 1986.
65. J. Tedstrom, 'Managing price reform in the Soviet Union', in *Radio Liberty Research Bulletin*, RL 319/88.
66. Y. Ligachev in *Pravda*, 1986.
67. Chubakov, *Voprosi ekonomiki*, 59, January 1987.
68. J. Tedstrom, 'Recent trends in the Soviet economy' in *Report on the USSR*, 3 February 1989.
69. T. Zaslavskaya cited in *Comparative Economic Studies*, Vol 31, No 1, Spring 1989.
70. J.L. Porket, *Communist Economies*, Vol 1, No 2, 1989.
71. A. Aganbegyan, *Newsweek*, 13 March 1989.
72. J. Tedstrom, 'Recent trends in the Soviet economy'.
73. *Trud*, 25 July 1989.
74. *Guardian*, 4 October 1989.
75. *The Times*, 3 October 1989.
76. *The Times*, 2 October 1989.
77. *Izvestia*, 16 August 1989 (morning edition).
78. *BBC Summary of World Broadcasts*, 1989, SU/0524.
79. *Guardian*, 4 October 1989.
80. *Guardian*, 4 October 1989.
81. *Guardian*, 11 September 1989.
82. *Sobesednik*, No 39, September 1987.
83. *Sobesednik*, No 39.
84. *Sobesednik*, No 39.
85. *Radyanska Ukraina*, 10 August 1989.
86. Donetsk Scientific Centre report cited in *Report on the USSR*, No 36, 8 September 1989.
87. *Los Angeles Times*, 18 September 1988.
88. *The Times*, 11 September 1989.
89. *BBC Summary of World Broadcasts*, 1989, SU/0568.
90. *BBC Summary of World Broadcasts*, 1989, SU/0568.
91. *BBC Summary of World Broadcasts*, 1989, SU/0568.
92. See this book, Chapter 3, 'The upsurge in the national republics.
93. M. Walker, *Guardian*, 4 November 1989.

3 The Upsurge in the National Republics

The 1990s opened with an upsurge of nationalist movements in the Soviet Union. The Kremlin was obliged to send the Soviet army into Azerbaijan to contain the instability unleashed by fierce internecine strife between Azeris and Armenians in the oil centre of Baku and in the disputed Armenian enclave of Nagorno Karabakh. Gorbachev himself visited Lithuania in an attempt to head off the movement for independence in the Baltic republics, and was forced to concede local demands for a referendum on the secession of the local Communist Party from the Soviet party. Meanwhile, in the Ukraine, the second most populous and economically important Soviet republic, the bureaucracy itself has encouraged the revival of the nationalist movement as well as the long-dormant Uniate Church.

The re-emergence of nationalist movements in the Soviet Union is a result of chronic economic stagnation and the decline of central bureaucratic control. The crisis of the Soviet system under Gorbachev has encouraged the various national republics to move even further away from Moscow's influence to pursue their own course of development. The tendency of the local bureaucrats to turn to nationalist movements to strengthen their own legitimacy in face of the collapsing authority of the Stalinist order has only exacerbated the process of fragmentation. The consequences have been different in different areas of the Soviet Union, according to the extent of social and economic disintegration, the relative strengths of the bureaucracy and nationalist movements and the influence of diverse local cultural traditions. However, the decisive factor in provoking nationalist tensions to the point of violent conflict has generally been the role of the local Stalinist bureaucracy.

We can divide the Soviet Union's fractious national minorities into three broad camps. In the Baltic republics of Estonia, Latvia, and Lithuania, the steady spread of market forces has created a substantial base of support for strongly pro-capitalist nationalist movements which have pushed the local bureaucrats towards breaking links with Moscow and building closer ties with the West. In the core republics – Byelorussia and, most importantly, the Ukraine – local bureaucrats themselves have taken the initiative in reviving relatively weak nationalist movements as a means of containing popular revolt against austerity. In the Caucasian republics of Georgia, Armenia and Azerbaijan, the weakness of the local bureaucracies has led them to cultivate militant nationalist and religious sentiments in an attempt to contain high levels of popular discontent at the disastrous local consequences of Gorbachev's perestroika programme. The effect in Azerbaijan was to unleash a wave of sectarian animosity against the generally more prosperous Armenian minority, which rapidly degenerated into pogroms and chaos.

The working class plays an important role in the republics, but generally in a subordinate relationship to the nationalist movements and the local bureaucracy. The effect of rising nationalism is to create even further division and confusion in the ranks of the Soviet proletariat. In Azerbaijan, for example, industrial action by Azeri railworkers effectively cut off Armenia in 1989, keeping nationalist hysteria on both sides at fever pitch. In the Baltics, by contrast, the substantial Russian working class has taken strike action for their own voting and language rights in defiance of the staunchly anti-working-class nationalist movements. In the Ukraine, the victory of the miners' strike in the summer of 1989 was a major factor in pushing the bureaucracy to promote the unifying propaganda of Ukrainian and pan-Slav nationalism.

More than 70 years after the Russian Revolution offered the right to national self-determination to the national republics, the national question has again come to the fore in the Soviet Union. This is a direct consequence of the violation of this principle and the cynical manipulation of national minorities in the Soviet Union throughout the Stalinist period. The impact of perestroika has been to encourage the tendency towards the Balkanisation of the Soviet Union, its fragmentation into 15 separate national republics and more than 100 ethnic minorities. If this tendency continues it can only strengthen the capitalist world at the expense of the Soviet Union and weaken the potential unity and common purpose of the Soviet working class. Let's look more closely at the process of national fragmentation in the three areas we have identified.

The Baltic republics

Gorbachev's dramatic plea in January 1990 to the people of Lithuania not to begin the breakup of the Soviet Union by voting to leave the Soviet Communist Party revealed the growing threat of Baltic nationalism to the Soviet state. The underlying problem facing Gorbachev is that Kremlin rule enjoys no legitimacy in any of the republics of Estonia, Latvia or Lithuania. This is the result of the historical legacy of Stalinist rule and the particular impact of the Gorbachev reforms in a region which was never fully incorporated into the Soviet state.

The Baltic states provide a classical illustration of the difference between the Leninist approach to the national question and the Stalinist approach. In 1920, the newly established Bolshevik government endorsed the right to self-determination of the bourgeois republics of Estonia, Latvia and Lithuania. Lenin's aim was to promote good relations with these states and increase the influence of revolutionary politics in their working class movements. These states remained independent until 1940 when they were occupied by Stalin after his non-aggression pact with Hitler's Germany. For Stalin, the national rights of the Baltic states and the concerns of the working class in the area were subordinate to the immediate tactical requirements of the regime in Moscow. When Hitler subsequently turned to attack the Soviet Union they were taken over by the Nazis until they were re-occupied by Soviet forces in 1944. As part of the post-war agreement among Churchill, Truman and Stalin, the Baltic republics were incorporated into the Soviet Union. Thus Soviet rule in these areas was not the result of revolution or popular choice, but the outcome of military occupation and superpower diplomacy.

The Soviet command economy model was imposed on the Baltic states in the 1940s and 1950s, but much less rigorously than it had been in the Soviet Union a decade earlier. In the climate of East-West Cold War, Stalin was more concerned with ensuring political stability by deporting potential opponents than he was with transforming economic and social relations.[1] Indeed the collectivisation of agriculture did not begin until 1949, and it then proceeded in a rather half-hearted manner:

> By the end of 1950 90 per cent of all farms in Lithuania were collectivised, but the collectivisation drive could hardly be termed a success. A surprising number of kolkhozy [collective

farms] were only nominally collective, for their members continued to work exclusively on their former land, using their own agricultural implements, draught horses and other inventory.[2]

Hence the private sector was never liquidated in the Baltic states in the same way as it had been in the Soviet Union. Throughout the 1950s, three-quarters of the annual average income of a Lithuanian collective farmer came from his private plot.

When the Soviet leadership turned, after Stalin's death in 1953, to investigate the potential of market reforms to revive its flagging economy, the Baltic states were a natural choice for experiments in reform. In 1958 Estonia became the first place in the Soviet Union where money wages were paid to kolkhoz workers. In 1967, when 390 *sovkhoz* (state farms) in the Soviet Union were put on a self-management experiment, all Estonia's 168 *sovkhoz* were involved (43 per cent of the total). By 1972, the income of Estonian collective farmers had surpassed that of urban workers for the first time. The source of their wealth was not agriculture, however, but light industry. It formed 14 per cent of Estonia's total 'agricultural' production that year:

By 1970, many Baltic collective farms derived most of their profits from mills, canneries, wine factories, and mineral-water bottling. They made furniture, bakery products, barbed wire, special rails, and various wooden and metal consumer goods ... Some kolkhozes built their own stores in the cities. The kolkhozes were supposed to use only their own labour and agricultural raw materials but in practice successful farms often bought raw materials from other farms and brought in city labour ...[3]

Compared with other regions of the Soviet Union, the Baltic economies have flourished. Estonia, Latvia and Lithuania all produce manufactured goods and export them to the West. They have all built up close economic ties with the Scandinavian countries.

The long-established traditions of private enterprise and industry in the Baltic states encouraged the emergence of a substantial social layer of relatively prosperous managers of collective farms and industries. This section of society inevitably resented Moscow's incompetent and bureaucratic interference and increasingly looked across the Baltic Sea towards Scandinavia as a more attractive model of development. However, the forces pushing towards greater autonomy for the Baltic states were also sympathetic towards that section of the Soviet bureaucracy which sought to extend market forces throughout the Soviet Union – the section that brought Gorbachev to power in 1985.

Unlike elsewhere in the Soviet Union, in the Baltic states Gorbachev's perestroika merely ratified an economic system that had already informally come into operation. Hence it was greeted here with enthusiasm by the emerging middle strata and, at least at first, it caused little disruption or controversy. Indeed Gorbachev encouraged Baltic moves towards greater economic autonomy. For Moscow the highly market-oriented economies of the Baltics, with their relatively well-stocked shops and well-fed people, offered a model of the potential of perestroika for the rest of the Soviet Union. The Kremlin was only too keen for local entrepreneurs to take some of the load off the stagnating centre by extending the role of the local economy. This convergence of interests between Moscow and the Baltic states ensured that a fairly harmonious relationship prevailed in the early days of perestroika.

However by 1987 the failure of the policies of perestroika in the Soviet Union were widely apparent in continuing stagnation and the disintegration of central planning. The result in the Baltic states was rising nationalist sentiments and growing resentment towards Moscow. Whereas Baltic entrepreneurs in 1985 and 1986 were willing to give Gorbachev a chance, by 1987 and 1988 their growing frustrations with the failures of reform and their aspirations for closer relations with the West were expressed in the re-emergence of powerful nationalist movements.

In response to the declining legitimacy of the beleaguered Soviet leadership, local Baltic bureaucrats increasingly adapted to the dynamic nationalist movements. In the spring of 1989, the Estonian Popular Front refrained from putting up candidates to the new Soviet parliament when the local Communist Party agreed to represent its views. When even official Communist Party papers could increase their circulation by echoing nationalist criticisms of the Party, it was not surprising that there was little demand for independent papers.[4] By the end of 1989 the Estonian Communist Party was well on its way to transforming itself into the party of the Estonian middle class.

There remain, however, three important obstacles to the Baltic states' drive towards independence, one strategic, one economic, the other social. The strategic difficulty facing the Baltic states is the question of how they would defend their national security if they were no longer under the protection of Moscow. The fear of a return to their traditional vulnerability to local power struggles underlines their hesitancy in proclaiming independence from the Soviet Union in matters of defence and foreign policy. The economic obstacle is the extent to which the Baltic states have become integrated into the Soviet Union. Though the Stalinist yoke fell less heavily on Estonia, Latvia and Lithuania than other parts of the Soviet Union, they have been tied into the Soviet economy much more tightly than the countries of Eastern Europe. Thus these republics are heavily dependent on the Soviet Union for their energy and raw material requirements.

The social obstacle is the working class, the majority of which is made up of Russian immigrants. Ethnic Russians constitute more than a quarter of the population of Estonia, nearly one third that of Latvia and less than 10 per cent that of Lithuania. Though nationalists have accused the Soviet government of a deliberate policy of 'Russification', most immigrants over the past 20 years have come voluntarily in response to an acute labour shortage in the Baltic states, either spontaneously or in response to recruitment campaigns offering housing as well as jobs.[5] The result, at least in Estonia, appears to have been more 'Estonianisation' than 'Russification' as Russian workers have settled, inter-married and assimilated.[6] Nor have Russian workers received any special privileges; on the contrary, a Western account of Kopli, the Russian part of Tallinn, describes it as a 'ghetto' where people live in a state of 'obvious poverty' that doesn't exist elsewhere in the 'well-groomed' Estonian capital.[7]

Despite the anti-immigrant prejudice that has long flourished in the Baltic republics, Russian workers were at first sympathetic to the nationalist movements because of their strongly anti-bureaucratic rhetoric. However, as relations between Moscow and the Baltic states deteriorated, two factors caused a shift in workers' allegiances. First, increasing nationalist hostility towards the Soviet leadership led to Estonian insistence that factory managers should be appointed in Tallinn, not Moscow, and that they should speak Estonian. This move, due to have taken effect from early 1990, was a direct threat to the livelihood of a substantial number of Russian managers. They responded by backing the pro-Moscow 'Interfront' movement. Second, given the increasingly anti-communist and pro-capitalist direction of the nationalist movements, they also began to express a more explicitly anti-immigrant and anti-working-class outlook. In Estonia, for example, the pro-nationalist

the toughest nationalists to agree to a softening of the congress resolutions.'[12]

The Kiev moderates also persuaded the Western Ukrainians to accept concessions on the language question for the sake of collaboration with the miners' committees in the Donbas. Miners' representatives further warned the conference that 'if the Ukrainian nationalist symbols of the blue and yellow flag were adopted, the movement would be rejected by the Russian-speaking Donbas.'

The success of the Ruch congress convinced the Kiev bureaucrats that the nationalist movement could help them regain their grip over the working class. A satisfied Gorbachev commented on the September events in the Ukraine: 'Either we recognise the right of others to independent thought and actions and engage in vigorous activities to win over public opinion ... or we shall become an isolated organisation while claiming a leading role.'[13]

Before the miners' strikes the Kiev bureaucracy was concerned that there were too many nationalists in the Ukraine. Now they found that there were too few, especially in the Eastern Ukraine. Gorbachev has shown no qualms about stirring up the atavistic chauvinism of the Western Ukraine to further his own interests.

The revival of the Uniate Church in Ukraine is another feature of the Gorbachev strategy to improve the local prestige of the Stalinist bureaucracy. Suppressed by Stalin in 1948 because of its support for Ukrainian nationalist resistance to Soviet domination, the Uniate Church went underground. It continued to follow its orthodox rituals while giving allegiance to Rome, with a loyal following confined largely to older peasants in the Western Ukraine, and the support of anti-Soviet expatriates in the West. However, one week after the Ruch congress in Kiev, tens of thousands of Western Ukrainians were permitted to demonstrate in Lvov, demanding the legalisation of the Uniate Church. Moscow relaxed proscriptions on the Uniates to prepare the way for Gorbachev's trip to the Vatican and an audience with Pope John Paul II in November 1989.

If all goes according to plan, Ruch and the Uniate Church will duplicate the role of Solidarity and the Catholic Church in neighbouring Poland. Gorbachev hopes that they will act as a force for moderation among the Ukrainian masses, and provide useful allies for the Kiev bureaucracy. A representative of the new Solidarity government in Poland, Adam Michnik, was allowed to attend the Ruch congress by the authorities, in a heavy-handed hint to ensure that the local bureaucrats got the Kremlin's message: nationalist unity is the only available way to contain working-class resistance. The fact that the Soviet bureaucracy has been forced to adopt the high-risk strategy of promoting the potentially hostile forces of Ukrainian nationalism is evidence of its profound unease at the prospect of further working-class unrest.

Whereas Baltic nationalism expresses the fragmentation of the Soviet bureaucracy, the nationalist resurgence in the Ukraine has been deliberately sponsored by the central bureaucracy. Though there is a possibility that a genuine Ukrainian nationalist movement may take off, there is no social basis for it at present in any part of the Ukraine. On the other hand, there is a basis for uniting bureaucrats and nationalists around a pan-Slav platform to force through perestroika against working-class resistance. According to historical tradition, pan-Slavism emphasises the union of Russia and the Ukraine, and holds that Moscow is the 'Third Rome' (after Rome itself and Constantinople). The fact that the working class in the Ukraine is the direct object of political attack for the new nationalist alliance underlines the urgency of strengthening the unity of the Soviet working class through resisting the divisive propaganda of pan-Slavic nationalism.

The Caucasian republics

The most explosive conflicts in Moscow's national republics have been in the Caucasian regions of Georgia, Armenia and Azerbaijan. Here the manipulative role of the local Stalinist bureaucracies in relation to the nationalist movements has been most apparent and most destructive in its consequences. The dangers of inter-communal strife are particularly acute in the Caucasian republics because of the relative lack of ethnic homogeneity of each country. All three republics contain substantial minorities of the other nationalities as well as numerous other linguistic and religious groupings. In Georgia, for example, there are substantial numbers of Armenians, Russians and Azeris as well as Ossetians, Abkhazians and others. The division between the predominantly Christian Georgians and Armenians and the Muslim Azeris raises a religious conflict with wider implications for the republics of Soviet Central Asia and the whole of the Middle East.

It is ironic that the Caucasian republics should have become the focus of demands for secession from Moscow, because all three republics have strong traditions of loyalty to the Soviet Union going back to the 1917 Revolution. Many leading Bolsheviks were Armenian and even a hostile Armenian émigré is prepared to acknowledge the extent of local sympathy for the Revolution:

The communist dictatorship in Armenia encountered after 1921 and into Stalinist times less resistance than in Russia ... The bulk of the intellectuals served the Soviet Armenian authorities and many of them seemed to have been converted to communism. In Armenia (and Georgia) there were more native communists than in other non-Slav republics of the Soviet Union.[14]

After centuries of oppression and the experience of mass slaughter at the hands of the Turks in 1915, the Armenians have found greater security and national recognition within the Soviet Union than at any time in their history. As late as 1976 more than 10 per cent of Armenians were card-carrying Communist Party members, the second highest rate in the Soviet Union – after Georgia.[15] Of course, Stalin himself was a Georgian, as is the former Soviet foreign minister Eduard Shevardnadze. Azeris in Soviet Azerbaijan have long enjoyed higher living standards and greater civil liberties than their compatriots in Turkey or Iran; the Stalinist-sponsored 'socialist republic' incorporating the Azeri population of northern Iran in the 1940s enjoyed lasting local popularity.

The Caucasian republics were fully integrated into the Soviet system from the 1930s onwards. Market relations were eradicated, agriculture was collectivised and industrialisation launched. All three republics suffered the resulting prolonged economic stagnation and tendencies towards economic autarchy throughout the post-war period. One response to the chaotic character of the Soviet economic system that became particularly highly developed in the Caucasian republics was the black market. Through informal trading, largely in consumer goods, a significant number of traders amassed substantial fortunes while the majority endured shortages and hardship. In Georgia, for example, between 1960 and 1971 national income grew by 102 per cent, the third lowest rate of any region in the Soviet Union. However in 1970 the average Georgian savings account stood at nearly twice the Soviet average. According to the American academic R.G. Suny, the discrepancy was attributable to 'a vast network of illegal economic operations and exchanges, which produced great private wealth for some citizens while their republic grew insignificantly'.[16]

The informal economy in the Caucasian republics had a quite different character from the flourishing market sector in the Baltic states. There, private wealth was based on the development of market relations outside the official economy and entrepreneurs remained aloof from the Stalinist bureaucracy. In the Caucasian

region, traders operated in a symbiotic relationship with the mainstream economy and maintained close relations with the local
party hierarchy. They thrived during the Brezhnev years of stagnation, while Moscow tolerated the expansion of the black market
activities, hoping that they would provide the sort of incentive to
higher productivity that the centralised economy could not. The
arrival of Gorbachev reversed relations between Moscow and the
Caucasian traders: his anti-corruption drive explicitly targeted
'southern millionaires' and scapegoated them for the wider failures
of the system.

Because of the particular character of the Caucasian economies,
the disintegration of the Soviet system in the late 1980s had a
more destabilising effect here than in the other republics. Though
the close links between the black marketeers and the bureaucracy
provided some protection for them, the Stalinist leaderships could
not soften the impact of the crisis on the masses. The absence of a
private sector in agriculture and industry meant that there was no
middle-class stratum that could act as a buffer between the bureaucracy and the increasingly impoverished masses. In the Azerbaijani
capital of Baku, the authorities were confronted in 1988 with
falling oil revenues, an unemployment rate of 12 per cent and
growing poverty:

> Unemployed villagers come to the city in search of jobs. Unable
> to get permanent employment or residence permits to live in
> the city, they have built a shanty town on the outskirts of Baku.
> More than 200,000 people – a quarter of the city's population –
> now live there in unauthorised structures that went up over-
> night and are unfit for human habitation ... Embarrassed city
> authorities have put up a high wall to hide it.[17]

Faced with economic decay and rising mass unrest, local Stalinist
leaders in the Caucasian states turned to the previously marginal,
intelligentsia-based, nationalist movements in an attempt to divert
and contain popular dissatisfaction.

In Georgia, the nationalist movement was so weak in 1988 that
it did not even attempt to contest the elections to the Supreme
Soviet. Instead nationalists recommended support for a sympathetic party candidate Aki Bakhradze. Yet it was in Tbilisi, the
capital of Georgia, that Soviet troops were involved in the first
major repression in the national republics in recent years, in April
1989. A nationalist demonstration was attacked by soldiers
wielding sharpened shovels and other improvised weapons,

leaving 20 dead. It was significant that the occasion of the demonstration was not to demand independence for Georgia, but to protest against the claims for autonomy within Russia from the Abkhazian minority on the Black Sea coast in the north.

In Armenia the local bureaucracy first took up the issue of Nagorno Karabakh, the disputed Armenian enclave in Azerbaijan, in January 1988 in response to Gorbachev's anti-corruption drive. Aimed at officials who took advantage of their positions to engage in profiteering, it was a direct threat to many party leaders. However, at a time of deepening economic crisis and mass alienation from the Soviet system, the bureaucrats' endorsement of nationalist protests demanding the return of Karabakh to Armenia unleashed forces beyond their control. Faced with escalating mass demonstrations in the Armenian capital of Yerevan, the Armenian leadership was forced to turn to Moscow to endorse martial law rather than risk an insurrection.

The early nationalist slogan 'Karabakh – the test of glasnost' soon changed to 'Perestroika through fascism' after Soviet troops attacked a demonstration at Yerevan airport in July 1988, killing one person. Though they began as moderates, the Armenian nationalists were pushed by the masses into an increasingly anti-Soviet direction. At the end of 1988 the authorities felt obliged to suppress the movement and in March 1989 they modified the electoral regulations to deal with the threat of a massive nationalist boycott. If playing the nationalist card in Armenia proved a high-risk strategy for the local bureaucracy, it had even more explosive consequences in neighbouring Azerbaijan.

In addition to sparking off conflict between Armenians and Azeris in Nagorno Karabakh itself, the mass demonstrations in Yerevan stirred anti-Armenian resentment throughout Azerbaijan, particularly in Baku, where many Armenians occupy relatively privileged positions in trade, industry and the professions. In February 1988 a savage anti-Armenian pogrom in the port of Sumgait near Baku left several hundred dead. Another pogrom in Baku itself in November 1988, just before the earthquake in Armenia, provoked anti-Azeri atrocities in Armenia. The result was a massive exchange of population as around 200,000 people fled in each direction seeking the safety of their own communities.

For its part the Stalinist leadership in Azerbaijan was not slow to take advantage of sectarian strife. When unemployment skyrocketed in the oilfields around Baku, the Azeri authorities sought to scapegoat the Armenian community. By manipulating ethnic tensions between Armenians and Azerbaijanis, Moscow has so far managed to keep control over the crisis while avoiding attracting any blame itself. In January 1989 Moscow imposed direct rule over Nagorno Karabakh only to hand control back to Azerbaijan in November, a move that could only exacerbate local tensions. When Armenians began to import arms on a large scale Azeri resentment multiplied. Industrial action by Azeri oil and transport workers over Nagorno-Karabakh finally broke Moscow's grip. When workers extended strike action to a blockade of Armenia, the Soviet economy itself began to feel the pinch. When the Soviet parliament voted to ban strikes in key industries in October 1989, both oil and rail were covered and special permission was granted to the Kremlin to use troops to break the Azeri blockade. The challenge of the popular front to Soviet rule brought the intervention of the army which showed little hesitation in crushing the nationalist revolt.

Two features of the Soviet clampdown in Azerbaijan were striking. The first was the way in which it appeared to legitimise the explicitly anti-Islamic prejudices that were increasingly expressed by the Soviet leadership through 1989. In February Soviet ideology spokesman Vladimir Efimov claimed that 'the Christian heritage is part of our national culture. It is not in contradiction with the socialist character of our society.'[18] In June Gorbachev asserted that Muslim fundamentalism had 'bared its teeth' after riots in the Muslim republic of Uzbekistan, and he frequently emphasises his concern about the Soviet Union's role in a 'common European home', leaving Moscow's vast Asian territories out of the picture. The Kremlin's formerly neutral pose in the Trans-Caucasian republics changed from that of 'peacekeeping referee' to that of 'Holy Moscow' fighting to protect the Christian Armenians against the forces of Islam.

The second feature is the way that Gorbachev's deployment of the army in Azerbaijan has won widespread support in the West. There is a general consensus among the Western powers that Gorbachev should be supported as the best way of maintaining stability in a potentially explosive region. This is not only because of a strong common prejudice against Islam and a common fear of the dangers of working-class revolt. There is also a strong tendency developing among those Western powers (the US, Britain, France) that are likely to lose out from any scramble for a disintegrated Eastern bloc to prefer that the Soviet bureaucracy remained in place, rather than let their rivals (West Germany, Japan) draw any benefits from its collapse.

Conclusion

The effect of the Gorbachev reform process in the Soviet Union's national republics has been to intensify the tendencies towards fragmentation that were always implicit in Stalinist adaptations towards regional nationalism. To maintain the interests of the Soviet bureaucracy Stalin was prepared to suppress national rights, as in the forcible incorporation of the Baltic states in 1940. He was also prepared to make substantial concessions to national minorities to stabilise relations with Moscow, by acknowledging minority languages and cultural customs and by promoting minority representatives to prominent positions in the local party hierarchy. In recent years the latter trend has come to the fore to such an extent that it would be difficult to talk of any systematic tendency towards Soviet oppression in the national republics: living standards are often higher than in Russia itself and, as we have seen, nationalist movements are not only tolerated but often sponsored by the local bureaucracies.

The major factor in the current eruption of nationalist sentiment in the republics is the role of regional Stalinist leaderships in promoting national demands as a means of overcoming their own unpopularity. Now that Stalinism has been discredited, nationalism is the only available alternative source of legitimacy. Thus the national movements in the republics do not simply represent the aspirations of local people to be free of Moscow's domination. In many cases national demands and national prejudices have been stirred up and manipulated by local Stalinist officials for their own purposes.

The fragmentation of the Soviet Union along national lines would unleash a process of Balkanisation and confuse the class struggle still further. Each republic would inevitably come under the control of its own national movement and then become subject to the depredations of rival imperialist powers – a return to the state of affairs that prevailed in the Balkans for 40 years before the First World War and throughout Eastern Europe in the interwar period. Nationalism would assume even greater prominence. Competition among the different countries over trade and natural resources would exacerbate national conflicts even more. The result would be a working class even more divided and confused than it is at present.

The solution to the national question in the Soviet Union lies in the creation of a federation of autonomous, self-governing republics, with equal rights in all aspects of political and cultural life. Such a federation can only be forged through a united action by workers in Russia and the national republics against the bureaucracy which continues to manipulate nationalist sentiment in an attempt to maintain its grip over the Soviet Union as a whole.

Notes

1. Both Britain and America were infiltrating agents into the Baltic until well into the mid-1950s. See T. Bowyer, *The Red Web*, Aurum Press, 1989.
2. K.K. Girnius, 'The Collectivisation of Lithuanian Agriculture', in *Soviet Studies*, Glasgow, July 1989, p. 461.
3. R.J. Misunias and R. Taagepera, *The Baltic States – Years of Dependence, 1940–80*, London: C. Hurst & Co., 1983, p. 220.
4. *New York Review of Books*, 28 September 1989.
5. Misunias and Taagepera, *The Baltic States*, p. 227.
6. See T.U. Raun, *Estonia and the Estonians*, Stanford, California: Hoover Institution Press, 1987, p. 205.
7. *Guardian*, 17 August 1989.
8. *Guardian*, 12 August 1989.
9. *Independent*, 30 August 1989.
10. *Guardian*, 10 May 1989.
11. *Newsweek*, 25 September 1989.
12. *International Viewpoint*, 16 October 1989.
13. *Morning Star*, 2 October 1989.
14. M. Sarkisyanz, *Modern History of Trans-Caucasian Armenia*, Nagpur, India: Udyama Commercial Press, 1975, p. 273–4.
15. David Lane, *Soviet Economy and Society*, Oxford: Basil Blackwell, 1985, p. 229.
16. R.G. Suny, *The Making of the Georgian Nation*, Indiana: Indiana University Press, 1988, p. 304.
17. Alex Amerisov, 'What About the Workers?', in *New Internationalist*, December 1988.
18. A. Taheri, *Crescent in a Red Sky*, London: Hutchinson, 1989, p. 180.

4 Eastern Europe in Ferment

The key ingredients for change in the Communist world are already well identified, the recipe lifted from a Western cookbook for democracy. Separate Party from State. Add opposition parties and free elections to State. Briskly mix in press, speech and travel freedoms. Top with rights to assemble, strike and form labor unions. Bake in oven turned to Free Enterprise setting. Then hope that the inevitable spillover of chaos – including the inevitable hard economic times – doesn't cause the Democracy Souffle to fall.[1]

In the late 1980s remarkable events became commonplace in Eastern Europe. These were times when a Soviet president could send a telegram congratulating a Communist Party on abolishing itself;[2] when a right-wing Catholic intellectual could become the first non-communist prime minister of an Eastern bloc country in 40 years;[3] when those who built the Berlin Wall could abolish the physical division of Germany overnight.

In the course of 1989 the Stalinist regimes simply crumbled one by one as a result of a remarkable combination of internal moral disintegration and mass popular pressure. In Poland the freest elections for 40 years resulted in the formation of a government led by the opposition movement Solidarity. In Hungary the Communist Party abandoned its leaders, its name and its factory cells and declared free elections in the hope of clinging on to power. In the German Democratic Republic the regime was forced to sacrifice its veteran leader, and then within weeks his successor; it was forced too to tolerate opposition parties and to organise free elections. In Czechoslovakia the old guard capitulated and opposition leader Vaclav Havel became president pending elections. In Bulgaria Premier Zhivkov was ousted and in Romania, Ceausescu was summarily shot at the height of a brief but bloody revolt.

In a few months the characteristics that had defined the countries of the Eastern bloc since the Stalinist post-war takeover were suddenly reversed. Dependence on Moscow was abandoned as each country pursued its distinctive course, with national flags prominently displayed in mass demonstrations. The leading role of the party was replaced with a new spirit of pluralism as old parties re-emerged and new movements took shape. The fusion of party and state was dissolved as party machines disintegrated. The climate of repression evaporated as open debate and free newspapers proliferated: only the old agents of the security apparatuses had much to fear. Market relations, long allowed only restricted operation, were now greeted as the vital forces of the post-Stalinist order. Before examining the forces behind these cataclysmic events, let's look more closely at some of the key aspects of the collapse of the Eastern bloc.

The collapse of the Eastern bloc

Once the reform process got under way in Eastern Europe in the late 1980s it rapidly became apparent that none of the long-standing characteristics of these societies was inviolable. Indeed, once the lack of legitimacy of these regimes became apparent the only constant feature was the speed of their passing.

The end of the party

Polish premier General Jaruzelski was typical of the new generation of Eastern European rulers who recognised the inevitability of reform and the need to adapt to the opposition movement. Hence the man who had imposed martial law to crush the Solidarity movement in 1981 had by 1988 become a staunch supporter of Gorbachev who was ready to do business with Solidarity leader Lech Walesa.[4] Spurred on by two major strike waves, the Polish party leadership agreed to 'round table' talks with Solidarity early in 1989. The talks led to a famous agreement to stage Eastern Europe's first partially free post-war elections.[5] However Poland's reforming Stalinists miscalculated the degree of popular hostility to their regime. Even in seats reserved only for official party candidates not enough people voted to put the Stalinists into the new parliament. Jaruzelski candidly admitted that 'our defeat is total, a political solution will have to be found.'[6]

Jaruzelski's solution was a coalition with Solidarity. After much haggling, Catholic intellectual Tadeusz Mazowiecki became Poland's first non-communist prime minister for more than 40 years. What had started out as a plan to stabilise the rule of the bureaucracy ended up almost destroying it. The communist monopoly of government power had been severely curtailed.

In Hungary the regime had led the way in introducing market reforms in the early 1980s. Figures in the reformist wing of the leadership like Imre Pozsgay put growing pressure on the old guard and even went as far as participating in the setting up of new opposition groups.[7] However the rapidity of subsequent change exceeded even the wildest expectations of the reformers. Hoping to avoid the Polish debacle, they decided to hold free elections but to enter them with a completely refurbished and de-Stalinised party. In the event the reconstitution of the old Hungarian Socialist Workers (Communist) Party turned out to be a disaster. The new product, rechristened the Hungarian Socialist Party, looked little different from the old as hardline Stalinist factions refused to leave. Its electoral prospects seemed little better than those of the Polish Stalinists.

The collapse of the East German Communist Party was in many ways the most remarkable. An official visit by Gorbachev in September 1989 met with widespread acclaim but also increased the pressure for change. A mass illegal exodus of refugees to the West via a liberalised Hungary revealed the extent of popular disillusionment and once again raised the spectre of the end of the East German state as a separate entity. Gorbachev publicly urged ageing hardline leader Erich Honecker to implement reforms before it was too late.[8] East Germany had long been seen as the core of a hardline anti-reform bloc within Comecon, including Czechoslovakia, Bulgaria and Romania. Even though all these regimes had introduced some reforms in an attempt to counteract economic decline, particular local circumstances precluded rapid political change along Polish or Hungarian lines.[9] Rulers of all four countries had always pursued harsh repressive policies to maintain domestic control. Sudden change risked serious instability.

In the end the East German regime was unable to resist the combined pressures of the refugee exodus and a wave of mass demonstrations. Honecker soon fell from power, leading to a succession of party purges in an attempt to shape a more credible ruling-party profile. As in Hungary and Poland attempts to stem the decline in the credibility of the ruling party soon led to open talk of more cooperation with respectable opposition forces like New Forum and the need for free elections. The opening of the Berlin Wall in November 1989 marked the end of East Germany's hardline reputation. The collapse of the remaining Eastern Communist Parties followed in rapid succession before Christmas.

The end of the absolutist state

There could be no more potent image of the collapse of the coercive Eastern European state than television pictures of people dancing through the Brandenburg Gate at the Berlin Wall on New Year's Eve 1989. What was once a section of the Iron Curtain to be breached only on pain of immediate execution had now become a symbol of the impotence of the old repressive apparatus.

The breaching of the Berlin Wall was anticipated by events in Poland and Hungary that were perhaps more difficult to capture on television, but no less dramatic. In these countries an end to the unified party-state machine followed closely after the introduction of pluralist democratic structures. At special conferences of the Polish Communist Party held early in 1989 to justify the coming round-table talks, party ideologues began to motivate a new separation between party and state. This was not just a cynical attempt to demonstrate the party's new-found democratic credentials. It also reflected the accelerating disintegration of the bureaucracy itself as it was forced to adapt to external events.[10] The new Mazowiecki coalition government began the task of destroying the party patronage machine which permeated every pore of Polish society. Everywhere the talk was of the need to reconstruct civil society – to recreate the informal social structures so long suppressed under the Stalinists.[11] When Hungary's HSWP abolished its party cells in workplaces in October 1989 it became clear that the old bureaucracy was preparing to relinquish its total control.

The reintroduction of the market

Events in Poland and Hungary showed that in the economic sphere developments were proceeding rapidly down the road to capitalist restoration. The Solidarity coalition government was quick to seek advice from experts on privatisation like the Thatcherite Adam Smith Institute which held a 'teach-in' in Warsaw in October 1989. The British government also promised to send out a team of 'privatisation experts' to advise on the transformation of the economy from communism to capitalism.[12] There was no argument within Solidarity about whether the capitalist market should be reintroduced. The only dispute was over the pace at which such a restoration should take place.[13] The first genuine signs of the new influence of the market in Polish life was the opening of several soup kitchens to feed the poor of Warsaw.[14]

The Hungarian socialists were not quite as radical in their economic prescriptions as the Polish supporters of a 'big bang' restoration of capitalism. The newly christened Hungarian Socialist Party merely called for the imposition of a 'mixed economy' with continued state intervention.

Forces for change

The most striking feature of the transformation of Eastern Europe in the late 1980s was the relatively low profile of mass popular resistance. Indeed the only country in which significant military activity – and consequent casualties – took place was Romania, the last regime to fall, at the very end of the decade. Mass demonstrations and industrial action were important components in the process of overthrowing the Stalinist regimes. In Poland for example, the 1988 strikes caused concern both to the government and to the leaders of Solidarity who feared losing control over the younger and more militant workers. In the GDR and Czechoslovakia daily demonstrations maintained public pressure on the regimes. However, these events were not decisive in initiating the disintegration of the old order. They simply accelerated an already existing crisis within the ruling bureaucracies.

It is important to note that the scale of popular upsurge in 1988–89 was generally smaller and more subdued than earlier Eastern bloc revolts. In the 1953 uprising in the GDR, workers burned police stations and party offices and even strung up secret policemen. The 1956 revolution in Hungary could only be put down when Soviet tanks devastated central Budapest and slaughtered 30,000 people. Even the Czechoslovak Prague Spring of 1968 and the Polish events of 1971 represented a qualitatively different kind of threat to the system. In all these cases uncontrollable mass movements either smashed the ruling bureaucracy or came very close to sweeping it away.[15]

The popular upsurges of 1988–89 were more restrained. There were no visible protest movements in Hungary – the first country to introduce radical changes – and only a small green movement in Bulgaria. In many cases the initiative for reform came from within the Stalinist bureaucracy itself and popular protest only gained momentum after the bureaucracy had made the first moves. Hungarian party politburo member Imre Pozsgay not only helped to form the oppositional Hungarian Democratic Forum, but he led the way in questioning the leading role of the party and demanding a public reassessment of the events of 1956.[16] Long before the 1988 strikes in Poland, Jaruzelski was pressing for the internal reforms in the Communist Party which cleared the way for a deal with the opposition and eventual elections.[17] In Czechoslovakia too changes were largely stage-managed as opposition leaders worked together with reformers inside the Party and a previous generation of purged Stalinists led by the former president Dubcek in an attempt to ensure a stable transition to a new order. Even in Romania, where workers took up arms alongside the army to fight against security forces loyal to Ceausescu, the short duration of the struggle – and the substantial element of continuity in the new caretaker regime – confirmed the strength of support for change within the old bureaucracy.

The sequence of events in East Germany, which triggered the removal of Bulgaria's Zhivkov and Czechoslovakia's Jakes within a week, provide a clue to the decisive factor in the events of Eastern Europe. Here it was Gorbachev's public warnings on an official state visit on the need for urgent change that encouraged the rise of the protest movement and the upheaval inside the party which led to the demise of Honecker. The transformation of Eastern Europe in 1988–89 was a direct consequence of the application of Gorbachev's approach of perestroika in the sphere of foreign policy.

Though Gorbachev came to power in 1985, changes in Soviet foreign policy took place only gradually following the consolidation of his position at home. However a meeting of top officials in July 1988 proclaimed Moscow's intention of making perestroika in diplomacy irreversible. The confrontational and interventionist style of the Brezhnev era was blamed for placing an excessive burden on the ailing Soviet economy. Gorbachev emphasised his determination to reduce Soviet expenditure abroad and his commitment to international peace and stability. While little real reform took place in the Soviet Union itself, Gorbachev rapidly became the darling of the Western media as he made one concession after another on his foreign visits.[18] The biggest challenge for the Soviet regime was to create a new relationship with Western Europe by promoting the process of reform in Eastern Europe.

Fearful that the Soviet Union and its Eastern bloc allies were being left out of the movement towards European integration, Gorbachev's new foreign policy strategists now argued that a future Soviet world role could only be built on the basis of renewed economic strength in Comecon itself.[19] They looked to Eastern Europe to provide a new conduit for modified diplomatic and economic arrangements with the West. Gorbachev hoped that modernised Eastern European regimes might provide the locomotive power to pull the whole bloc out of its state of decline.

Gorbachev was also concerned at growing signs of instability through Eastern Europe. Workers staged violent food riots at Brasov in Romania in 1987 and the scale of the 1988 Polish strikes threatened a rerun of events on the scale of the Solidarity upheavals of 1980–81. If Eastern Europe was to prove a secure ally and play its role in Gorbachev's new scheme of things, reform was needed to assure stability. The new line from Moscow therefore was to encourage each Eastern bloc country to follow its own path of development within the Warsaw Pact. But once it became clear that the Soviet Union would no longer intervene militarily to protect its client regimes against domestic revolt, their dependency on Moscow and their lack of legitimacy were exposed. It thus required only a slight push from below and they collapsed, virtually overnight. To appreciate the extraordinary fragility of the Eastern bloc regimes in the late 1980s it is necessary to look more closely at the emergence of the ruling bureaucracies, their relations with the Soviet Union and their own societies.

The origins of change

Western commentators have generally viewed the Eastern bloc as an unchanging monolith. The countries of Eastern Europe have long been regarded as faithful copies of the Soviet prototype, as stagnant and conformist societies ruled by austere and repressive bureaucracies and ultimately kept in line by the ever-present threat of Moscow's military might. Indeed the current realities of life and the post-war history of Eastern Europe all appear to confirm this impression. Television pictures of conditions in Silesia, Bohemia or Transylvania reveal societies in which time appears to have stood still for more than half a century. Khrushchev despatched the troops to Hungary in 1956 while his successor sent them into Czechoslovakia: Brezhnev gave his name to the doctrine which justified Soviet military intervention in Eastern Europe if Moscow considered that its interests were threatened. Only in the closing months of the 1980s did things seem to begin to change in Eastern Europe.

In fact the post-war history of Eastern Europe is more complex and diverse than the prevailing Western orthodoxy allows. Closer investigation helps to explain the extraordinary pace of events in 1988–89 and some key differences between the relatively slow impact of the Gorbachev reform process in the Soviet Union and its cataclysmic effects in Eastern Europe. We can discern five broad phases in the evolution of the Eastern bloc. In the first three years after the war, the Soviet Union consolidated its control. Between 1948 and 1956 there followed the classical period of Stalinist coercion. After the Hungarian revolution, the Soviet Union encouraged a process of carefully controlled reform; however, the onset of the world recession in 1973–74 exposed the economic stagnation of the whole Eastern bloc, forcing the Soviet bureaucracy into a desperate holding operation which continued until Gorbachev came to power in 1985 and the current phase of reform began. Let's look at each of these periods more closely.

The consolidation of Soviet control

The origins of the current shape of Eastern Europe can be traced to the February 1945 conference at Yalta which agreed on a 'friendly' division of the post-war world among the victorious Allied powers. American policy at Yalta was based on President Franklin D. Roosevelt's immediate preoccupation with maintaining good relations with the Soviet Union while the US had still to conclude its war in the Pacific. Roosevelt endorsed Stalin's plan for the integration of an Eastern Europe under Soviet domination into the post-war world order. His long-term perspective was that large-scale US aid to the Eastern bloc would gradually turn it capitalist.[20] However, as the US's position strengthened in the closing stages of the war, Roosevelt's successor Harry Truman went on the offensive against Stalin. The Potsdam conference in July 1945 reaffirmed Yalta but revealed growing Western pressure to reduce Moscow's sphere of influence. The subsequent pattern of Soviet domination of Eastern Europe was thus conditioned by growing American resistance.

Once Japan was crushed by the atomic bombs dropped on Hiroshima and Nagasaki in August 1945, US pressure on Stalin intensified. Eastern Europe now became a key focus of US foreign policy. The American propaganda war opened in early 1946 with the famous George Kennan telegram which codified US allegations of Moscow's expansionist tendencies. Churchill's 'iron curtain' speech at Fulton, Missouri in March 1946 merely gave Kennan's crude anti-Sovietism a more English literary gloss. The main themes in the subsequent Cold War that set the tone of East-West relations for the whole post-war period were that traditional-style diplomacy with the Soviet Union was impossible; that Western rearmament was justified by the necessity to protect the world from Soviet expansionism; and that any resistance to US interests amounted to communist subversion, and was probably directed from the Kremlin.[21]

In response to the US's mounting anti-communist hysteria, Stalin raised the stakes in Eastern Europe. He set out to forge a defensive buffer zone around the Soviet Union out of the states occupied by Soviet forces in their final counter-attack against Germany. While national peculiarities and widely varying conditions in post-war Eastern Europe need to be taken into account, all Stalin's puppet regimes had one thing in common. The communist governments which took power after the war were all a creation of the occupying Red Army: they had few roots in their societies.

Stalin was forced to rely on his military machine to consolidate a power base in Eastern Europe. As a result of a decade of fascist occupation, war and exile the influence of the old Communist Parties was at best tenuous. By the late 1930s most of the Communist Party leaders had fled to the Soviet Union, where they became victims of some of Stalin's most vicious purges. Almost all party activists with genuine roots among the masses were removed or even executed on Stalin's instructions, leaving only a servile rump in Moscow.

The Polish example was fairly typical. The Communist Workers Party of Poland (CWPP) has a long record of taking an independent stand against Stalin. In 1923 it had strongly opposed the Soviet bureaucracy's attempts to expel Trotsky from the Bolshevik party and openly denounced Stalin. The Soviet leadership was unable to stomach such a show of defiance and Stalin moved fast against the Polish party. Vulnerable because repression in Poland had forced many of its leaders into exile in Russia, the leadership was purged in 1924 without any consultation with the CWPP's own party congress. Subsequent purges took place in 1925, 1928 and 1932. In 1937–38 almost every Polish revolutionary in exile in Russia was either executed or jailed. Before the Second World War began the CWPP had effectively been destroyed.[22]

Together with the liquidation of the Communist Parties came the destruction of the world party of revolution. The Communist International, the Comintern of Lenin and Trotsky, was dissolved by Soviet fiat in 1943. Stalin replaced it with the more manageable Communist Information Bureau (Cominform) in October 1947.[23]

Even in those Eastern countries where there was a revolutionary upsurge at the end of the war, the remnants of the exiled Communist Parties had few links with the militant masses. Far from seeking to encourage the development of communist movements with genuine roots in the working class, Stalin was only interested in setting up regimes which were totally subservient to his defensive requirements.

In Bulgaria Soviet troops overturned a popular revolution, protected private property and supported an ex-fascist as head of a coalition government. In Romania the tame Communist Party was ordered into a coalition with ex-fascists, anti-Semites and persecutors of the left. Former fascists were permitted to join the party en masse. In Poland there was a revolutionary upsurge in Warsaw in August 1944 even before the German occupation forces had departed and when the Red Army was only 15 miles away. The programme of the leadership of the uprising called for agrarian reform, the socialisation of key industries and workers' control. This was too radical for Stalin who labelled it 'reactionary' and denounced the uprising as premature. The Red Army gave no assistance to the uprising and it was put down after 63 days with 240,000 killed. Stalin had allowed the destruction of the Polish uprising in order to facilitate his own eventual takeover.[24]

In circumstances of military devastation and economic collapse throughout Eastern Europe Stalin's forces proceeded to consolidate their position. In Romania, Bulgaria and Hungary the old ruling élites had been discredited by their alliances with the Nazi occupation forces. Poland's ruling class was decimated: 20 per cent of the entire Polish population was dead, its industry had been virtually destroyed and 45 per cent of Polish territory was absorbed by the Soviet Union. In all these countries war had put the state in command of the national economy. The situation was ripe for the imposition of Soviet-style states backed by the Red Army.

In the first step towards the goal of Soviet control communists entered so-called 'people's democratic' governments in coalition with other parties. The Communist Parties themselves generally held a minority of ministries but, with the crucial backing of the Soviet military, they kept control of key repressive machinery. The Stalinists gradually began to use their monopoly of terror to eliminate their opponents. Within three years of the end of the war a mixture of threats and bribes had ensured Communist Party control everywhere.

Recognising that the newly installed bureaucracies were isolated from the mass of the population, Stalin attempted to create a new social layer which would identify with the new parties and give them a more secure base. The Communist Parties were opened to all who wanted to join and they grew rapidly. Many also joined in response to the vision of progress promoted by the parties through state intervention. The relative political freedom permitted at the time contrasted favourably with the coercive nature of most pre-war regimes. The Communist Parties became vehicles through which to achieve social advancement as their leaders used them to play off different nationalities against each other and to grant privileges to some at the expense of others. Through such methods Stalin gained a temporary base of support for his newly imposed parties. More than 100,000 Germans were deported from Czechoslovakia and their property and land were given to Czech workers and peasants. In Poland too the party gained support through the redistribution of property and land regained from Germany.

By the end of 1947 Stalin's control over the Communist Parties of Eastern Europe meant control over the societies as well. Mass parties were temporarily created on the basis of a combination of repression and patronage. The economies of Bulgaria, Hungary and Romania were then nationalised and restructured in the Soviet image.[25]

However, the bureaucracy in Eastern Europe remained much weaker with a much narrower social base than that in the Soviet Union, a fact that has had a decisive bearing on recent developments. The Soviet bureaucracy began with the historic legitimacy of the Russian Revolution; while Stalin liquidated the last remnants of the Bolshevik tradition in the early 1930s he set about forging a new intelligentsia to provide a new base for the bureaucracy. Forced industrialisation and collectivisation created great scope for upward mobility through the party. By 1939 the Soviet intelligentsia, including their families, numbered some 10 million or 13 per cent of the population. A significant number of these had sufficient privileges guaranteed by the regime to give them a stake in its preservation. The persistence of this social base for the bureaucracy in the Soviet Union through the post-war period gave it a certain degree of immunity from the kind of rapid collapse experienced by the bureaucracies in Eastern Europe.

The period of classical Stalinism

The June 1948 rift between the Soviet Union and Yugoslavia marked a watershed in the development of Soviet domination over Eastern Europe. As a result of the success of the partisan resistance struggle during the Nazi occupation, the Yugoslav party enjoyed substantial domestic support and Tito's regime could take the most independent stand of all the Eastern European countries against Moscow. When Tito refused to submit to Stalin's master plan he was soon denounced as the pawn of Western intelligence services. Stalin regarded Tito's defiance as a dangerous precedent that could encourage nationalist resentment in every country dominated by the Red Army since 1945. Yugoslavia was expelled from the Cominform as the division of Eastern Europe hardened into what would become Nato and the Warsaw Pact.[26]

To avoid any sympathetic response, Stalin ensured that all Tito's potential sympathisers were expelled from Communist Parties throughout Eastern Europe. Tens of thousands of party members were purged, imprisoned and executed as whole sections of the bureaucracy were thrown out in a ruthless drive to enforce an unquestioning loyalty to Moscow. Anyone with an independent base in society had to go; only those who were subservient to Stalin were allowed to remain in power. These purges broke the last links between the Eastern European Communist Parties and pre-war struggles and destroyed their last vestiges of legitimacy.[27]

The relatively free political atmosphere immediately after the war ended with the Yugoslav schism. Eastern European regimes soon came to be distinguished by ruthless purges and the violent suppression of protest. The cynical show trials which affected every Communist Party in 1949 and 1950 recalled the methods which Stalin had used to secure his domination over the Soviet Communist Party in the 1930s. The judicial murders of the Hungarian foreign minister Lazlo Rajk, of Kostov in Bulgaria and of Slansky, Sling and others at the end of an anti-Semitic trial in Czechoslovakia were the forerunners of a long and shameful tradition.

The climate of intolerance and fear fostered by Stalinist rule was reinforced by widespread poverty. Living standards had in fact generally risen in Eastern Europe immediately after the war. However, after the imposition of Soviet-style central control and extensive development of heavy industry in 1948, Soviet-style stagnation soon set in. While total industrial production rose impressively to meet the targets of the first Five Year Plans, growth was heavily concentrated in heavy industry. Targets for consumer goods were abandoned and working-class living standards fell. The apparent successes of the Five Year Plans were largely the result of a massive increase in the total number of workers and the mass of resources thrown into production. Rural areas were 'collectivised', causing a huge migration of peasants into the ranks of the working class. But no increase in productivity accompanied the rise in the volume of production and quality standards declined sharply. In conditions of draconian labour discipline and ruthless speed-ups in the workplace, workers became more and more impoverished.

The fragility of the support for the Stalinist bureaucracies was openly revealed by a series of major upheavals during the 1950s: 1953 in East Germany, 1956 in Poland and Hungary. The credibility of the imposed leaderships had shrunk to nothing as living standards continued to decline. Open rebellion was often the only course open to the disenchanted population. The savage repression of these uprisings confirmed that the survival of the Stalinist regimes in Eastern Europe had come to rely entirely on coercion directed from Moscow.[28]

Managed change: 1956–74

The striking similarities between Budapest 1956 and Prague 1968 appear to confirm the unchanging character of Soviet tyranny over Eastern Europe throughout the post-war period. Yet, whereas the Hungarian events were the logical culmination of Stalinist policies in the 1950s, the events in Czechoslovakia marked a reluctant departure from the new course charted by the Soviet authorities in the 1960s. In fact the Soviet leadership learned important lessons from the Hungarian bloodbath which followed shortly after Khrushchev's celebrated denunciation of Stalin's past methods at the Twentieth Congress of the Soviet Communist Party. The failure of the command economies throughout the Eastern bloc was causing grave concern in Moscow as state repression and shortages of basic consumer goods provoked widespread unrest. Khrushchev was determined to find a new direction.[29]

To avoid further explosions Moscow sought to achieve the 'decompression' of Eastern Europe – a process of managed change in the economies and political structures of its satellites. Such changes were intended to be evolutionary, occurring strictly within the Soviet camp and under Moscow's control, with the constant threat of military intervention if things went wrong.

The East German experiment was an early example of the post-1956 strategy. Here the regime embarked upon a reform programme designated as a specific 'German road to socialism'. It aimed to modernise the economy, shake up the party apparatus and decentralise some economic and administrative activities. University reforms helped win some support for the regime from the intelligentsia. The government cultivated better relations with West Germany and an influx of Western economic assistance enabled a significant rise in living standards. From the mid-1960s onwards social stability seemed assured.

The crisis in Czechoslovakia was the result of the destabilising effect of reform process on the Stalinist bureaucracy itself. In the 1960s the distinctive feature of the Czechoslovakian regime was its slowness in implementing the sort of de-Stalinisation reforms advocated by Khrushchev. At a time when other Eastern European economies were undergoing a spurt in growth on the basis of loans and technology from the West, the Czechoslovak economy continued to stagnate and popular unrest grew. When public manifestations of dissatisfaction were brutally and ineptly handled by the Novotny regime, the party began to split between reformist and hardline Stalinist wings. When reformist Alexander Dubcek succeeded Novotny as party first secretary in January 1968, he was forced to appeal for public support to help purge the hardliners who still controlled the apparatus. This was the background to the 'Prague spring': it was a popular movement fostered by a section of the bureaucracy in pursuit of its own ends.

Moscow finally intervened only when events in Prague appeared to be getting out of control. The process of 'normalisation' which followed the removal of Dubcek may have been repressive but it had little in common with past Stalinist methods: the tanks went onto the streets of Prague but they did not devastate whole blocks of the city as they had in Budapest and there were few fatalities: even Dubcek survived to re-emerge as a popular focus in 1989. The manner in which the Soviet Union handled the Czechoslovak events was clearly in line with its post-1956 strategy of reform backed with the use of force only with reluctance and discretion.[30]

The real problem for Moscow was that the economic reforms instituted under its 'decompression' strategy had only short-term effects. Neither reforms nor normalisation succeeded in stopping the continuing economic slowdown of the Eastern bloc. The consequences of the slow decay of the Stalinist states were exposed when recession struck the capitalist world in 1973–74 and the influx of Western investment and technology slowed.

Holding operation: 1974–85

Even before Western credit began to run out the weaknesses of the new strategy started to become apparent. The bureaucracies in Eastern Europe were unable to assimilate new foreign technology for the same reason that they could not previously raise productivity. In the absence of conscious planning, new technology was introduced in an arbitrary manner. The result was massive waste: billions of dollars worth of investment were tied up in incomplete projects whilst operational plant was used at 20 to 50 per cent capacity. The bureaucracy was clearly incapable of overcoming inbuilt obstacles to increasing the productivity of labour in its system.[31]

Unlike the Soviet Union which was always much less reliant on trade with the West, dependence on imports of foreign technology made Eastern Europe far more vulnerable to fluctuations in the world economy. The international recession which set in from the early 1970s did not spare the Warsaw Pact countries. Romania and Czechoslovakia were forced to introduce rationing by the early 1980s. Attempts to make Polish workers pay for the crisis led to the upheavals there in 1980–81.

The Polish events were clear evidence of the limitations of the post-Hungary strategy. The limited reforms permitted by Moscow failed to satisfy an increasingly confident working class. In 1980–81 Polish workers organised in the free trade union Solidarity posed a real threat to stability of the regime. In late 1981 the regime clamped down by imposing martial law and imprisoning thousands of Solidarity activists. However the reality of the 1980s was that every Eastern European regime embarked on a holding operation, marking time and hoping something would turn up. In 1985 it came – in the form of Mikhail Gorbachev.

After 1985: the era of reform

In 1987 Gorbachev's senior foreign affairs spokesman Gennady Gerasimov proclaimed the replacement of the Brezhnev doctrine with what was soon dubbed the 'Sinatra doctrine': 'He has a song "I did it my way". Every Eastern European country decides on its own which road to take.'[32]

The Soviet Union now intended to encourage the pursuit of a reform strategy in Eastern Europe which had much in common with the programme of the Prague Spring. When asked to clarify the differences, Gerasimov tersely replied 'nineteen years'. Now Moscow was itself to be the inspiration for radical reform in Eastern Europe.[33]

One model for future relations between the Soviet Union and Eastern Europe favoured by Gorbachev himself was that pursued by Finland after the Second World War: 'Finlandisation' became a familiar term in the late 1980s debates. While never directly dominated by the Soviet Union or formally included in the Warsaw Pact, Finland has maintained a loose working relationship with Moscow since 1945. A treaty between the two countries even stipulates mutual military assistance in the event of foreign attack. This special relationship has never however prevented Finland's economic integration into the world market. Finland was Gorbachev's dream solution for Eastern Europe: a successful capitalist economy – but within the Soviet sphere of influence.

Soviet commentators contrasted Finnish dynamism and prosperity with the inertia and decline of Moscow's more domesticated Warsaw Pact satellites.[34] The Comecon countries presented a depressing picture. As economic decline intensified, mutual antagonism turned into open feuding between partners. While trade relations in the West were increasingly characterised by moves towards protectionism, in the Eastern bloc export restrictions were the order of the day as governments attempted to prevent an outflow of scarce consumer goods to their equally hard-up neighbours. A ring of Finland-style states around the Soviet Union appeared to Gorbachev to be an infinitely preferable option to the ramshackle collection of economic failures organised in Comecon.

When the new Soviet leader dictated reforms in Eastern Europe in line with his own policies at home, the leaders of the Warsaw Pact regimes were obliged to follow. But reforms along the lines proposed by Gorbachev had already been tried in the 1970s and had proved an expensive failure. The people of Eastern Europe were in no mood to tolerate a further round of experiments which could only result in further austerity measures. This time the bureaucrats were forced to make changes of a far more radical and thoroughgoing nature. However, given the tenuous connection between the bureaucracy and ordinary people, the changes resulting from these reforms were of an explosive and unpredictable nature.

The reform process unleashed by Gorbachev in the East took off on a scale that astonished observers around the world. What had long appeared to be a cohesive bloc disintegrated over a few months; in some countries – GDR, Czechoslovakia – the bureaucracy took weeks to crumble, in others – Romania, Bulgaria – it happened within days. The tidal wave of change that swept through East Germany was perhaps the most spectacular. In what appeared the most stable economy and society in the Eastern bloc, the mass movement forced the bureaucracy to dismantle the Berlin Wall and replace the old party leadership, and it did not stop until it had forced the bureaucracy itself effectively to abdicate power.

The rapidity and scale of these changes contrasts starkly with the relative slowness of reform in the homeland of glasnost and perestroika: Gorbachev's Soviet Union. Here little seems to have changed at all in spite of the clear need for urgent solutions to rampant economic and social crises. Such minor economic reforms as have taken place are in no way comparable to the major advances of market forces in Hungary or Poland. In Moscow political reform has merely served to strengthen the hand of the leadership clique around Gorbachev himself. While giving rise to destabilising tremors throughout the Soviet Union, glasnost did not weaken the hold of the Stalinist bureaucracy and precipitate a collapse of the entire post-war order as it did in the Eastern bloc.[35]

While Gorbachev's Soviet bureaucracy was still fairly securely in control at the end of the 1980s, its Eastern European counterparts had clearly lost the will to continue to rule in the old way. The haste with which many members of the old *nomenklatura* tried to ditch their old parties and took cover behind new political colours showed that they were experiencing a fundamental crisis of identity. They had lost faith in their own system. Such was their internal moral collapse that they were even prepared to countenance the dissolution of their own rule.[36] The profundity of the crisis of the bureaucracy in the East confirmed the extent of their lack of domestic legitimacy and their dependence on the Soviet Union. Once Gorbachev indicated that the Soviet Union would no longer back the Eastern regimes, they collapsed like a house of cards.

Conclusion: problems of transition

The problem is, the pace and scale of change in Eastern Europe makes a rigorous analysis of the implications extremely difficult. Couldn't it still all end in tears? The continued benign reaction of the Soviet Union to the unbundling of its empire cannot be taken for granted.[37]

As the relative certainties of Soviet domination come to an end, the future paths of development of different Eastern European countries become more and more difficult to foresee. The rules of the game in a typical Stalinist regime no longer apply. Furthermore the rapid collapse of all the regimes has increased the pace at which the old system is disintegrating. With direct Soviet control gone, few mechanisms remain to restore stability and the future looks increasingly uncertain.

The basic demands of every popular movement in Eastern Europe sound fairly similar. Everywhere there are cries for an end to the domination of 'communism' and for the rapid destruction of one-party rule. Now that democratic regimes are set to take the place of the Stalinist autocracy, the parliamentary systems of Western Europe and North America seem to many to be the way forward. Everywhere too there are calls for the restoration of market relations. Stalinist command planning has clearly collapsed. For everyone from Polish shipyard workers to Gorbachev's economic advisers, the free play of market forces seems to be the panacea and a necessary underpinning for the democratic structures desired by the masses.

In theory too everybody from George Bush through Margaret Thatcher to the workers of Leipzig wants to heal the post-war division of Europe and to see an end to East-West confrontation. Western investment in Eastern markets is held to be the locomotive force which will pull the backward East into Gorbachev's united and prosperous new 'Common European Home'.

However the achievement of all these goals depends not so much on what happens in Eastern Europe itself as on events elsewhere. All the Eastern bloc countries have for too long been dominated by a system without any internal dynamic. Change cannot come about merely as a result of their own efforts. The fate of Eastern Europe is therefore intimately bound up with the way in which the big international players – the major Western powers and the Soviet Union – decide to move.

As we have seen Gorbachev was the main mover in the process that has swept away the Stalinist bureaucracies of Eastern Europe. His emphasis has always been on political cooperation with the West through a reformed Warsaw Pact rather than a continued reliance on military solutions. However political stability within the Pact itself depends more and more on the West's capacity and willingness to bolster up the East. This is where the problems really start. A collapsing Eastern bloc, eager for Western capital and assistance, ironically comes face to face with a Nato alliance which is increasingly in disarray and less and less capable of playing the locomotive role desired by Gorbachev's strategists.

Concerned at the growing problems within their own system, both Western governments and private investors are reticent when it comes to offering major assistance to the East. Western aid has consequently been predicated on further belt-tightening in Eastern bloc countries, in which many people are already on the brink of starvation. All eyes are on relatively well-off East Germany as the area which will point the way to future investment possibilities. But there are problems here too. As an American business magazine recently pointed out: 'The danger is that an economically reunited Germany will throw the European balance of power out of whack.'[38] There will be winners and losers among Western powers in any new wave of investment in the East. In such uncertain times, nobody is in a hurry to alter the increasingly delicate post-war balance. Conservative Western leaders who have long called for the end to the division of Europe are now amongst its firmest defenders. Fear of a major change now far outweighs the need to maintain the old anti-communist rhetoric.

Stringent preconditions for Western financial assistance will also cause problems. Attacks on living standards to satisfy Western bankers can expect to meet further resistance from workers fed up with years of queuing, economising and going without basic necessities. Such measures could well lead to rapid reversals in the promised democratic experiment. More repression, further resurgences of nationalism and major social breakdown cannot be ruled out in such circumstances. It is even possible to envisage a return of old-style Soviet control. However as a Western commentator has argued: 'It is easier to envision the emergence of army-backed dictatorships. Eastern Europe might then revert to the fractious and divided region it has been throughout most of its history.'[39]

The fate of Eastern Europe is intimately bound up with the changing international order. Gorbachev has shown that he is prepared to countenance almost anything in the interests of assuring the survival, in at least some form, of the traditional Soviet sphere of influence. Even the secession of parts of the Warsaw Pact cannot be ruled out provided that this is seen as having some benefit for the Soviet Union. For their part, the Western powers are unlikely to do anything in the short term which might undermine the precarious stability of the bloc.

However the best-laid plans of the major powers could soon run into trouble. Rapid change has unleashed forces which are difficult to control. The disintegration of the old forms of rule has taken place faster than anyone could have predicted. While in the short term the forces of reaction are likely to benefit, the ground has been cleared for significant struggles to come. Stalinism is in its death throes and the working class of Eastern Europe can enter battle on its own account for the first time in more than 40 years.

Notes

1. 'There goes the Bloc', *Time*, 6 November 1989.
2. Newly elected Hungarian President Rezso Myers said that Gorbachev was the first to congratulate him: 'Gorbachev conducts very fast diplomacy. They gave me his telegram within two hours of my election.' Ian Traynor and Susan Viets, 'Hungarian reformers pull back from the split', *Guardian*, 10 October 1989.

3. Catholic intellectual, Tadeusz Mazowiecki, nominated as Poland's first non-communist prime minister since the Second World War by President Jaruszelski.
4. 'Breezes from Moscow', *Time*, 18 April 1988.
5. See Timothy Garton Ash 'Revolution: The Springtime of Two Nations' in *New York Review of Books*, 15 June 1989 and Russell Osborne 'Poland in transition' *Confrontation*, 5, London: Junius, 1989, for a description of the Polish reform process which led to the elections.
6. Michael Meyer, 'Solidarity's stunning win', *Newsweek*, 19 June 1989.
7. Joan Phillips, 'Hungary: the party that tried to bury its past' in *Confrontation*, 5.
8. 'The flight to freedom', *Newsweek*, 16 October 1989.
9. 'Breezes from Moscow', *Time*, 18 April 1989.
10. Radio Warsaw reports of discussions at the PUWP central committee plenums of December 1988 and January 1989, and a special 'National, theoretical and ideological' conference in February 1989 clearly indicated this tendency.
11 On the concept of civil society in Eastern Europe see Timothy Garton Ash, 'The opposition', *New York Review of Books*, 13 October 1988.
12. At the seminar Dr Madsen Pirie, President of the Adam Smith Institute, and Oliver Letwin, head of Rothschild's international privatisation unit, both espoused the 'big bang' theory of privatisation – do it and see what happens. Reported in David Hencke, 'Right way forward for Poland's economy', *Guardian*, 24 October 1989.
13. Osborne, 'Will Poles pay Walesa's price?', *Living Marxism*, 12 October 1989.
14. John Kampfner 'A poverty crisis grips Poland's cities', *Sunday Telegraph*, 5 November 1989. Zygmunt Szymaniak, General Secretary of the Polish Committee for Social Aid estimated that one in four citizens was in need of some help to stave off hunger. His organisation alone planned to open up 52 new soup kitchens.
15. Francois Fejto, *A History of the People's Democracies*, Harmondsworth: Penguin, 1977, p. 490. Attempts at reform in Poland from 1 January 1971 led to cuts in living standards and violent protests in Gdansk, Gydnia and Szczecin with hundreds killed by the army.
16. Phillips, 'Hungary: the party that tried to bury its past'.
17. Osborne, 'Poland in transition'.

18. Gorbachev's revelations on the Hungarian uprising of 1956 and the Prague spring of 1969 were typical. In discussions with the then Hungarian leader, Karoly Grosz, he was quoted by Grosz as arguing that 'all possible safeguards should be provided so that no external force can interfere in the domestic affairs of socialist countries.' This was taken to be a repudiation of the Brezhnev doctrine of limited sovereignty for Soviet satellites. Leslie Collitt, 'Gorbachev pledge on E. Europe creates stir', *Financial Times*, 31 March 1989.

19. 'Breezes from Moscow', *Time*, 18 April 1988 'Gorbachev is counting on a reform-inspired upswing in the stagnant East European economies to stimulate the economy of the more backward Soviet Union. Faced with the reality that even modest results from reform may take years to materialise in the vast Soviet system, Gorbachev is hoping that his policies will be vindicated more quickly in the smaller and more advanced economic laboratories of Eastern Europe.'

20. Stephen E. Ambrose, *Rise to Globalism*, Harmondsworth: Penguin, 1973, Chapter 4, 'The beginnings of the cold war'.

21. 'The objectionable feature of their foreign policy is that they are attempting in foreign affairs to do precisely what they have been doing at home for nearly 20 years.', John Foster Dulles, May 1946, quoted in Daniel Yergin, *Shattered Peace – the Origins of the Cold War and the National Security State*, Boston: Houghton Mifflin, 1978, Chapter IX.

22. Fejto, *A History of the People's Democracies*, p. 69.

23. F. Claudin, *The Communist Movement From Comintern to Cominform*, Harmondsworth: Penguin, 1975, Chapter 6, 'The Cominform'.

24. Gabriel Kolko, *The Politics of War – The World and United States Foreign Policy 1943–45*, New York: Vintage Books, 1968.

25. Claudin, Chapter 6.

26. Claudin, Chapter 7, 'The Yugoslav breach'.

27. Claudin, Chapter 7.

28. Imre Nagy, *The New Course*, Praeger, 1957, on the first Hungarian Five Year Plan.

29. Olga Narkiewicz, *Eastern Europe 1968–1984*, Croom Helm, 1989, on the 'dualism' of Soviet policy towards the Eastern bloc.

30. Fejto, Chapter 11, 'The Czechoslovak tragedy and its implications'.

31. The Polish case is well described in *Poland: the State of the Republic*, London: Pluto, 1981.

32. Gennady Gerasimov, *The Economist*, 4 February 1989.
33. *Time*, 18 April 1988.
34. 'Survey on Finland', *Financial Times*, 18 December 1989.
35. Frank Richards, 'New suit same old system', *Living Marxism*, November 1988.
36. The example of the Hungarian party, the HSWP, is particularly illuminating. HSWP 'reformers' even played a key role in setting up new opposition groups like the Hungarian Democratic Forum, source: Radio Free Europe 'Hungary Reports' 1989.
37. 'Breaking down the wall', Report by Union Bank of Switzerland Phillips & Drew, 20 November 1989.
38. 'The shape of Europe to come', *Business Week*, 27 November 1989.
39. 'Yes, he's for real', *Time*, 6 November 1989.

5 China: the Road to Tiananmen Square

Mark Wu

Introduction

Observers of the transformation of China in the 1980s from all sides of the political spectrum have discerned a decisive break from the dogmatic Stalinist traditions of Mao Zedong. Yet even a cursory glance at the policies followed by the Chinese Communist Party from the proclamation of the people's republic in 1949 to the adoption of an 'open door' approach towards foreign investment in 1978 reveals a complex mixture of often contradictory measures. For example, the 'great leap forward' policy pursued by Mao between 1958 and 1960, with its mass mobilisations and the formation of huge communes, is often selected as a typical illustration of the methods of Chinese communism. However, this approach ignores the partial decollectivisation of agriculture and the reopening of rural markets that followed the collapse of the 'great leap forward'. Mao's China was always governed more by pragmatism than by dogma.

The distinctive feature of the 1980s lies not in the specific reforms encouraging various forms of private enterprise, but in the fairly consistent pursuit of these measures over the decade. As a result, the changes in the social relations of Chinese society have been more substantial than in any earlier period and the prospects of capitalist restoration have become proportionately greater. To assess the current crisis of China and the prospects for the 1990s it is necessary to begin with a brief overview of the first 30 years of the people's republic and the forces which pushed the regime into embarking on a programme of reform in the 1980s. We can then look in more detail at the impact of reforms in different areas of society and the problems unleashed by the extension of market forces that provoked growing unrest in 1988, culminating in the protest movement that was savagely crushed in Tiananmen Square in Beijing in June 1989. We can then, in conclusion, assess the trends likely to influence the course of events in China in the 1990s.[1]

China under Mao

The Chinese Communist Party came to power on a platform of national unity and independence, not communist revolution.[2] The vagueness of the party programme, based on Mao's doctrine of the 'new democracy' developed a decade earlier, enabled the CCP to unite diverse social forces in support of the new regime. Proclaimed as the 'people's democratic dictatorship' in 1949, Mao's government openly accepted 'a certain degree of capitalist development'.[3] The regime's economic strategy was to encourage growth through protecting the private property of the 'national bourgeoisie' and farmers. In the early months after Mao's takeover, the new government was more concerned about 'cadre excesses' and 'leftist deviations' – direct action by workers who took the idea of worker's control at face value – than it was by the activities of the old bourgeoisie. One capitalist later declared that 'the communists provided the best business climate we had ever known.'[4]

The outbreak of war in Korea in 1950 brought an abrupt end to the favourable international climate that had allowed Mao's regime to pursue a moderate course without fear of external interference. The large-scale US military commitment to South Korea raised real fears of a US-backed counter-revolution in China. Launched in June 1950, Mao's agrarian reform programme aimed centrally to break the power of the landlords, who might be expected to sympathise with imperialist subversion. The redistribution of land was not specifically intended to benefit the peasantry, though a significant layer of better-off peasants emerged through buying land after it had been removed from the landlords. Hence redistribution was balanced by concentration; in a similar way subsequent waves of collectivisation were always followed by periods in which decollectivisation and the re-opening of rural markets took place. Capitalist social relations were gradually abolished in China, not by the actions of the working class but by bureaucratic confiscation. Many Chinese capitalists managed to keep control of their enterprises until 1956 and some continued to receive fixed interest payments on their old businesses until the outbreak of the cultural revolution in 1966.[5] But, once the capitalist market had been suppressed, how was economic activity to be regulated? Here the Chinese leadership turned to the Soviet experience for guidance, but conditions there were very different from China. In Russia, the working class had played the leading role in the 1917 Revolution and in the early Soviet state it had at least the potential to play a direct role in managing a planned economy. In China, by contrast, the proletarian base of the CCP had been destroyed in the 1920s; the absence of working-class participation in the revolution meant that there was no possibility of workers' management of the economy once capitalist social relations had been abolished. Mao's alternative was to emulate the methods pursued by Stalin in the 1930s once his regime had liqui-dated working-class involvement in the Soviet state. Stalinist bureaucratic economic policies were particularly evident in the first 'Five Year Plan' (1953–58). There was however a basic conflict between Stalinist-style command management and traditional Maoist policies, which were essentially anti-bureaucratic and dependent on the mobilisation of the generally compliant masses in support of the regime's objectives. Indeed despite promoting the first 'Five Year Plan' under the slogan 'be modern, be Soviet', the Chinese regime never succeeded in developing the large and coherent bureaucracy that was the key to Stalin's administration of Soviet society. Mao admitted the virtual disappearance of planning during the 'great leap forward':

> By doing away with planning, I mean they dispensed with overall balances, and simply made no estimates of how much coal, iron and transport would be needed. Coal and iron cannot walk by themselves; they need vehicles to transport them. This I did not foresee.[6]

Whereas Stalin turned the intelligentsia into a base of support for the regime, Mao's distrust of the intellectual élite grew through the 1950s, to reach its zenith in the 'cultural revolution' (1966–1968). For example, he effectively suspended the official statistical bureau, which by 1981 employed only 193 workers at national level.[7] Throughout the 1950s and 1960s, the US-led trade embargo forced China to pursue an isolationist course of development. Unable to import modern technology, the Chinese leadership reverted to the policy of 'self-reliance' it had pursued in the bitter struggles of the 1930s: 'At the national level it made a virtue out of the inability to trade; at the local level, it was a substitute for both a domestic market and administrative planning.'[8] The problem of resource allocation was minimised by making even small units as self-sufficient as possible. The result was the familiar example of the 'backyard' steel furnaces: millions were established, each capable of producing only a few hundred tons of steel a year, most of which was of such poor quality as to be useless. What were the effects of these contradictory policies on China's economic development? Most Western analysts refer disparagingly to the 'stagnation' of the first 30 years of the people's republic and contrast this with the rapid growth of the 1980s. They regard the 'achievements' proclaimed by apologists for the regime with suspicion if not disbelief.[9] On the other hand, many radical observers lament the passing of the Mao era and the golden age of the 'Chinese road to socialism'. Fortunately there is now a large amount of statistical information available which allows a more rational assessment of the Mao era.[10] Between 1952 and 1979 China's gross national product grew at 8 per cent a year, the value of its industrial output increased at 11 per cent a year, and national income increased at 6 per cent a year. Meanwhile annual inflation remained at less than one per cent.[11] In spite of this extraordinary record of growth, average income, which was equivalent to US$28 in 1950, by 1978 had increased to the equivalent of US$188 according to Chinese sources, and to US$230 according to the World Bank.[12] Of course such averages mask dramatic fluctuations: the immediately catastrophic effects on growth and living standards of the 'great leap forward' and, to a lesser extent, the cultural revolution, are not revealed. According to the Stalinist model, high growth rates were achieved by massive investment in plant and raw materials. While labour productivity almost tripled between 1952 and 1978, output per yuan of capital fell to about three-quarters of its 1952 value.[13] According to a 1985 World Bank study on China's state-owned industry, productivity increased between 1952 and 1957, then stagnated or declined between 1957 and 1982.[14]

Even many anti-communist commentators believe that the peasants have been major beneficiaries of the Chinese Revolution. Indeed the CCP's claim that only socialism could feed China's vast population is crucial to its legitimacy. How does this claim stand up? Grain production figures show that output per head increased during the early 1950s with the formation of mutual aid teams and small cooperatives. However the forced creation of communes during the 'great leap forward' led to a sharp drop in agricultural production resulting in widespread famine between 1959 and

1961, virtually exclusively in the countryside: up to 30 million died.[15] Faced with this crisis, the state continued to export grain, and it was not until the following year that grain imports began to alleviate the problem. Chinese agriculture did not recover until the 1970s, and as late as 1978 around 100 million peasants were still living on the brink of starvation.[16] The state has proved either incapable or unwilling to resolve the problem of transporting grain: interprovincial grain transfers dropped from more than 5 per cent of total output in 1953 to less than one per cent in 1978.[17]

The differential between town and country in the availability of grain also applied to other commodities. The collectivisation of agriculture and the nationalisation of industry during the first Five Year Plan increased the gap between urban and rural areas. A household registration system prevented peasants from moving to the cities to improve their lot. Although urban wages fell by 17 per cent in real terms between 1957 and 1977, this decline was offset by subsidies in the price of grain and edible oil, housing, education, pensions and health care.[18] According to statistics distrusted by many experts, by 1975, city dwellers could expect to live to reach the age of 72, whereas in rural China life expectancy was 57 years.[19] Although government policy generally favoured the working class over the peasants, workers were not indulged with any luxuries. For example, in housing, the average amount of floor space per urban inhabitant declined from 4.5 square metres in 1952 to 3.6 square metres in 1978.[20]

By the end of the cultural revolution the CCP had reached an impasse. The genuine popular support which the CCP had enjoyed in 1949 had been dissipated by nearly three decades of twists and turns in policy which often appeared arbitrary and damaging to workers and peasants. The regime could no longer attempt to tackle its problems through the mobilisation of the masses. The bureaucracy was paralysed, its individual members fearful of making the incorrect decision that could mean job loss, public humiliation or physical assault. It was also becoming increasingly apparent that the periods in which the market had been used to regulate the economy were more successful than those periods in which mass mobilisation was used. Although he came under increasing criticism, Mao's prestige was such that only after his death in 1976 was it possible to correct what later became known as the 'left errors' of the cultural revolution and turn China back towards Western capitalism.

The reform decade

The era of reform was officially inaugurated at the historic Third Plenum of the Eleventh Central Committee of the CCP in December 1978. After a period of indecision following the death of Mao, Deng Xiaoping emerged as undisputed leader empowered to reform all aspects of Chinese society. Given continuing uncertainty within the leadership about the scope to be allowed to the reform process, there was at first little attempt to provide a fuller explanation of the new strategy. Three years later, in the key document 'On questions of party history' the leadership still preferred to keep things vague: 'since [1978] our party has gradually mapped out the correct path for socialist modernization suited to China's conditions. In the course of practice, the path will be broadened and become more clearly defined.'[21] The 'principal contradiction', identified by the 1981 document, was 'that between the growing material and cultural needs of the people and backwardness of social production'.[22] The document was explicit in directing the blame at 'the influence of "left" deviationist errors ... [which] ... resulted in the various correct measures aimed at enlivening enterprises and developing socialist commodity economy being regarded as "capitalist"'.[23] The long-established tradition of hostility towards the expansion of capitalist forces was now labelled a left deviation as the leadership sought a free hand to promote the market. It was not until 1987 that party leader Zhao Ziyang felt confident enough to attempt to justify the reforms. Zhao argued that the free market, stock exchanges and such practices as inefficient firms being allowed to go bankrupt could not be considered exclusive to capitalism, but could also exist in a society such as China, which had entered the 'primary phase of socialism' and was now in the process of attaining a fully modern economy.[24] Zhao's thesis defended the Chinese leadership against an alternative view that since China had never gone through a capitalist stage of development it was now necessary to return to capitalism with the aim of achieving socialism at some later stage – a theory that pointed logically to the liquidation of the CCP.[25]

Though the reform measures introduced by the regime number several hundred, there has never been any systematic programme. Some of the most important measures have legitimised changes that have already taken place, others have either been ignored or have provoked such opposition that they have been postponed or shelved indefinitely. The process of reform can be divided into three stages.[26] From 1978 until 1984, the decollectivisation of agriculture and the extension of markets in rural produce and the 'open door' policy towards foreign investment appeared to be going well. These successes gave the CCP the confidence to embark on more drastic reforms in agriculture and to start the shake-up of industry and planning. Over the next three years, some problems began to emerge, but the regime was confident that it could solve them. After October 1987, however, the CCP increasingly lost control over the economy and indeed the whole of Chinese society. Let's look in more detail at the impact of reform in three areas: agriculture, the 'open door' policy, and industry and planning.

Agricultural reforms

In 1979 the Chinese government issued two key documents promoting agricultural reform: 'Regulations on the work in rural people's communes' and the 'Decision of the central committee of the CCP on some questions concerning the acceleration of agricultural development'. In retrospect, these documents seem fairly bland. There is no mention of the decollectivisation of agriculture which was to take off so rapidly in the early 1980s. Although they refer to the need to combat egalitarianism by implementing a policy of 'from each according to his ability, to each according to his work', they expressly forbid the fixing of output quotas or the distribution of land to individual households. Subsequent official statements were progressively more radical, but they often amounted to the state giving its seal of approval to events that had already taken place spontaneously.

The state sanctioned two new forms of land ownership which led to the rapid disintegration of the communes which had become the basic unit of local administration in the early 1960s. By 'contracting output to the household', a fixed amount of land and a target output were allocated to the household, and final income was then distributed as previously, on a work-point system. In the more radical process of 'contracting everything to the household' production and distribution were made the responsibility of the individual household. Draught animals, farm tools and other equipment were distributed among households which could then freely dispose of any surplus income left over after paying taxes and quotas.

After 1981, contracting everything to the household became the main form of organisation and by the end of 1984, the communes had virtually disappeared. The higher prices paid by the state for grain and other agricultural goods to stimulate production also encouraged the privatisation of agriculture.

How successful was the first stage of agricultural reform? Riskin has pointed out that total agricultural output grew by 8.9 per cent in 1978 and 8.6 per cent in 1979, before the household responsibility system had begun to take effect. These increases were the results of the state taking pressure off the communes and allowing peasants to specialise and diversify according to local conditions. As Riskin observes, this 'raises the broader question why the party decided to bring back individual farming rather than permit and encourage autonomy for the collectives'.[27] Although it is difficult to quantify, it appears that much of the early increase in output was attributable to the technological and infrastructional improvements of the Maoist era – including massive irrigation, flood control and land-levelling schemes and the purchase of 13 large-scale Western fertiliser plants.[28]

Part of the growth was simply the result of peasants shifting from growing rice to producing higher-priced products. However, it seems reasonable to conclude that growth rates were exceptionally high between 1978 and 1984, if not quite as high as most Chinese economists claim. The success of the first stage of reform, reflected in the bumper harvest of 1984, encouraged the regime to press on with more radical measures, which were first announced in October 1984. Up to this time the reforms that were implemented were variants of methods which had been tried in earlier drives to improve agricultural output. However, 'Document No. 1, 1985', released on 1 January 1985, marked a decisive breakaway from the state's 30-year-old monopoly of purchasing and marketing. From now on farmers would 'learn to swim in the ocean of the commodity economy'. In the hope that the market would prove a more effective regulator of supply and demand than the state, the prices of all agricultural goods except grain and cotton were de-regulated. The government also hoped that this would reduce the growing burden of the subsidies it had to pay out to keep down grain prices in the cities. Just as the more radical measures were being implemented, problems began to emerge. At first the reforms had the effect of narrowing the gap between city and countryside, but by 1986 it had increased again to 2.3:1, worse than in 1981.[29]

Within the countryside itself, society became increasingly polarised. As one observer writes, 'Before 1979, the most significant differentials were those between localities with different ecological conditions or proximity to urban markets, whereas income within villages was distributed quite evenly.'[30] Since 1979, large differentials have appeared within the same locality, which is obviously more divisive. Official statistics suggest that there has been a marked reduction in the number of poor households and a rapid rise in well-off ones.[31] But this leaves out of the picture many landless peasants who have migrated to the cities in search of work and do not therefore appear in the statistics. A survey of 21,000 'prosperous' households in Shanxi Province showed that 34 per cent were cadres or former cadres who had therefore been in a favourable position when land and resources were allocated. Some 42 per cent were recorded as 'educated youth' or demobilised soldiers, while only 5 per cent were peasants.[32]

Early advances in production and in peasant living standards have not been sustained. Peasants' income stagnated in the mid-1980s, culminating in a drop in income in 1988.[33] State investment in agriculture declined rapidly throughout the reform period, and most peasant households have not been able to accumulate the necessary surplus for investment.[34] Where they have managed to accumulate funds, they have preferred to invest in housing, often built illegally on land intended for agriculture.[35] Because of their doubts about the long-term security of their land tenure, peasants have often not maintained the land that they have contracted. There has also been a gradual deterioration in the agricultural infrastructure especially irrigation and flood control.[36] Peasants are increasingly unwilling to do the work necessary to maintain the projects of the Mao era.

As the cost of agricultural inputs – fertiliser, diesel oil, pesticides and high-yield seeds – has increased, the return on grain has declined. Many peasants have switched from grain to more profitable agricultural products or have left farming altogether. Though state grain procurement prices have been constantly raised to encourage peasants to grow more, they have never been raised enough. However, rising grain prices meant a steadily increasing urban grain subsidy.[37]

In 1985, grain production fell from 407 to 379 million tons, the second largest drop in the history of the people's republic. Production recovered in the late 1980s, probably reaching around 400 million tons in 1989, but it is now clear that the record harvest of 1984, which gave the CCP the confidence to launch the second phase of reform, was more the result of good weather than one of party policy.[38] A target of 445 million tons for 1990 has already been cut to 425 but even that seems unlikely to be achieved; in the winter of 1988–89, some 20 million people faced near famine conditions.[39] China imported about 15–16 million tons of grain in 1989, mostly from the US. With a population increasing by 15 million a year and available land decreasing by 200–300,000 hectares a year, China's inability to raise the productivity of the land makes the possibility of famine very real. There can be no better illustration of the failure of the CCP's policies than the fact that after 40 years China still cannot feed its own people.

The 'open door' policy

The Shanghai Communique, signed by China and the US in 1972, brought the long post-war embargo to an end and foreign trade increased dramatically in the 1970s. The decentralisation of control over foreign trade in 1978 led to an upsurge in both imports and exports, and soon prompted stabilising measures from the state. Less than a year later a foreign investment control commission was set up to restore some control over access to foreign exchange. A similar cycle of reforms, followed by an explosive increase in imports, followed in turn by the re-imposition of central control was repeated in 1984–1985. The overall trend in overseas trade was, however, steadily upwards.[40] Zhao Ziyang explained that the aim of the 'open door' policy was that 'by linking our country with the world market ... we can use our strong points to make up for our weak points through international exchange on the basis of equality and mutual benefit.'[41] Although Japan had assiduously cultivated China as a trading partner since the 1960s, in the 1980s Hong Kong took the lead.

China's Largest Trading Partners

	1988		1983
Hong Kong (*US$ billion*)	30.2		(5.3)
Japan	19.0		(9.1)
US		(4.0)	
W. Germany	4.9		(N/A)
USSR	3.3		(0.7)
S. Korea	3.0		(0.3)

Whereas in the 1970s China stood aloof from the world market, by the end of the 1980s it was as dependent on the international capitalist order as any Third World country. Before China embarked on the 'open door' policy, the World Bank had noted approvingly how low its imports were as a proportion of GNP.[42] As late as 1983, China was a net exporter of capital; a decade later the situation had completely changed. China joined the World Bank and the International Monetary Fund (IMF) in 1980, followed by the Food and Agricultural Organisation; in 1986 it joined the Asian Development Bank and applied to join GATT. Between 1979 and 1987 China received a total of US$37.5 billion (US$26.5 billion in loans plus US$9 billion in direct investment).[43] China has used the Tokyo stock market extensively to float bonds.[44]

One of the key features of the 'open door' policy was the establishment of four 'special economic zones' (SEZs) in Guangdong and Fujian provinces to attract foreign capital into joint ventures. Whereas the CCP could present the increase in foreign trade as an ideologically neutral process, this was more difficult with the overtly pro-capitalist SEZs. However the central role played by Chinese capitalists living in Hong Kong, Taiwan and Singapore obscured the renewed imperialist penetration of China after 40 years of independence. Zhao Ziyang insisted that the aim of the SEZs was 'to promote China's socialist modernization; we should adhere to the characteristics of the socialist system in our work in the special zones, and the workers, staff and other inhabitants should be imbued with socialist morality.'[45] Zhao's warning revealed the Chinese leadership's recognition that introducing foreign investment carried the risk of introducing capitalist social relations.

The position of the SEZs is highly significant. Shenzhen is directly across the border from the British colony of Hong Kong, Zhuhai is adjacent to the old Portuguese colony of Macao, while Xiamen faces Taiwan, the island refuge of the defeated national bourgeoisie after 1949. The fourth SEZ, Shantou, has traditionally been an area of high emigration: some four million Shantou Chinese are scattered throughout South-East Asia. While there was no coherent plan or statement of objectives for the SEZs, they were intended to encourage foreign investment in enterprises which could manufacture products for export, to attract advanced technology, and to teach the Chinese Western-style management and business methods. The first four SEZs have now been joined by a fifth, Hainan Island, and by 14 'open cities' and three 'golden deltas'. The result is a 2,000 mile strip of open areas from Dalian in the north to Hainan Island in the south. The SEZs have, however, proved a disappointment both for foreign investors and for the Chinese leadership. Setting up a joint venture company is still a complex procedure taking up to five years. Productivity is higher than in the rest of China, but it is still lower than in Hong Kong or Macao, and complaints about supply shortages and changes in costs are frequent. Although firms are formally allowed to hire and fire workers, in practice the state controls the supply of labour and makes dismissal difficult. These problems are partly the result of a deliberate attempt to keep joint ventures separate from the main economy, and partly the consequence of the different objectives of the Chinese regime and foreign investors in the SEZs. The main function of the SEZs for the regime is to attract foreign exchange and technology by offering cheap labour to produce goods for export. For foreign investors, the main attraction is gaining access to a market of nearly 1.2 billion people. In this clash of interests the investors have come out on top: in 1985 only one-third of SEZ production was exported.[46] Even worse news for China is that much of the investment has not gone into developing industry but into building hotels, golf courses and other services.[47]

The SEZs have provided some of the most spectacular examples of the corruption which is now endemic in China. The most celebrated example occurred in Hainan Island, where party officials used foreign exchange to buy 2.86 million colour televisions, 252,000 video cassette recorders, 122,000 motor cycles and 10,000 cars and mini-buses. These were then sold on the mainland at double or triple the original prices.[48] The local bureaucrats had obviously taken to heart Deng's celebrated aphorism 'To get rich is glorious.'

Industry and planning

Reforms in industry and planning slowly gathered momentum in the early 1980s. Central ministries began to give greater autonomy in budgeting to the provinces, abandoning both mandatory fiscal targets and the practice of adjusting inter-provincial revenue-sharing each year which made budgeting more than 12 months in advance impossible. At local level the province rather than central government became the centre of administration. At the level of the province, the uniform system of fiscal relations with central government was replaced by five different budgeting arrangements depending on the prosperity of the province. At one end of the spectrum Guangdong was given freedom to decide its own budgets, so long as it remitted a fixed sum to the centre. At the other, the metropolitan provinces of Beijing, Tianjin and Shanghai had to negotiate with central government an annual revenue-sharing rate.[49]

In 1984 the regime stepped up the pace of reform. Though the 'Decision of the central committee on reform of the economic structure' did not detail the specific measures to be taken, it was of crucial importance as an official declaration of intent to promote market forces in wider areas of Chinese society. Budgeting now became the responsibility of provinces and localities rather than central government and a new commitment to specialisation replaced the old Maoist notion that enterprises should be self-sufficient. The key theme was that of 'linking projects to the market'; price reform, long the most contentious issue was now to be 'energetically and steadily pursued'. Though private enterprise had been legalised in 1978, entrepreneurs were still formally banned from engaging in the 'exploitation of others' and their activities remained restricted until the more favourable climate created by the 1984 reforms gave them new confidence to expand.

Central planning and financial control were further reduced in 1985 and 1986 as seven more major cities gained a large measure of independence from central government. There were more changes in tax legislation and local profit retention. The practice of allocating funds directly to enterprises was replaced by low interest bank loans, combined with the threat of bankruptcy for enterprises that consistently recorded losses. Because the implementation of these and other measures has been so uneven, with frequent reversals, rather than looking at the sequence of reform it is more useful to concentrate on the results of the reform process – what one writer aptly describes as a 'strange hybrid, a novel category of market stalinism'.[50]

One of the effects of reform has been to strengthen the position of the bureaucracy:

> In response to every innovation, a corresponding office has been designated or a new one created within the state bureaucracy to act as a sort of broker. As a consequence, the pre-existing power of state bureaucratic organs and their cadres is readily being translated into market power ... The market power of the state bureaucratic organs and their cadres rests on control over key supplies and large facilities and especially on '*guanxi*' or personal relationships formed over many years of manoeuvring within the state planned economy.[51]

While the national workforce grew by 20 per cent between 1982 and 1988, the number of state and party officials expanded by 51 per cent, from 6.1 million to 9.71 million.[52]

Though there were no immediate increases in industrial production to compare with those in the agricultural sector, there has been a change in the balance of contributions between the state factories and the emerging cooperative and private sector. While the gross output of state industry doubled between 1978 and 1987, the state's share in total output fell from 78 per cent to 60 per cent. This was due almost entirely to the expansion of cooperative industry, which increased its share from 19 per cent to 27 per cent.[53] Private industry, though probably underestimated, contributed less than 3 per cent in 1978 and had only reached 5 per cent by 1988. By the end of 1988 when all limits on the number of workers who could be employed were finally scrapped, some 225,000 firms with eight or more employees were officially registered.[54]

Reform also encouraged a shift towards light industry and the production of consumer goods and a reduction in mandatory planning. Thus while heavy industry grew by 7 per cent a year between 1978 and 1985, light industry registered an 11 per cent annual growth rate. In 1978, 40 per cent of the gross value of industrial output was provided through mandatory planning; this was halved by 1987. Over the same period the number of commodities produced according to planned quotas was cut from 120 to 60. By 1987 the prices of only 26 raw materials were still fixed by the state, compared with 20,000 fixed by Gosplan in the Soviet Union.[55] Though bankruptcy has become technically possible, most loss making enterprises are still subsidised by the state from its contracting income. In 1988 subsidies were estimated at more than US$11 billion, more than half of total industrial profit.[56]

The most controversial aspect of the process of deregulation was the proposal to remove responsibility for workers' social welfare from the work unit. Because all social services, including housing, are organised around the work unit, the regime's threat to 'break the iron rice bowl' was a real danger to social stability that caused widespread dissension within the CCP.

The developing crisis

The October 1987 party congress marked the zenith of the reform movement. The new central committee was younger and better educated; the old 'mobilizers and ideologues' were increasingly being replaced by managers and technocrats.[57] However, the reformers did not get it all their own way as Li Peng and other conservatives were also promoted. Zhao Ziyang's keynote speech emphasised the new formula of 'the state regulating the market and the market stimulating the enterprises', which opened up the prospect of mass unemployment as 'surplus workers' were squeezed out of the factories. Zhao responded to mounting opposition within the CCP by stepping up the pace of reform, declaring that price deregulation was to be 'energetically and steadily pursued' in 1988. But the contradictory economic consequences of the earlier reforms were already causing problems for the regime.

While agriculture stagnated, industrial output exceeded targets; growth in 1988 was 20.7 per cent compared with a target of 8 per cent. The growth rate for province-run industries in 1988 was more than 35 per cent and that of industries at village level was even higher.[58] One result was intense competition for resources – both energy and raw materials. A survey of Hainan Island bluntly advised American investors either to install their own electricity generators or postpone investment.[59] Whole sectors of industry were afflicted by shortages of raw materials and by fierce competition for supplies, between the state and producers and among different provinces and enterprises. Although price fixing had been sharply reduced, the prices of key raw materials were still regulated. Some commodities had three different prices – a state fixed price, a negotiable price and a free market price – giving unscrupulous bureaucrats considerable scope for making money by switching between the different systems.

One of Mao's proudest boasts was that the people's republic had wiped out the rampant inflation of the pre-1949 era. Reform brought it back, as retail prices rose by 7.4 per cent a year between 1985 and 1987, and then by twice that rate in the first half of 1988.[60] Rising prices and the threat of further price reforms produced a series of runs on the banks, panic buying and hoarding by individuals and enterprises. There was also a wave of strikes, riots and sabotage which led to the formation of special armed mobile police units in many cities.[61]

Another consequence of reform was to intensify interprovincial rivalry. Though the traditional policy of state redistribution in favour of the poorer provinces was only partly successful, it did ensure that the more backward provinces of the interior had higher industrial growth rates than the more industrialised coastal provinces. Nevertheless it often proved difficult for the state to impose its budget demands on the richer provinces, which were expected to give up most of their income. This policy provoked both passive noncompliance and active defiance; in the Maoist era provincial first party secretaries were particularly liable to be purged and replaced by outsiders.[62] Since the reforms, rivalry over resources has replaced conflict over targets as the main focus of interprovincial strife.[63]

In the late 1980s regional trade barriers became widespread. Guangdong in particular was repeatedly denounced by poorer provinces because of its protectionist policies. The state however acquiesced to the demands of the more affluent provinces and municipalities for more autonomy and the right to retain a greater share of locally collected revenues. The opening up of the coastal provinces as largely autonomous entities in 1988 marked the regime's recognition that it could not direct the development of China as a whole. It justified this policy with the dubious claim that wealth would 'trickle down' to the poorer interior provinces. This policy is also likely to increase the gulf between the Han Chinese of the coast and the national minorities of the interior and thus exacerbate racial tensions. When a bill giving Shenzen SEZ in Guangdong the right to pass its own laws was discussed at the National People's Congress in April 1989, nearly half the delegates voted against or abstained – an extraordinary result for a body which normally unanimously supports government policy.[64]

In the course of 1988 Li Peng came to the fore as the leading critic of Zhao Ziyang's reforms. By summer the scale of popular discontent forced the government to make concessions and slow the pace of reform. The September central committee meeting effectively marked the end of the reform decade. The leadership now postponed further price reforms, cut back investment in fixed assets and consumption funds, imposed controls on the issue of currency, clamped down on arbitrary price increases and launched a campaign against corruption. However, as the corrective measures began to take effect, the economic situation continued to deteriorate. To make matters worse measures taken to restore control over the economy were applied indiscriminately and insensitively; thus cuts in electricity supply were enforced in the same way as cuts in spending on business entertainment.

Li Peng's report to the March 1989 National People's Congress was a direct attack on the reform policies of Zhao and Deng:

> Instead of taking vigorous measures in good time to stabilise finance and control prices when inflation was already rather conspicuously felt, we relaxed control over, and readjusted the prices of more commodities, only to intensify the panic of the masses over the price hikes and evoke a buying spree and a drop

in savings deposits in many localities ... our work over the past six months has helped slow down the economic growth rate, weakened price hikes, alleviated people's panic over prices, and more or less stabilized urban and rural markets.[65]

This was a considerable exaggeration. The reduction in enterprise funds led to defaults on debts both to other enterprises and to banks. There was also a sudden rise in unemployment: 5 million construction workers were laid off and returned to their villages or roamed the streets looking for work; in the first three months of 1989 around 2.5 million unemployed peasants came into Guangdong looking for work.[66] According to a Japanese report 81,000 enterprises had gone bankrupt by January 1989 as inflation accelerated to between 25 and 50 per cent; for some commodities prices were rising even faster.[67] State industries were obliged to raise wages to enable workers to survive.

After months of deepening economic instability and growing popular dissatisfaction, students took to the streets in April 1989, using the death of party leader Hu Yaobang as a pretext. It soon became clear that the scale of the 1989 protest movement was much greater than that of student demonstrations in 1986 and 1987. For the first time the working class, dubbed 'ordinary citizens' in the Chinese press, became involved. Though the experience of the cynically manipulated mass mobilisations of the 'cultural revolution' had made many older Chinese workers suspicious of any kind of political activity, a new generation, formed in the reform decade, was now willing to take action. Young workers and students could not reconcile their experience of inflation, unemployment and threats to subsidies on essential goods with party propaganda about the achievements of reform. An official survey in 1988 candidly revealed that 'the masses' expectations of the benefits that they can gain from the reform keep rising in a straight line' while 'the level of the masses' subjective appraisal of the improvement of their living standard keeps decreasing.'[68] By 1989 the CCP had become synonymous with corruption; a 'reformer' was regarded as someone on the make. A survey of 12 townships in Jiangsu province between May 1987 and May 1988 recorded 381 incidents of the 'masses taking revenge on village cadres'.[69]

There were two significant features of the protests which culminated in the 4 June massacre in Beijing's Tiananmen Square.[70] The first was the extraordinary paralysis which gripped the bureaucracy throughout May: even the proclamation of martial law on

20 May was followed by nearly two weeks of indecision. The second was the diffuse character of the protest movement. Though Western observers characterised the movement as 'pro-democracy' and drew parallels with events in Eastern Europe, the Chinese participants were far from clear that their aim was to introduce Western-style democracy, of which China has no traditions or experience whatever. Nor indeed are there any neighbouring countries which might act as a model for democracy in China. On the contrary, the most appealing model for many is that of the economically successful regimes run by Chinese capitalists in Hong Kong, Taiwan and Singapore on authoritarian lines. Some reformers in China have openly championed a 'new authoritarianism' led by an 'enlightened autocracy' which would 'force ahead with the reforms with an iron fist ... and eventually ... bid farewell to authoritarian politics and thus release economic prosperity and political development'.[71] Western liberals found this approach rather disconcerting, observing that a policy of promoting reform 'while at the same time terrorising intellectuals and implementing a regime of political repression is inherently contradictory'.[72]

China after Tiananmen Square

The Tiananmen Square massacre led to a widespread questioning of the likely subsequent course of Chinese policy both abroad and at home. Would the grisly events relayed to the world by television delay the process of integrating China into the world economy that had accelerated so dramatically over the previous decade? Did the military clampdown portend a return to the rigid conformity and the Stalinist command economy of the Mao period?

Early Western reactions to the 4 June massacre were muted expressions of embarrassment rather than condemnation.[73] While Britain's *Financial Times* pontificated that the 'The world demands a high price for a return to normality', former US president Richard Nixon, who had restored relations with China in 1972, suggested that the price should not be too high: he begged the West not to 'shut the door on China'.[74] When Nixon subsequently visited Beijing as Bush's unofficial envoy, he was humiliated by an unrepentant Deng, who blamed the US for fomenting 'counter-revolution' and demanded that Washington take the initiative in restoring links.[75] The President of the US–China Business Council summed up the pragmatic response of the West:

We must of course deplore the suppression and wanton killing of the demonstrators and find appropriate ways to respond. But we must also resist the temptation to respond emotionally. It would be unwise to take any actions which would undermine our long term interests or those of the people of China whom we wish to support.[76]

The US was so successful in resisting the temptation to respond emotionally that work on a project to upgrade China's antiquated F8 fighter aircraft, which was suspended in June, began again after a couple of months.[77]

From China's point of view, the most serious threat was that of a suspension of its substantial foreign loans.[78] The bureaucrats need not have worried. Within a few months one commentator observed that 'although new lending activity is well below the level before 4 June, the resumption of lending is a barometer of how quickly business sentiment has turned around in a market still regarded as profitable.'[79] Another expert commented that 'China has undoubtedly learned much from Tiananmen, in particular the significance of a high credit rating in the Western economic and financial systems.'[80] World Bank officials continued working on their existing projects in China and were anxious to resume lending. Even at the height of the June crisis foreign bankers were active in Beijing.[81] By early 1990, David Wilson, Britain's man in Hong Kong, was cordially shaking hands with Deng, and Douglas Hurd, newly appointed foreign secretary, was pleading that 'it's not for us to tell the Chinese how China should be run.'[82] The message from the West was clear: mass murder and repression in China were no obstacle to doing business as usual.

How is China likely to be integrated into the world economy in the 1990s? At present China accounts for nearly 2 per cent of world trade and about 5 per cent of trade in the Pacific region.[83] In the past relations with the US have always been the key to China's international role and since the 1970s the US has been keen to strengthen links. As President Bush summed up the perspective from Washington, 'if you look at the world and understand the dynamics of the Pacific area, good relations with China are in the national interest of the United States.'[84] The US has two major objectives in China. The first is strategic: China has proved very helpful to the US in tying down a large part of the Soviet army on the Eastern front. The second is economic: the lure of the world's biggest market is a long-standing theme in US business journals. Ever since the US 'lost China' with the defeat of the Guomindang in 1949, China has assumed almost mythical significance.[85] However, the shifting pattern of great power alliances and the global decline of US power are already diminishing the importance of relations between the US and China. The recent improvement in US–Soviet and Sino–Soviet relations has reduced the importance of the strategic component of the alliance. The dynamic East Asian economies are becoming more important to China than the stagnant US.

China's relations with its neighbour and historic enemy Japan remain complex and often contradictory. On the one hand, China complains constantly about Japan's reluctance to invest and to import China's shoddy products and its policy of vetoing Japanese high-tech exports to China. On the other hand, traditional hostility to Japan remains intense, fuelled by frequent press reminders of past Japanese occupations and accounts of its rapidly increasing military budget.[86] Japan too is ambivalent about its relations with China. While Tokyo is keen to exploit the massive Chinese market, it fears that if capitalist development really took off in China the sheer size of its economy could soon allow it to overwhelm Japan.[87]

It is most likely that the 'four small dragons' of Hong Kong, Singapore, Taiwan and South Korea will increase their trade and investment stake in China at the expense of both Japan and the US. Hong Kong is likely to continue to be the most important partner for China. After the formal return of Hong Kong to China in 1997 most local capitalists can be expected to continue to keep their financial interests in China. The substantial investment by Hong Kong in China already gives rise to the question 'will the tail wag the dog?' after 1997. More than 3 million Chinese in Guangdong are already employed by Hong Hong manufacturers.[88] But Chinese investment in Hong Kong is also on a large scale, though impossible to quantify. Taiwan shares Hong Kong's advantage of having an indigenous Chinese capitalist class, without the disadvantage of impending territorial fusion, and its currency reserves are currently the world's second largest.[89] China has offered special treatment for Taiwan investors in its SEZs, including exclusive use of a special industrial zone near Shenzen.[90]

South Korea would appear an unlikely candidate for a close relationship with China. It has no expatriate Chinese business community and the legacy of the Korean War and the partition of the country preclude any formal alliance with China. Yet, whereas in the past North Korean protests have blocked joint projects, they are unlikely to continue to do so as diplomatic relations improve;

indeed North Korea has itself set up an SEZ. South Korea is very close to the northern Chinese provinces of Shandong, Jiangsu, Hebei and Lioning, and its 'medium' level technology is more appropriate to China than the high-tech of Japan. Rising labour costs and working-class militancy at home make investment in China an attractive proposition for South Korean capitalists; between 20 and 50 Korean firms have invested in China and at the end of 1989 more than 80 joint ventures were under discussion.[91] Because most trade is conducted indirectly through Hong Kong, it is difficult to estimate its true extent. Unlike Japan, South Korea is not tarnished with a record of imperialist conquest and it is not yet so strong that it presents a threat to China. Japan has promoted relations between South Korea and China, hoping to deflect cheap South Korean goods to China.[92]

One possible consequence of recent trends which has been widely discussed in China is the disintegration of the country into a loose federation of provinces each under the influence of a particular capitalist power. Some Chinese commentators consider that this has already happened and that the country is 'split into about 30 dukedoms, with some 2,000 rival principalities'.[93] Before 4 June, the state attempted to rein in the most autonomous provinces, but because of the essential role of provinces like Guangdong in attracting foreign exchange it made little headway. [94]

Western capitalists took a sober view of the June clampdown, regarding it as the inevitable domestic cost of restoring market relations. However, many journalists portrayed it as a dramatic reversal of the trends of the previous decade, as a 'conservative backlash' which meant a return to 'Maoist orthodoxy'. Indeed it is easy to confuse the post-June drive 'to energetically seek out counter-revolutionaries' with numerous waves of repression launched by the regime since the 1950s. The injunction to all work units and colleges that Deng Xiaoping's typically banal statement to the nation on 9 June must be 'thoroughly discussed' was strikingly reminiscent of the days of Mao.[95] In its attempt to restore the legitimacy of party rule the Chinese leadership resorted to the rhetoric of the Mao era to justify coercing the students, workers and especially party members who supported the protest movement. At the same time harsh disciplinary measures were imposed: already miserable holiday leave was cancelled, some workers suffered cuts in subsidies worth up to 50 per cent of wages and others were forced to spend up to 100 per cent of their wages on bonds in their own industries.[96]

It is important however not to confuse the form of the government campaign with its content. Maoist rhetoric is the only language of political debate in China and the regime has no alternative but to attempt to justify its policies in these terms. But there is no possibility of a return to Maoist orthodoxy in today's China; the object of the clampdown is to stabilise the process of capitalist transformation, not to reverse it. The reforms have acquired too great a momentum, they have achieved too great a transformation of social relations and China has become too integrated into the world economy for the whole process to be turned backwards. The bureaucracy itself has no intention of retreating because, more than any other section of society, it has gained from the reforms. At the lowest level, party cadres benefited from land allocation when the communes were split up. At higher levels, officials control the distribution and allocation of scarce resources. At the very top the blatant corruption of the bureaucrats and their integration into capitalist ventures is common knowledge.[97]

The social and political changes in China are such that even if the CCP wanted to turn back the clock to the 1960s it lacks the base of support from which to rally the sort of mass mobilisations that enabled Mao to consolidate his rule. This was true even before the 4 June massacre destroyed its last vestiges of legitimacy. The party also faces the problem of replacing the ageing Deng in the near future. Since the death of Mao, Deng has performed a fairly successful balancing act in producing a degree of consensus among political interest groups in the bureaucracy. While at first backing Hu Yaobang and Zhao Ziyang in speeding up the pace of reforms, Deng was ready to jettison them when they moved too fast and upset the balance. Yang Shangkun is the most obvious choice, but at 82 he may not even outlive Deng. The younger generation of leaders, who have risen through the ranks by patronage or nepotism, seem to lack the dynamism or charisma required to emerge as 'paramount leader'.[98]

The most important question, however, is not who succeeds Deng but the manner of the succession. If the transition is not managed smoothly then there is the real possibility of a military coup, though there is no evidence that any faction of the army has any particular political aspirations. The army's apparent vacillation after the proclamation of martial law probably reflected conflicts within the bureaucracy rather than the military. The authorities decided to use troops from six of China's seven military regions, not because of fears of mutiny, but to spread the responsibility as widely as possible.

There can be little doubt that the move towards capitalist restoration will continue after the state has regained some control over the economy. In October 1989, on the occasion of the 40th anniversary of the foundation of the people's republic, Jiang Zemin, who replaced Zhao as CCP general secretary, inadvertently provided a striking description of the likely direction of events:

> If we do not uphold socialism in the future but instead, as some people advocate, turn back to the capitalist road, using the blood and sweat of our working people to cultivate and fatten a new capitalist class ... it will only result in the majority of people once again being reduced to extreme poverty. Such a capitalism could be only the old style comprador capitalism, implying that every race in China would once again sink to becoming the twin slaves of foreign capital and a domestic exploiting class.[99]

Instead of taking this sort of rhetorical anti-capitalism at face value, in the manner of some Western commentators, it is more useful to look at the practical measures taken by the Chinese leadership after June 1989. It is significant that there was no widespread purge of the CCP, even though whole sections of the party were openly involved in the demonstrations in May and June. Nor were there any signs of a return to centralised command management, which as we have seen, was never highly developed in China even in the Mao era. Events since Tiananmen Square confirm that the regime in China has no alternative but to carry on down the capitalist road.

Both Western and Chinese authors often blame the absence of any coordinated plan of market reforms for the chaos and unrest that resulted. Indeed there can be no doubt that the failure of the Chinese leadership to control the allocation of financial and material resources encouraged inflation and corruption. But if the Chinese rulers could plan their system, then it would not be necessary to introduce the market; introducing the market into a Stalinist economy inevitably has a destabilising effect. Two major obstacles remain to be confronted. First, though many prices have been deregulated, sooner or later market forces must be allowed free rein, which will mean sharp increases in the prices of grain and other essential goods. It is unlikely that the state will be able to continue subsidising urban living standards even at present levels. Second, the application of capitalist principles to China's labour market will mean making redundant hundreds of millions of 'under-employed' workers. The process of reform has already increased differentials and polarised Chinese society in a way unprecedented since 1949. The hesitancy of the old leadership in the weeks leading up to the 4 June massacre revealed the difficulty of the Mao generation in coming to terms with the consequences of reform. The emerging Chinese ruling class, composed largely of those with connections to the bureaucracy at home and Chinese capitalists abroad, will probably have to resort to military rule to cope with the social upheaval involved in the full-scale restoration of capitalist social relations in China.

The main obstacle to the Chinese bureaucracy's plans for further capitalist development is the working class – the biggest urban proletariat in the world. After Tiananmen Square the working class has become the target of an intense wave of repression as the bureaucracy struggles to regain control. The response of the working class to these events remains unclear. One of the most striking features of the protest movement was its failure to develop a political dimension beyond immediate concerns such as inflation and corruption. On the other hand, the CCP has now lost all legitimacy and, unlike Eastern Europe, in China the protest movement did not acquire a right-wing pro-capitalist bias. It is worth noting that the overseas Chinese capitalists seem to have exerted little influence over the protest movement. Even those in Taiwan, traditionally the most hostile to the regime, did not take advantage of the Tiananmen clampdown to launch their usual anti-communist tirade.

Given the extent of working class disillusionment with the CCP it is unlikely that in the short term many workers will look to Marxism to provide the way forward. Yet in 1984, when censorship was relaxed, an extraordinary number of publications appeared calling for genuine working-class control. The Chinese working class has a long tradition of struggle, dating back to the famous 4 May 1919 protests when workers joined students on the streets of Shanghai. Within eight years, the working-class movement was strong enough to threaten to seize state power in the civil war of 1927, an opportunity squandered as a result of the Stalinist policies of the international communist movement.[100] The resulting defeat and the virtual liquidation of the working-class base of the Chinese communist movement ensured that the 1949 revolution had a more national democratic than a proletarian character. Though the 1949 revolution was a major blow to the world capitalist order, it did not put power in the hands of the Chinese working class which remained the object of Maoist propaganda rather than the force leading the transformation of society. Forty years later, the Chinese working class is stirring again. Many workers supported a movement which challenged the regime without offering an alternative political focus or national leadership of its own; just as in Russia in 1905, defeat was inevitable. But just as the Russian workers returned with strong organisation and decisive political direction a dozen years later, so the Chinese working class can learn the lessons of Tiananmen Square and win their own victory.

Mark Wu is a research microbiologist at a London hospital. His long-standing interest in China has developed through extensive discussions with his Chinese relatives.

Notes

Journals:
Business China
Beijing Review
China Newsletter
China Business
China Analysis
China Review
China Quarterly
Far Eastern Economic Review
Problems of Communism
Studies in Comparative Communism
C Riskin, *Political Economy of China* 1987

Translations and abstractions:
Foreign Broadcast Information Service (US), China.
BBC Summary of World Broadcasts (UK), Far East/China.

1. Thanks are due to Professor Rhoads Murphey, University of Michigan, Ann Arbor and a postgraduate student from Beijing Normal University who wishes to remain anonymous, for useful comments and discussion of earlier drafts of this chapter.
2. The best introduction to the period before 1949 is the *Cambridge History of China*, Vol 12: Republican China 1912–1949 pt 1, edited by J.K. Fairbank, Cambridge University Press, 1983; and Vol 13: Republican China 1912–1949 pt 2 edited by J.K. Fairbank and A. Feuerwerker, Cambridge

University Press, 1986. The bibliographical essays are especially useful. For a stimulating discussion on how the CCP won support during the Second World War, see Chen Yung Fa, *Making Revolution, the communist movement in Eastern and Central China, 1937–1945*, Berkeley: University of California Press, 1986. Alan Harding's 'China: Stalinism and national liberation' in *Confrontation*, No 5, Summer 1989, also provides a useful background.

3. Mao Zedong, *Selected Works Vol II*, Beijing: Foreign Language Press, 1967, pp. 305–334.

4. Cited in T.B. Gold, 'Urban Private Business in China',*Studies in Comparative Communism*, Vol XXII, 2/3, p. 187–201, 1989.

5. *Beijing Review*, 28 April 1980, pp. 19–21.

6. C. Riskin, *China's Political Economy*, Oxford: Oxford University Press, 1987, p. 127.

7. Sun Ye Fang in *Foreign Broadcast Information Service China*, March 1981, L4–L9.

8. See Riskin, *China's Political Economy*, pp. 201–22 for a comprehensive discussion on the precise meaning of the term 'self-reliance' and its application at different levels of administration.

9. See for example Joint Economic Committee of Congress, *An Economic Profile of Mainland China*, Washington: 1967.

10 For example World Bank, *China: Socialist Economic Development*, Vol I–III, 1983 and subsequent reports. Chinese statistics collected by the State Statistical Bureau are published in the *Statistical Yearbook* and the most important in *Beijing Review*.

11. *China Statistical Yearbook 1984*, Beijing: Chinese Statistical Publishing House, 1984.

12. World Bank, *World Development Report*, 1987.

13. See Riskin, *China's Political Economy*, pp. 257–83

14. Cited in M. Selden *The Political Economy of Chinese Socialism*, New York: ME Sharpe, 1987.

15. This figure includes both those who starved to death directly and those who died prematurely as a result of the famine. See Ashton et al., 'Famine in China 1958–1961', *Population and Development Review*, 4, 1984. Estimates of the numbers of people who died in the famine have continually been revised upwards. Ironically, even the estimates by anti-communist Westerners, which were widely ridiculed at the time as gross exaggerations, turned out to be underestimates.

16. Jiang et al., 1980, cited in Riskin, *China's Political Economy*, p. 262.
17. N. Lardy, 'Prices Markets and the Chinese Peasant', *Discussion Paper No 428*, Yale Economic Growth Centre, 1982.
18. *China Statistical Yearbook 1982*, Beijing: Chinese Statistical Publishing House, 1982.
19. See M. Selden, 'City versus countryside' in *Political Economy of Chinese Socialism*, for an interesting discussion on urban bias in CCP policies and a comparison with the achievements of large rural backward capitalist countries such as India.
20. Yok-Shiu F. Lee, 'The urban housing problem in China' *China Quarterly*, 115, 1988, pp. 387–407.
21. 'On Questions of Party History – Resolution on certain Questions in the History of our Party since the founding of the People's Republic of China' (1981) is the reformists' attempt to reassess the record of the Maoist era and the errors of the 'great proletarian revolutionary Mao Zedong'.
22. 'On Questions of Party History'.
23. See M. Oksenberg, 'China's 13th Party Congress', *Problems of Communism*, Nov–Dec 1987, pp. 1–17.
24. Zhao Ziyang, 'Advance along the road of socialism with Chinese characteristics', *Beijing Review*, 9 November, 1987, pp. 23–49.
25. See M. Oksenberg, 'China's 13th Party Congress', *Problems of Communism*, Nov–Dec 1987, pp. 1–17.
26. Liu Guogang, one of China's leading economists in an article entitled 'the sweet and sour decade ' calls the first period 'sweet' and the second 'sour'; unfortunately this leaves him with no adjective to describe the third period; 'bitter' which is the commonest Chinese metaphor would scarcely be politically acceptable. *Beijing Review*, 2 January 1989, p. 22–9.
27. Riskin, *China's Political Economy*, p. 298.
28. B. Stone, 'Developments in Agricultural Technology', *China Quarterly*, 116, 1987, pp. 767–822.
29. J. Fewsmith, 'Agricultural crisis in China', *Problems of Communism*, Nov–Dec 1988, pp. 78–92.
30. Riskin, *China's Political Economy*, pp. 306.
31. Y.Y. Kueh, 'Food consumption and peasant income in the post-Mao era', *China Quarterly*, 116, 1988, pp. 634–670.
32. *Beijing Review*, 49, 3 December 1984.

33. J. Fewsmith, 'Agricultural crisis in China', and *Far Eastern Economic Review*, 13 July 1989.

Table: Changes in annual per capita income of peasants

1978–84 (average)	+17.6
1985	+11.8
1986	+6.9
1987	+5.5
1988	–6.3

From Fewsmith, 'Agricultural crisis'.

34. A. Watson, 'Investment issues in the Chinese countryside', *Australian Journal of Chinese Affairs*, 22, 1989, pp. 85–126.
35. A. Watson, 'Investment issues in the Chinese countryside', p. 114
36. B. Stone, 'Developments in agricultural technology', *China Quarterly*, 116, 1988, pp. 767–822. Stone explains how the extent of this deterioration may have been unintentionally exaggerated, see especially pp. 771–83.
37. *Far Eastern Economic Review*, 13 July 1989.
38. *Far Eastern Economic Review* and Fewsmith 'Agricultural crisis in China', p. 78–92.
39. 'Li Peng stresses the importance of population control' in *BBC Short Wave Broadcasting Far East, China*, FE/0400/B2/2 1989.
40. China's trade turnover has increased from US$ 15 billion in 1978, through US$ 44 billion in 1983 to US$ 103 billion in 1988. See S. Nakajima, 'The Chinese economy in 1988', *China Newsletter*, 79, 1989 p. 19–20 and N. Lardy, 'Prices Markets and the Chinese Peasant', p. 4.
41. Zhao Ziyang, *China's Economy and Development Principles*, Beijing: Foreign Language Press, 1982, p. 47.
42. *World Bank*, 1983, Vol II, p. 139.
43. 'Special Report: Chinese bonds in the introduction of foreign capital', *China Newsletter*, 82, 1989, pp. 9–15.
44. Between 1982 and the end of 1988, China floated US$ 25 billion; 21 of the 39 issues were floated in Tokyo. See 'Special report: China's hard currency problems', *China Newsletter*, 82, 1989, pp. 2–8.
45. Zhao, *China's Economy and Development Principles*, p. 49.
46. *Far Eastern Economic Review*, 11 October 1984.

47. China has probably spent more on the infrastructural investment of the SEZs than it has gained. *Far Eastern Economic Review*, 7 March 1985. See D. Philips and A.G.O. Yeh, *Special Economic Zones in China's Regional Development*, ed. D.S.G. Goodman, London: Routledge, 1989, pp. 112–34.
48. *Beijing Review*, 12 August 1985.
49. J. Tong, 'Fiscal Reform, elite turnover and central provincial relations in post-Mao China', *Australian Journal of Chinese Affairs*, 22, 1989, pp. 1–28.
50. Cyril Lin, *Guardian*, March 1989
51. D. Solinger, 'Capitalist Measures with Chinese Characteristics', *Problems of Communism*, Jan–Feb 1989, pp. 19–33.
52. *Far Eastern Economic Review*, 9 November 1989.
53. Much of the 'co-operative industry' was essentially private, but registered as co-operative for reasons of caution.
54. *Beijing Review*, 16 January 1989, pp. 42–3.
55. J.S. Prybla, 'China's economic experiment: back from the market', *Problems Of Communism*, Jan–Feb 1989, pp. 1–18.
56. Cited in Solinger, 'Capitalist Measures with Chinese Characteristics', p. 20.
57. See L. Cheng and L. White, 'The Thirteenth Central Committee of the Chinese Communist Party from mobilisers to managers', *Asian Survey*, XXVIII, 4, 1989, pp. 371–99.
58. SSB figures quoted in *China Newsletter*, 81, 9, 1989, p. 8.
59. *China Business Review*, Jan–Feb 1989, p. 30.
60. SSB figures quoted in *China Newsletter*, 81, 9, 1989, p. 8. Previously an upper limit of seven had been enforced, apparently because of a passing comment in a letter from Marx to Engels, which mentioned seven employees as the number above which an employer becomes a capitalist.
61. Compare *BBC Short Wave Broadcasting* and *Foreign Broadcasting Information Service* (US) reports for 1987 with 1988; in particular see *Foreign Broadcasting Information Service* 36, 6 September 1988, and 21, 29 August 1988.
62 *Beijing Review*, 16 January 1989, pp. 42–3.
63 See for example A. Watson et al, 'Who won the "wool war", a case study of rural product marketing in China', *China Quarterly*, 118, pp. 213–41.
64. *Independent*, 5 April 1989.
65. K. Yamanouchi, 'China's economic reforms meet with difficulties', *China Newsletter*, 81, 1989, pp. 8–12.
66. Yamanouchi, 'China's economic reforms meet with difficulties'.

67. *Financial Times*, 12 December 1989.
68. *Foreign Broadcasting Information Service*, 6 October 1988, p. 17.
69. *Foreign Broadcasting Information Service*, 26 September 1988, p. 12.
70. Numerous day-by-day accounts are now available. The best journalistic account is M. Fathers and A. Higgins, 'Tiananmen: The rape of Beijing', *Independent*, 1989. The most comprehensive and balanced account is in the 'China Quarterly Chronicle and Documentation April–June 1989', *China Quarterly*, 119, pp. 666–734.
71. *New York Times*, 28 Febuary 1989, and *Independent*, 29 March 1989.
72. See J.P. Burns, 'China's Governance: Political reform in a turbulent environment', *China Quarterly*, 119, pp. 481–518.
73. For a summary see *China Quarterly*, 119.
74. *Financial Times*, 30 June 1989.
75. *Financial Times*, 1 and 2 November 1989.
76. *China Business Review*, 8 July/August 1989.
77. *Far Eastern Economic Review*, 16 November 1989.
78. For a discussion on conflicting estimates of China's debt see 'Special Report: China's hard currency problems', *China Newsletter*, 82, 1989, pp. 2–8. See also *Business China*, 11 Sept 1989, p. 11; *China Review*, Sept 1989 p. 4.
79. *Far Eastern Economic Review*, 2 November 1989, p. 48.
80. 'Special report: Chinese bonds in the introduction of foreign capital', *China Newsletter*, 82, 1989, pp. 9–15.
81. *Far Eastern Economic Review*, 2 November 1989, p. 48.
82. *Guardian*, 20 January 1990.
83. IMF, *Directory of World Trade Statistics Yearbook*, 1985.
84. *Guardian*, 28 June 1989.
85. See Burns, 'China's Governance'. Burns makes the point that the 'mythic dimensions of China's economic significance often prevail over the hard facts'. He cites a recent US Government report whose compilers included both Brezinski and Kissinger which projected that by 2010 China would rank third in the world , behind the US and Europe with a GNP of just under US\$ 3 trillion – about the same as Japan. In 1988, China's GNP was only US\$ 372 billion.
86. *Beijing Review*, 6 March 1989, pp. 12–15.
87. Japan's Ministry of International Trade and Industry tried to block Hitachi's application to transfer video cassette recorder 'head' technology to China which would enable China to manufacture its own VCRs (*Wall Street Journal*, 10

the exchange of products, technologies and ideas, and wide-ranging contacts among people'.[8]

If, according to the new thinking, the East-West class struggle is obsolete, then so also is old-style anti-imperialist struggle in the Third World. According to Primakov

a thorough change is also appropriate for the Marxist theory of class struggle – this also must find a way out of the critical situation and find ways in which a social renewal of the world in the extremely complex new situation can be found.[9]

The director of the Soviet Union's African Institute puts the point more bluntly. 'For all practical purposes,' says A. Vasilyev, 'the age of national-liberation wars is over.'[10] The Soviet Union now seeks to avoid confrontations with Western powers in the Third World. As Andrei Kolosovsky, Soviet assistant deputy foreign minister, argued, 'the Third World is not an arena for an East-West showdown.'[11]

Rather than take advantage of anti-Western hostility the Soviet leadership is keen to work out a joint approach to solving regional problems. This is what Gorbachev meant when he said that he hoped 'that the common struggle against international terrorism will broaden in the years to come'.[12] The Soviet bureaucracy is particularly eager to cooperate with the US in the Third World. As one Soviet foreign ministry official explained: 'Generally speaking, the promotion of new political thinking has enabled us to devise a common approach to regional conflicts, an approach making the Soviet position more balanced and flexible than before.'[13] In July 1989 new KGB chief Vladimir Kryuchkov, announced his enthusiasm for joint work with the CIA against terrorism and drug-trafficking.[14]

The second feature of the Soviet new thinking on foreign policy is the striking way the Gorbachev leadership appears to have accepted some of the key themes of traditional Western Cold War ideology. Moscow now freely admits that instability and conflict in the Third World have often been the result of its own actions. It seems that the idea of the 'Soviet threat' – a cold war myth – has been internalised and now re-emerges as a component of Soviet foreign policy doctrine. For example, Soviet analysts have come to accept the Western view that it was the Soviet invasion of Afghanistan, rather than American propaganda, that triggered the second Cold War.

Gorbachev has been highly critical of the way past leaders have handled international affairs. In *Perestroika* he sharply criticises

Nikita Khrushchev, a Soviet leader known for his anti-Western rhetoric, and describes him as 'an emotional man'.[15] Gorbachev goes on to claim, however, that it is nonsense to argue that Lenin expounded a doctrine of world revolution. The idea that the Soviet Union is behind national liberation movements he describes as 'a malicious lie'.[16]

Despite Gorbachev's reservations the view that Moscow was to blame for much Third World conflict in the past is widespread among Soviet commentators. A typical article explains how past Soviet policies have justified Western fears of Soviet expansionism:

> It has to be admitted that ... the continuing direct and indirect Soviet support for some forces and regimes in the Third World prone to use force to settle international problems prompted propagandistic accusations that the Soviet Union was bent on expansion and intended to use the lessening of tensions in Europe to gain an edge on the West in the Third World .[17]

The object of such breast-beating confessions of past misdemeanours is to emphasise the commitment of the Gorbachev regime to keep out of Third World conflicts. As early as 1987, Primakov noted the positive diplomatic results of this policy:

> The situation today is far from what it was two or three years ago. It is becoming more and more difficult for anti-Sovieteers in the West to maintain their artificially created image of the USSR as a bellicose, undemocratic state that threatens the West and thinks about nothing but expansion.[18]

It is a short step from arguing the need for cooperation with the Western powers to the acceptance of capitalism as a dynamic force in the Third World. This third theme of the new thinking on Soviet foreign policy has been described by one Western commentator as its 'conditioning principle'.[19] Having recognised the fact that its own system does not offer a viable model for development at home or abroad, the Soviet leadership has come around to an acknowledgement of the vitality of capitalism. So, according to Kolosovsky,

> we believe ... that the experience of successful and rapid development of many countries in Asia, Latin America and in Africa for that matter, and the astonishing progress achieved in solving the food problem in such densely populated countries as India

and China, debunk the apocalyptical view of the world economy as being in deep crisis.[20]

Some Soviet commentators are even more explicit about the supposed merits of capitalism. Andrei V. Kozyrev, a prominent official in the Soviet foreign ministry, has reversed the old orthodoxy that the Eastern bloc and the Third World have a common interest in resisting the West. Instead he argues that the Third World shares an interest with the West in developing capitalism:

> The myth that the class interests of socialist and developing countries coincide in resisting imperialism does not hold up to criticism at all. The majority of developing countries already adhere to or tend toward the Western model of development and they suffer not so much capitalism as from a lack of it.[21]

Even traditional targets of Stalinist abuse have been rehabilitated: one writer argues that it is necessary to avoid 'a one-sided evaluation of the activity of Transnational Corporations and of the recommendations of the IMF, the World Bank and other international organisations'.[22] The Soviet bureaucracy has come full circle to the traditional right-wing Western view that the problems of the Third World result from not enough capitalism rather than too much.

The conclusion of the new thinking in Soviet foreign policy doctrine is the need to remove ideology from international relations. In the past, whatever the state of military tensions between East and West, the Soviet bureaucracy has always had a distinct and coherent ideology. By the late 1980s the moral collapse of the Soviet Union had gone so far that Gorbachev explicitly rejected Moscow's claim to have a distinct world view. At a speech in Rome in 1989 he said:

> we have abandoned the claim to have a monopoly of truth; we no longer think that we are always right, that those who disagree with us are our enemies. We have now decided, firmly and irrevocably, to base our policy on the principles of freedom of choice, and to develop our culture through dialogue and acceptance of all that is applicable in our conditions.[23]

Gorbachev's explicit renunciation of the distinctive outlook promoted by the Soviet Union for more than half a century means that there is no longer any basis even for ideological rivalry between East and West. In the past the Soviet Union often disguised conservative policies behind radical rhetoric.[24] In practice the Soviet Union long ago made peace with the West in the economic and military spheres. But this did not preclude denunciations of the capitalist system or the promotion of the Soviet model when international circumstances were opportune. Today Gorbachev is an overt conservative who has actively disclaimed all radical pretensions for the Soviet Union. For him 'the psychological and ideological struggle should be a thing of the past.'[25]

Many of the arguments of the new thinkers are presented more or less openly as attacks on the activist foreign policy of the Brezhnev era which is widely blamed for the problems the Soviet Union is facing today. Several prominent new thinkers have come to the fore at the expense of former Brezhnev foreign policy ideologues.[26]

Yet the key ideas of new thinking had already begun to emerge in the later years of Brezhnev's rule. First advanced in specialist journals such as *Vosprosy filsofii* and *Vosprosy ekonomiki*, the new concepts gradually permeated the Soviet foreign policy establishment.[27] The term 'new thinking' was first used in 1983 during the brief interregnum of Yuri Andropov.[28] In *Moscow's post-Brezhnev Reassessment of the Third World*, published in February 1986, Francis Fukuyama anticipated many of the foreign policy changes that were to occur under Gorbachev.[29] By this time the Soviet Union had virtually given up a confrontational posture with the West even in such cases as Afghanistan, Angola, Ethiopia and Nicaragua.[30]

The existence of the main themes of new thinking under Brezhnev shows that the foreign policy shift cannot be understood solely in terms of the ideas of Gorbachev. New thinking only became popular among the Soviet leadership because of the changing conditions facing the country in the 1980s. Indeed the shift in Moscow's foreign policy behaviour predates the widespread acceptance of new thinking. To grasp the relationship between the new thinking and the conduct of foreign policy it is necessary to look at the impact on the Soviet Union of international developments in the late 1970s and early 1980s.

Patterns of Soviet foreign policy

Brezhnev could pursue an activist foreign policy in the 1970s because of a string of setbacks for the West in the Third World. The devastating defeat of the US in Vietnam in the early 1970s was the catalyst for a series of Third World uprisings. Laos and Cambodia soon followed. In southern Africa, the remains of the Portuguese empire in Angola and Mozambique collapsed and radical nationalist movements came to power in 1975; Zimbabwe followed in 1979 and South Africa itself was shaken by internal revolt. In Latin America, the Sandinistas overthrew US stooge Anastasio Somoza in Nicaragua and in the Middle East, another vital US ally, the Shah of Iran, was deposed by a mass popular upsurge.

The Soviet Union played little or no part in the Third World revolt against imperialism in the 1970s. Radical nationalist movements were forced to fight alone against the superior military forces of the Western powers. The result was the devastation of economic life in wide areas of South-East Asia and southern Africa and insuperable problems for the new regimes. In other cases, such as Nicaragua and Iran, the Soviet Union backed the corrupt old dictators up to the bitter end.[31] Nevertheless, Moscow was quick to take advantage of the collapse of these regimes and quickly built up close relations with the new radical governments.[32] At the CPSU congress in 1981, Brezhnev could look back with satisfaction: 'comrades, among the important results of the Party's international activity in the period under review we can list the visible expansion of cooperation with countries that have liberated themselves from colonial oppression.'[33]

Moscow's relative success in the Third World in the late 1970s reveals the responsive character of its foreign policy. The Soviet Union has generally been reluctant to promote instability in the Third World, but when the West is in trouble it is always ready to take advantage. Nationalist revolt against overstretched and declining imperialist powers provided the opportunity for Brezhnev's activist foreign policy. Soviet spokesmen spouted radical anti-colonial rhetoric and the Kremlin dispatched economic and military aid to radical regimes and nationalist movements.

By the late 1980s the Soviet Union's approach to the Third World had undergone a dramatic reversal. It shifted from activism to retrenchment, drastically cutting back its provision of resources to Third World clients. In the diplomatic sphere the Soviet Union presented itself as more of a partner than an antagonist of the West. This reversal of policy can only be explained by internal economic disintegration of the Soviet Union which reduced its ability to intervene in the Third World.[34] Boris Piadyshev, the editor-in-chief of the Soviet foreign policy journal *International Affairs*, admitted that Moscow could not cope with its existing overseas commitments: 'the positions of Soviet foreign policy were stretched to the utmost all over the world. We were involved in a whole number of problems having little relevance to our key national interests.'[35] One striking example of Moscow's weakness was its inability to provide Ethiopia, a Soviet client, with famine relief in 1985. The impoverished African state had to turn to the West instead.[36]

The Soviet leadership soon discovered that it was much more difficult to sustain its links with Third World regimes than it was to establish them at moments of imperialist defeat. Accurate estimates of the cost of Moscow's Third World initiatives are difficult to find. According to one source the cost of supporting its allies rose from $13.6 billion to $21.8 billion in 1971, to $35.9 billion to $46.5 billion in 1980.[37] These funds were concentrated in a small number of post-revolutionary regimes. Of the $23.2 billion worth of weapons and equipment sent to the Third World between 1975 and 1979 some $19 billion went to 17 'revolutionary democracies'.[38] Eduard Shevardnadze, the Soviet foreign minister, later conceded that the diversion of resources abroad under Brezhnev was a severe drain on the domestic economy: 'We frequently cooperated and at times even provoked enormous material investments in hopeless foreign policy projects and tacitly encouraged actions that in a direct and indirect sense have cost the people dearly even to this day.'[39]

In the 1980s it became increasingly difficult for the Soviet Union to play the role of a global power. Domestic stagnation forced Moscow to cultivate better relations with the West as the price of gaining access to vital new technology. By cooperating with the West in the Third World Moscow hoped not only to reduce the burden of overseas aid, but also to gain tangible economic advantages at home. The shift in Soviet foreign policy is well illustrated in two spheres of great strategic significance for the Western powers: the Middle East and South Africa.

The Middle East

In general the Soviet Union's policy towards the Middle East has always been dominated by its concern to neutralise potential threats to its southern border, while maintaining friendly relations with other countries in the region. This is how the 1987 World Oil report summed up the Soviet outlook:

The Soviets have been far more concerned about developments among their immediate neighbours than among Arab states further to the south. In this context, it is perhaps interesting that the expression 'Middle East' is very rarely used in Soviet publications and statements. Instead reference is made to 'the Near East' and the 'Central East' (i.e., the northern tier including Turkey, Iran and Afghanistan). To the Soviets developments in Afghanistan and, particularly, Iran have a far more direct influence to their vital national interests than events in Kuwait or Saudi Arabia.[40]

Despite the continuity in the underlying motivation of Soviet actions the specific forms of its Middle East policy have changed dramatically over the years. In the wake of the Suez Crisis of 1956 the Soviet Union pursued a highly activist foreign policy throughout the region. In contrast its reaction to the Gulf War of the 1980s was one of clear retrenchment.

In 1955 the US and Britain linked up with Iraq, Iran, Turkey and Pakistan in the Baghdad Pact, part of the Western strategy of 'containing' the Soviet Union. The Soviet Union perceived this move as a direct threat to its security and stepped up arms sales, via Czechoslovakia, to Egypt. When the West responded by imposing sanctions the radical Egyptian leader, Gamal Abdel Nasser, nationalised the Suez Canal. Britain and France launched a joint attack on the Suez Canal with Israel. Washington, however, infuriated by the unilateral action of its junior partners, quickly forced them to withdraw. The Suez episode boosted anti-Western feeling in the Middle East and gave the Soviet Union an important opening. Rivalries among the Western powers and their inability to contain the upsurge of radical Arab nationalism gave the Soviet Union considerable room to manoeuvre. Its main achievement was the emergence of Egypt, then the most important Arab state, as a client.

By the early 1970s Egypt accounted for nearly 30 per cent of all Soviet aid to the Third World.[41] Yet Moscow could still not consolidate its relationship with this emerging Third World country. Whereas the West could offer its clients investments, loans, high technology and consumer goods – the Soviet Union could only sell weapons and poor-quality industrial plant. In 1972 Nasser's successor Anwar Sadat decided to move back into the Western camp: 15,000 Soviet military advisers were summarily expelled. The relative ease with which Egypt detached itself from the Soviet Union underlines the lack of a durable foundation for Soviet policy in the Third World.

In the 1980s the Gulf War and the Palestinian–Israeli conflict created ample opportunities for Soviet intervention in the Middle East. But in neither of these situations did the Soviet Union have the capacity or the inclination to damage Western interests. From the beginning of the Iran–Iraq war the Soviet Union was by far the largest arms supplier to Iraq, which also enjoyed tacit Western backing. Like the West, Moscow's main concern was to contain the radical movement in Iran. In 1987 the Soviet Union was the first power to agree to reflag Kuwaiti tankers in the Gulf after the West had initially refused.[42] This move provided the impetus for the West to send its task force into the Gulf. Iran's acceptance of a ceasefire in August 1988 was also partly a result of Soviet pressure.[43] Only after the war ended and Tehran adopted an openly conservative path did the USSR sign an accord with Iran promising 'good-neighbourliness'.[44]

The contrast between Soviet policy in the 1950s and in the 1980s is also apparent in its relations to other countries in the region. After Suez, Moscow developed close relations with radical regimes and political movements. During the Gulf War it allied itself with the most conservative forces in the region. The Soviet Union has strengthened links with a now securely pro-Western Egypt and in 1985 established diplomatic relations with the United Arab Emirates and Oman.[45] More recently Gorbachev has worked closely with the West in Lebanon, to the chagrin of former Soviet allies, and has publicly called for a ceasefire.[46] In 1986 the Soviet Union paid its contribution to the United Nations Interim Force in Lebanon (Unifil) for the first time. In 1987 Moscow announced that it would pay the bill for past UN peacekeeping operations in the region and Gorbachev made a detailed proposal for strengthening the UN.[47]

Gorbachev has also shifted away from Moscow's traditional sympathy for the Palestine Liberation Organisation in favour of improving relations with Israel. At a dinner in honour of Syria's President Hafez Assad in the Kremlin he stated that the lack of diplomatic relations between Israel and the Soviet Union 'cannot be considered normal'.[48] Consular relations were established in 1987 and the first joint Israeli–Soviet enterprise, an agricultural project, has been established. It became easier for Israeli tourists to visit the USSR and Soviet Jews to leave the country.[49]

Today the Soviet Union's clients in the Middle East tend to be the most marginal states, like Libya and South Yemen. Syria is the only significant remaining Soviet client in the region, giving Moscow a foothold which it can use to participate in the Middle East 'peace process'. Yet Moscow's capacity to support Syria with huge arms supplies is dwindling. Shevardnadze warned of the dangers of a regional arms race and Alexander Zotov, the Soviet ambassador to Damascus, has warned that the 'strain of military expenditures is quite obvious in all Arab countries ... and in Syria too.'[50]

Southern Africa

Though the Soviet Union played a minimal role in Africa before the anti-imperialist revolts of the mid-1970s it subsequently extended significant support to the radical regimes in southern Africa and to resistance movements such as SWAPO in Namibia and the ANC in South Africa itself. Yet by the mid-1980s the Soviet Union's declining capacity to sustain its African activities coincided with drastic South African economic and military destabilisation of the frontline states. Moscow's response was to pull away from its former clients and seek closer relations with the apartheid state and its Western allies.

The Soviet Union has cut back on its support for the frontline states. Mozambique has been forced to move closer to South Africa – particularly after the signing of the Nkomati Accord in March 1984.[51] Angola has been forced to fund its war against South African-backed Unita insurgents from its oil revenue rather than Soviet backing. Moscow played a key role in the talks that culminated in the 1988 United Nations accord on Namibia, signed by Cuba, Angola and South Africa. *The Times* congratulated the Soviet Union for smoothing the way for the diplomacy of Chester Crocker, the US Assistant Secretary of State for African Affairs: 'It is now clear that Moscow intervened to an unprecedented degree to persuade its allies to accept his overtures'.[52]

The Soviet leadership has put heavy pressure on the ANC to come to terms with Pretoria. At a round-table meeting in Moscow in March 1989 organised by the Novosti press agency, Yuri Yukalov, head of the Soviet foreign ministry's Africa department, openly contradicted ANC leader Oliver Tambo's call for an intensification of the armed struggle against apartheid: 'We don't emphasise the need to enhance the armed struggle. There are other means such as trade and economic sanctions.'[53] Moscow's improving relations with the apartheid regime at first brought it into conflict with the South African Communist Party (SACP). Boris Asoyan, a leading Soviet specialist on Africa, wrote in *Pravda* that 'extreme radicalism in the black community' and 'white extremism' bore an equal responsibility for the conflict. He also wrote that 'Within the black community rapid stratification is taking place, and a rather substantial middle class is emerging; this middle class is interested in stability and in peaceful ways of resolving the existing conflict. Skin colour is losing its significance as a factor in economic life.'[54] The article was vehemently denounced by SACP Secretary-General Joe Slovo.

The consequence of the shift in Soviet policy was to undermine the position of its former allies. Whereas previously Moscow had talked about isolating the apartheid regime, its new policies had the effect of isolating the movements fighting against it. South African ministers were happy to receive cordially an official delegation from Moscow at a time when Gorbachev's foreign policy was helping them in their drive to push the ANC into abandoning the struggle to overthrow the apartheid regime in favour of becoming a legitimate opposition movement. In August 1989, the ANC leadership in Harare endorsed a document written by imprisoned leader Nelson Mandela agreeing to talks with the apartheid regime to negotiate a political settlement. In a notably conciliatory tone the Harare document agreed to suspend hostilities in return for concessions from the government. Subsequent talks under the direction of the new president F.W. de Klerk culminated in the February 1990 announcement of the legalisation of the ANC, the SACP and other formerly outlawed organisations, as well as the imminent release of Mandela from prison.

South African foreign minister Pik Botha was not slow to remind ANC leaders of how changes in the Soviet Union and Eastern Europe had left them with little alternative but to come to terms with the apartheid regime: 'It's time the ANC discovered that their brother comrades, along with their ideologies in Eastern Europe are gone.'[55]

For his part, SACP leader Joe Slovo was now ready to recognise that 'we have to face up to our failure in Eastern Europe' and he urged his party to embrace pluralism and a mixed economy in a new South Africa.[56] Following the official recognition of the ANC and the SACP, the Pretoria regime was in a powerful position to take advantage of the weakness and isolation of the anti-apartheid movement.

Today the Soviet Union is not interested in exploiting instability in the most stagnant Third World countries. Indeed its own economic weakness gives it an incentive to improve relations with relatively dynamic 'newly industrialising countries' such as India, Brazil, Mexico, Argentina, Singapore, Thailand, Tunisia, Sri Lanka and Malaysia.[57] Moscow's expanding relations with India, in particular, are regarded by Gorbachev as the new model for relations with Third World states.[58] Gorbachev has also pursued several initiatives to persuade the more dynamic East Asian states, including the anti-communist regimes of South Korea and Taiwan, to take part in the development of the Soviet Far East:

> The East, specifically the Asia and the Pacific region, is now the place where civilization is stepping up its pace. Our economy in its development is moving to Siberia and to the Far East. We are therefore genuinely interested in promoting Asia–Pacific co-operation.[59]

The Soviet Union's desperation for technology from the newly industrialised countries (Nics) is a telling indictment of the decline of a nation that for 40 years after the Second World War was generally preceived as a global superpower on a par with the US.

The Third World

The dramatic reversal of Soviet foreign policy in the 1980s has had a profound impact on the Third World. The shift of radical regimes to the right and the retreat of radical movements cannot be attributed to the success of a Western containment strategy. In diverse forms anti-imperialist revolt has simmered throughout the 1980s in Lebanon and on the West Bank, in the Caribbean and Latin America, in the Philippines and southern Africa. If anything, the potential threat to the Western order was even greater than in the 1970s. The two key factors which strengthened conservative trends in the Third World and saved the day for imperialism were growing disillusionment with the Soviet model of development and the effects of Moscow's policies of retrenchment and collaboration.

By the late 1980s the chronic stagnation of the Eastern bloc was apparent for all to see. The explicit admissions of the Gorbachev leadership that the Soviet system was bankrupt and that the only hope for progress lay in introducing the capitalist market finally crushed the hopes of two generations of Third World radicals that this system offered an escape from the tyranny of imperialist domination. Throughout the post-war period most Third World economies had stagnated while the West boomed. In Malaya, Vietnam, Kenya, Algeria and numerous other European colonies, the masses continued to suffer the barbarities of Western rule. The apparent success of the countries of the Eastern bloc in achieving industrialisation, full employment and reasonable living standards suggested that Stalinism was a viable alternative to the capitalist system. In the 1980s, however, the Nics revealed a new capitalist dynamism in the Third World, while the Eastern bloc decayed and Soviet-backed Third World regimes slumped into deeper poverty and famine. After 1985 Gorbachev finally admitted openly what had increasingly become evident: the Soviet model was viable neither in the Soviet Union nor anywhere else. Though it was true that much of the capitalist Third World was also becoming more impoverished, Vietnam or Guinea Bissau did not appear to offer much of an alternative.

The limitations of the Soviet model in the Third World are now universally acknowledged. According to one Soviet academic:

First of all we must recognise that our model of development, toward which these other states have been oriented, has failed to produce the desired effect in their conditions, and quite frequently has impeded economic growth and caused new problems.[60]

Western commentators are not slow to draw negative conclusions:

In the 1950s and 1960s, many first generation leaders of former colonies sought rapid economic development through heavy industrialization on the Stalinist pattern: the steel mill was a symbol of modernity. The USSR's willingness to help finance and construct industrial projects in the public sector dovetailed with the new leadership's vague beliefs in the efficacy of a centralised, planned, highly nationalised urban-oriented economy, which they saw as the salient characteristics of the Soviet model. Hopes for a quick end to poverty, as well as their belief that a capitalist colonial system had kept them in bondage, predisposed them to socialism and to the Soviet experience.[61]

Disillusionment with the Soviet model has been felt most acutely in Third World states themselves. Take Vietnam. After fighting a war to rid itself of American influence the Soviet model seemed the natural choice. But Vietnamese visitors to the Soviet Union rapidly discovered the inadequacies of the Soviet system. For example, an article in *Tien Phong*, a Vietnamese magazine, reports that in many Soviet factories 'their production tools are obsolete and break down frequently.' One shoe factory had been using 'the same old production line ... since Lenin's time'.[62] Vietnam soon turned to doi moi, its version of perestroika, as a way of reintroducing capitalism.

In addition to the negative example of the Soviet economy, Moscow's foreign policy has also helped to promote Third World conservatism. Whereas in the past the Soviet Union always acted as a counterweight to the West, it is now inclined to cut back or avoid any financial commitment to radical forces and to cooperate with the West in containing potential instability. Moscow's foreign aid budget for 1990 was 20 per cent down on the 1989 figure.[63] The most direct effects have been on the Soviet Union's most dependent client regimes.

Cuts in Soviet support for Cuba and Vietnam have put pressure on them in turn to reduce their commitments abroad, leading to troop withdrawals from Africa and Cambodia. Cuba is now particularly susceptible to Western pressure as its $4.5 billion yearly handout from Moscow represents about half of all Soviet assistance to the Third World.[64] Like other previously uncompromisingly Stalinist regimes, Cuba has been forced to introduce pro-market reforms. Fidel Castro's execution of some of his former allies on drug charges was a significant concession to the US's anti-drug crusade.[65] Even North Korea, with a reputation as one of the most unreconstructed Stalinist regimes, has opened the door slightly to foreign capital. In 1985 Pyongyang introduced a foreign joint venture law similar to that already operating in China. Today foreign firms are creeping into North Korea's manufacturing and tourism sectors.[66] Nevertheless the division of Korea still provides the basis for strong anti-imperialist rhetoric in the North.

Soviet foreign policy has also affected the more radical capitalist regimes in the Third World, pushing them in a more conservative direction. In the 1970s, for example, Michael Manley in Jamaica and Ali Bhutto in Pakistan had a reputation for radical rhetoric and fraternal relations with Moscow. By the late 1980s, Manley and Bhutto's daughter Benazir had been elected on much more moderate programmes, with regimes that leant much more towards Washington than towards Moscow.

Gorbachev's conservative diplomacy has reinforced moderate trends in radical nationalist movements, encouraging them into negotiations with the imperialist powers. One of the most striking examples was that of Swapo in Namibia. For more than two decades Swapo fought an armed struggle against the South African Defence Force. But it was only when the Soviet Union joined the negotiating process that Swapo agreed to a settlement. Soviet pressure was also crucial in the 1988 decision of the PLO to recognise the state of Israel. In 1989 Nelson Mandela, the long-imprisoned ANC leader, had his first meetings with two successive South African presidents. Joaquin Villalobos, a top commander of the FMLN in El Salvador has recognised that 'We can't at this time aspire to an armed revolution that the Soviet Union will subsidise.'[67]

The Soviet Union has both responded to and played a part in promoting the new conservatism in the Third World. The success of the West in containing radical nationalism has limited the opportunities open to the Soviet Union. But at the same time the disintegration of the Soviet Union and its retrenchment in foreign policy played an important element in promoting the conservative mood of the 1980s. The crisis of Stalinism has deprived many Third World nationalist movements not only of money and weapons, but also of the ideology which has long enabled them to win mass popular backing. As a result they are more isolated than ever and more vulnerable to the pressures of the imperialist order. Whereas in the past Soviet backing allowed them to survive in difficult times and to rally mass support when circumstances were more favourable, today's Soviet retreat compounds the isolation of nationalist movements and forces them into accepting negotiated settlements on terms favourable to their oppressors.

In the early 1990s it is clear that the old order, forged by the Second World War, is in an advanced state of decay. For different reasons, neither the US nor the Soviet Union can carry on in the old way. In the short term these developments have strengthened the forces of reaction in the Third World. In the longer term the declining ability of the Soviet Union to contain conflicts can only be beneficial.

Notes

1. V. Kubalkova and A. Cruickshank, *Marxism and International Relations*, paperback edn, Oxford: Oxford University Press, 1989, p. 260. Alex Pravda makes the point that 'all the major concepts' of new thinking 'have been adapted by the Soviet foreign policy community from Western literature'. A. Pravda, 'Is there a Gorbachev foreign policy?' in W. Joyce et al. (eds), *Gorbachev and Gorbachevism*, London: Frank Cass 1989, p. 108.

2. M. Gorbachev, *Perestroika*, updated edn, London: Fontana, 1988, p. 140.

3. Gorbachev, *Perestroika*, p. 144.

4. *US News and World Report*, 9 May 1988. For a more extensive discussion of his views on Soviet foreign policy in the Third World see Y. Primakov 'USSR policy on regional conflicts', *International Affairs*, June 1988. All references to *International Affairs* in this chapter are to the Soviet journal rather than the British periodical of the same name.

5. *Izvestia*, 24 May 1989. In *Current Digest of the Soviet Press* (*CDSP*), XLI, 21, 21 June 1989.

6. Gorbachev, *Perestroika*, p. 145.

7. Gorbachev, *Perestroika*, p. 147.

8. *Financial Times*, 1 December 1989.

9. *Izvestia*, 3 February 1989. *CDSP*, XLI, 5, 1 March 1989.

10. M. Muchie and H. van Zon, 'Soviet foreign policy under Gorbachev and revolution in the Third World' in M. Kaldor et al. eds, *The New Detente*, Verso: London, 1989, p. 189. For Gorbachev's redefinition of the concept of national liberation, see M.N. Katz 'The Evolution of the Brezhnev Doctrine under Gorbachev' in K. M. Campbell and S. Neil MacFarlane (eds), *Gorbachev's Third World Dilemmas*, Routledge: London, 1989, p. 39.

11. A. Kolosovsky, 'Risk zones in the Third World', *International Affairs*, August 1989, p. 49.

12. Gorbachev, *Perestroika*, p. 173.

13. R. Turdiyev, 'The USSR and the Third World', *International Affairs*, December 1988, p140.

14. *Guardian*, 15 July 1989.

15. Gorbachev, *Perestroika*, p. 150.

16. Gorbachev, *Perestroika*, p. 151.

17. C.R. Saivetz, '"New Thinking" and Soviet Third World Policy", *Current History*, October 1989, p. 326.

18. S. Sestanovich, 'Gorbachev's foreign policy', *Problems of Communism*, Jan–Feb 1988, p. 9.

19. T. McNeill, 'Gorbachev's first three years in power', *Radio Liberty Report*, 2 March 1988, p. 3.

20. Kolosovsky, 'Risk zones in the Third World', pp. 45–6.

21. *International Herald Tribune*, 9 Jan 1989. For an attempt to give theoretical coherence to this view see A. Kiva, 'Developing countries, socialism, capitalism', *International Affairs*, March 1989.

22. Muchie and van Zon, 'Soviet foreign policy under Gorbachev', p. 193.

23. *Time*, 11 December 1989. For a discussion of de-ideologisation see A. Kozyrev, 'East and West: from confrontation to cooperation and co-development', *International Affairs*, October 1989.

24. F. Furedi, *The Soviet Union Demystified*, London: Junius, 1986, chapter 10.

25. *Guardian*, 4 December 1989.

26. S.N. MacFarlane, 'The Soviet Union and Southern African Security', *Problems of Communism*, March–June 1989, pp. 73–4.

27. H. Hamman, 'Soviet Defector on Origins of "the New Thinking"', *Report on the USSR*, 20 October 1989, p. 14 and A. Pravda 'Is There a Gorbachev Foreign Policy?', p. 109.
During the Brezhnev era the foreign ministry under Andrei Gromyko oversaw relations with the West while the International Department of the CPSU central committee, led by Boris Ponomarev, had primary responsibility for the Third World. Under Gorbachev the old ideologues of the International Department, Ponomarev and Rosti Ul'yanovsky, have been replaced by diplomats Anatoliy Dobrynin and Georgiy Korniyenko. The International Department has been downgraded in importance and a new International Policy Commission, headed by Aleksandr Yakovlev, created.

28. D. Wedgewood Benn, 'On from Marx and Lenin', *World Today*, May 1989, p. 91.

29. F. Fukuyama, *Moscow's Post-Brezhnev Reassessment of the Third World*, Santa Monica: Rand, 1986.

30. D.E. Albright, 'The USSR and the Third World in the 1980s', *Problems of Communism*, March–June 1989, p. 66.

31. J. Steele, *The Limits of Soviet Power*, revised edn, Harmondsworth: Pengun, 1985, p. 167.

32. F. Furedi, 'Superpower Rivalries in the Third World', in K. B. Hadjor (ed), *New Perspectives in North–South Dialogue*, I.B. Tauris: London, 1988. J. Steele, *The Limits of Soviet Power*, p. 167. For a list of countries 'lost' to the West during different phases after the Second World War see F. Halliday, *Beyond Irangate*, Amsterdam: Transnational Institute, 1987, p. 12.

33. Steele, *The Limits of Soviet Power*, p. 163.

34. Symptoms of its economic weakness include a budget deficit equivalent to 12 per cent of gross national product

and hard currency reserves in mid-1989 of $24 billion, of which $18 billion was needed to service its debt. See *The Independent*, 4 July 1989. On the internal economic crisis also see chapter 2 in this volume.

35. B. Piadyshev, 'Perestroika, the 19th Party Conference and Foreign Policy', *International Affairs*, July 1988, p. 5.
36. MacFarlane, 'The Soviet Union and Southern African Security', p. 76.
37. Fukuyama, *Moscow's Post-Brezhnev Reassessment of the Third World*, pp. 1–2.
38. Albright, 'The USSR and the Third World in the 1980s', p. 58.
39. Sestanovich, 'Gorbachev's foreign policy', p. 3.
40. Kleinwort Grieveson Securities World Oil report, April 1987, p. 6. For a sophisticated account of Islam in the Soviet Union, see Martin Walker in *Guardian*, 13 April 1988.
41. K. Dawisha, 'The Soviet Union in the Middle East' in E.J. Feuchtwanger and P. Nailor (eds), *The Soviet Union and the Third World*, London: Macmillan, 1981, p. 124.
42. *Middle East International*, 1 May 1987; and P. Shearman, 'Gorbachev and the Third World', *Third World Quarterly*, Vol 9 No 4, October 1987, p. 1105.
43. F. Halliday, 'Mikhail and the Mullahs', *Marxism Today*, February 1989, p. 24.
44. *Guardian*, 22 June 1989.
45. *Financial Times*, 1 June 1989.
46. *Independent*, 26 August 1989.
47. Goodman and Ekedahl, 'Gorbachev's "new directions" in the Middle East', p. 580.
48. M.A. Goodman and C. McGiffert Ekedahl, 'Gorbachev's "new directions" in the Middle East', *Middle East Journal*, 42, 4, Autumn 1988, p. 576.
49. *Middle East International*, 6 October 1989. For an account of Israel improving relations with the Soviet Union, see Z. Irwin, 'Israel and the Soviet Union: a slow thaw', *World Today*, May 1989. A cooperation agreement in science and technology between the two countries was reported on the Voice of Israel at 0500 gmt 12 Jan 1990. See *BBC Summary of World Broadcasts* (SWB) SU/WO112 A/15 26 Jan 1990. For a protocol creating the legal basis for trade and economic relations between the two countries see SWB SU/0671 ii 25 January 1990.
50. *Financial Times*, 20 November 1989.

51. Fukuyama, *Moscow's Post-Brezhnev Reassessment of the Third World*, p. vii.
52. *The Times*, 28 November 1988.
53. *Guardian*, 18 March 1989. For an account of the development of Soviet foreign policy in southern Africa in the mid-1980s see Howard Barrell's interview with Victor Goncharov in *Work in Progress*, No 48, July 1987. For a more recent account see A. Bovin, *Izvestia*, 28 July 1989 in *CDSP*, XLI, 31, 30 August 1989.
54. *Pravda*, 20 August 1989, in *CDSP*, XLI, 33, 13 September 1989. Reply by Joe Slovo in *Pravda*, 1 October 1989, in *CDSP*, XLI, 39, 25 October 1989.
55. *Newsweek*, 29 January 1990.
56. *Observer*, 21 January 1990.
57. Albright, 'The USSR and the Third World in the 1980s', p. 62. MacFarlane, 'The Soviet Union and Southern African Security', p. 73. Muchie and van Zon, 'Soviet foreign policy under Gorbachev and revolution in the Third World', pp. 199–200.
58. Gorbachev, *Perestroika*, pp. 185–6. For accounts of Gorbachev's offensive in East Asia see *Financial Times*, 19 Sept 1988; *Economist*, 24 September 1988; and *US News & World Report*, 6 February 1989.
59. Gorbachev, *Perestroika*, p. 180.
60. Y.B. Arefyera interviewed in *Izvestia*, 10 July 1989, *CDSP*, XLI, 28, 9 August 1989.
61. A.Z. Rubinstein, 'Soviet success story: the Third World', *Orbis*, 32, 4, Fall 1988, pp. 555–6.
62. *Far Eastern Economic Review*, 10 November 1988.
63. *Financial Times*, 31 October 1989.
64. *International Herald Tribune*, 3 April 1989.
65. *Independent*, 3 August 1989.
66. *Guardian*, 5 April 1989.
67. *Time*, 2 October 1989.

7 Farewell to Eurocommunism

> Eric Hobsbawm: We are talking at a more or less historical moment, an historical turning point: the Eastern European systems have collapsed, there is a dangerous situation in the USSR, we have become aware that a whole tradition, to which we dedicated part of our lives, has come to an end: the tradition dominated by the October Revolution. Do you agree?
>
> Achille Occhetto: Yes.
>
> (*Guardian*, 26 January 1990)

This gloomy exchange between Britain's leading Stalinist historian and the general secretary of the Italian Communist Party well sums up the impact of the events in the Soviet Union and Eastern Europe in the late 1980s on the Western communist parties. The crisis of identity unleashed by these events revealed that, despite the lengths many of the European parties – notably the Italian party – had gone to distance themselves from the Soviet system, they remained heavily reliant on the legacy of the Russian Revolution and the prestige of the Soviet Union. The state socialist policies and bureaucratic methods of Stalinism had remained at the core of the programmes and practice of Western communism. Once the head of the Soviet state himself had acknowledged the bankruptcy of the Soviet system and embraced the capitalist market, the Western communist parties were faced with a major crisis of identity and direction.

British Communist Party leader Martin Jacques summed up the dimensions of the crisis facing his party in a keynote speech to the party congress in November 1989:

> It is the end of the road for the communist system as we have known it: the central plan, the authoritarian state, the single-party system, the subjugated civil society. Stalinism is dead, and Leninism – its theory of state, its concept of the party, the absence of civil society, its notion of revolution – has also had its day.
>
> (*Marxism Today*, January 1990)

Lacking any coherent proposals for an alternative programme for the British Communist Party, Jacques merely hinted that the party might consider following the Italians and attempt to accelerate its merger with the wider forces of European radicalism by changing its name.

At the close of the 1980s the European communist parties were in an advanced state of decline and fragmentation, a process that seemed more likely to be exacerbated by the pursuit of increasingly opportunist alliances. In Italy, the once mighty PCI fell behind the socialist party for the first time in local elections in 1989; in France the PCF's residual base in the municipalities crumbled still further in the March 1989 elections. In Spain, the communists managed a slight increase in votes in the 1989 general election at the expense of an unpopular socialist government, but only by dissolving the party in a radical left coalition. In Holland the communists achieved the same result by entering a 'green left' coalition. The project of opportunist alliances went furthest in Greece, where in June 1989 the communists joined a coalition government with the same conservative forces that had waged a bloody civil war against them after the Second World War.

The pervasive pessimism of the European communist parties in the early 1990s stands in stark contrast to the confidence of these parties only a decade ago. In the mid-1970s the tide of Eurocommunism was in full flood and it seemed to many that the communist parties had finally succeeded in casting off the legacy of Stalinism.[1] In southern Europe, in particular, the communist parties appeared to have broken out of the electoral and social ghetto which they had occupied since the Cold War period of the late 1940s and early 1950s. After looking briefly at the rise and fall of Eurocommunism, we'll concentrate on the responses of the communist parties, particularly in France and Italy, to the failures of the Eurocommunist strategy and then assess the prospects of the communist parties as they look towards the 1990s.

The rise and fall of Eurocommunism

Two factors were crucial in the emergence of Eurocommunism. The first was the recession which struck the Western world in the early 1970s. The capitalist drive to restore profitability demanded raising unemployment, holding down wages, cutting welfare spending and restricting trade union militancy. These measures had to be imposed on working-class movements that had built up strong and stable organisations over two decades of post-war expansion. While workers turned to their traditional political organisations to defend jobs and living standards, governments looked to the same labour movement parties to persuade the working class to make the sacrifices required to maintain national capitalist interests. Where social democracy was traditionally weak – in southern Europe – the communist parties were called upon to mediate the growing conflict between capital and labour.

In the same period, the relaxation of East–West tensions allowed the communist parties to overcome, to a degree, the anti-Soviet prejudice that had long provided the right with its central propaganda weapon against the left. The era of détente from the Soviet invasion of Czechoslovakia in 1968 to the occupation of Afghanistan in 1979 was the second factor in the rise of Eurocommunism. The collapse of military dictatorships in Spain, Portugal and Greece in the mid-1970s was an additional element which added momentum to the Eurocommunist project.

In the early 1970s all the Western communist parties, to a greater or lesser extent and with more or less enthusiasm, embraced the doctrines of Eurocommunism. In fact there was little new in the theory of state monopoly capitalism and the strategy of advancing towards socialism through alliances with other class forces within the framework of bourgeois democracy. These notions had deep roots in Stalinist adaptations to social democracy from the 1920s onwards.[2] The only novel feature of the 1970s was the extent to which the communist parties went in explicitly repudiating fundamentals of Marxism-Leninism ('the dictatorship of the proletariat', 'democratic centralism') and in criticising the policies of the Soviet state (its repressive treatment of dissidents and the Eastern bloc). These measures were deemed necessary to win legitimacy and popular support in Western democracies and appeared to be vindicated by the successes of the communist parties in the mid-1970s.

The Spanish Communist Party, under the leadership of Santiago Carrillo, a pioneering force in the Eurocommunist movement, emerged from exile and clandestinity as the central focus of opposition to the caretaker regime installed upon the death of General Franco in November 1975. In France, the Common Programme agreed by the PS and the PCF in 1972 appeared little different from the PCF's own programme, and the Union of the Left made dramatic advances in the 1974 presidential elections. The party's twenty-second congress in 1976 was hailed as the triumph of Eurocommunism and it was widely expected that the PCF would coast to power in alliance with the PS in the elections due in 1978. In Italy, the PCI pursued the strategy of seeking a 'historic compromise' with the conservative Christian Democracy (DC) to save the nation from economic and social collapse. Between 1972 and 1976 it advanced from 27 to 34 per cent of the popular vote and the attempts of the corrupt ruling regime to exclude the PCI from a share of government power appeared increasingly forlorn. Yet the promise of Eurocommunism was not to be fulfilled.

At critical moments in 1977 and 1978 Eurocommunism experienced setbacks which presaged its demise. In June 1977, in the first free elections held in Spain since the Civil War, the PCE won less than 10 per cent of the vote. Felipe Gonzalez' PSOE, a party that had scarcely existed three years earlier, won 29 per cent. Carrillo's recognition of the monarchy, his adoption of the monarchist flag in place of the republican tricolour, his outspoken criticisms of the Soviet Union, his cringing moderation in all matters – all these concessions had failed to convince the middle classes that the PCE could be trusted to modernise Spanish capitalism. In September 1977 the PCF broke off talks with the PS over updating the Common Programme for the 1978 elections. Communist party leader Georges Marchais was concerned that unless the PCF took a more independent line Francois Mitterrand's PS would extend its already significant gains among PCF supporters. In the event the PCF suffered heavy losses and social democracy overtook Stalinism at the polls for the first time in the post-war period.

In Italy, the critical setback came in March 1978 when, after months of negotiations and PCI concessions, the DC leadership pushed the PCI into endorsing what amounted to a reshuffled DC-dominated coalition with unreconstructed DC policies. Though the subsequent ultra-left kidnap and assassination of DC chief Aldo Moro plunged Italy into a prolonged national crisis which distracted attention from the humiliation of the PCI, this moment marked the effective end of the strategy of the 'historic compromise'. Over the next two years the PCI experienced its first serious electoral reverses since the 1950s. By the early 1980s the 'crisis' of Eurocommunism was the subject of general debate.[3]

There were two aspects of the crisis of Eurocommunism. The first was that, from the point of view of the capitalist classes in southern Europe, by the late 1970s the communist parties had largely served their purpose in containing working-class resistance during the first phase of the recession. Despite its electoral setback in June, in September 1977 the PCE was the key signatory to the

Moncloa pact, through which the labour movement acquiesced to rising unemployment and falling wages in the national interest. In January 1977, Berlinguer launched an appeal to Italian workers to accept a similar austerity programme which was publicly endorsed by the communist trade union leader Luciano Lama. Twelve months later, in an agreement signed at the EUR conference centre outside Rome while Berlinguer's negotiations over the 'historic compromise' continued, Italian unions agreed to continuing austerity in return for measures to tackle unemployment and poverty in the south of the country.

In France, the full impact of the recession came slightly later and the capitalist class placed less reliance on the mediating role of the official labour movement. However the imposition of the 1976 Barre Plan, which promoted a shakeout of traditional industries as well as broader austerity policies, benefited from the PCF's influence in the main union federation, the CGT. Preoccupied with the Union of the Left strategy, the PCF discouraged localised rank-and-file resistance in favour of national 'days of action'.[4] It emphasised that the election of a radical coalition government was the only real solution to the economic difficulties facing the working class. (It was not until after 1981, when four members of an electorally humbled PCF accepted junior ministerial posts in Mitterrand's socialist government, that the PCF was seriously compromised with its supporters as a result of its support for a brutally anti-working-class counter-crisis programme.)

In their determination to win legitimacy at a time of national crises, Eurocommunist leaders preached restraint and discouraged militancy. By the late 1970s the result was rapidly rising unemployment, stagnating living standards and growing working-class demoralisation. If the capitalists could achieve all this without bringing communist parties into government or even introducing major reforms, then why bother? Sidney Tarrow sums up the role of the PCI in the period when it was closest to government office:

> The party remained tangential to the cabinet; it was exploited for its usefulness in reining in organised labour and for spreading among its supporters a moral revulsion against terrorism that helped the government to adopt more serious police measures; but it was largely ignored when it made even modest reform proposals.[5]

By the end of the decade the communist parties in Spain, Italy and France had served their purpose, the pressure was off and the capitalist classes had little need to grant further concessions, let alone bring communists into coalition governments.

The second aspect of the crisis of Eurocommunism was that the communist parties' pursuit of the policies of class collaboration not only failed to consolidate middle-class support, but began to alienate traditional working-class voters, supporters in the unions and even party members. The origin of today's problems of electoral and organisational decline can be traced to the heyday of Eurocommunism. In France and Italy a clear pattern is discernible in the electoral sphere. In the early days of Eurocommunism, the communist parties' new approach enabled them to reach beyond their traditional proletarian heartlands, to win support from wider layers in the cities, from voters in rural and provincial regions where communist support was historically weak, and from women and young voters. However, the parties' support for capitalist austerity policies and their apparent willingness to make any concession to win the approval of middle-class public opinion led to growing alienation among working-class supporters from the late 1970s onwards. By the early 1980s, disillusionment with communist policies at national and local level meant that the parties could neither hold on to their new voters nor guarantee the loyalty of traditional supporters.

Martin Schain's study of the French Communist Party in local government reveals the shifts in the party's support.[6] While the PCF share of the vote in national elections remained fairly steady at around 20 per cent throughout the 1970s, local pacts with the PS enabled the PCF to extend its municipal power considerably after 1972, at the expense of the centre-right. The PCF reached out from its traditional base in the solidly working-class Paris suburbs to any provincial towns with a more socially diverse population. By 1981, 42 per cent of the larger towns with PCF mayors were in the provinces, and only 14 per cent had a majority working-class population.[7] Yet when the PCF began to sustain its heaviest electoral losses in 1983, it was hit hardest where it had been in power longest – in the Paris 'red belt' – where working class disillusionment, reflected in abstentions and votes for other parties, was greatest.[8] The breakdown in cooperation with the PS also led to defeats in less secure towns and by the mid-1980s the PCF was driven back to an even weaker position than it had been in before its Eurocommunist phase began more than a decade earlier. In 1986 the PS won more votes in the Paris 'red belt' than the PCF.[9]

Surveys of the pattern of voting for the PCI in the 1970s reveal a similar trend. The PCI's breakthrough in 1976 was achieved through broadening the party's support from the 'red triangle' of Tuscany, Umbria and Emilia-Romagna to include areas of the south and northern cities in which the party had long been weak. When the PCI's fortunes changed in the late 1970s, its heaviest losses were often in its working-class heartlands.[10]

Stephen Hellman's detailed study of the results of the 1978 referenda on the public financing of political parties and on repressive 'anti-terrorist' legislation in the northern city of Turin provide local confirmation of the general trend.[11] In its desperate bid to prove its respectability, the PCI took what was widely regarded – even by loyal party supporters – as a reactionary line on both issues. The results showed that the lowest turn-outs and the highest proportion of spoiled votes were recorded in areas where the PCI was formerly strongest. It only succeeded in winning majority support for its line in its most loyal areas. The highest votes against the PCI line were recorded in the volatile council housing estates occupied by the poorest workers, where the party had only begun to win majority support in the early 1970s.

Hellman's conclusion was prescient: 'Most alarming of all, the areas of the greatest triumphs of the mid-1970s, the large urban centres, had produced results that were embarrassing in the immediate sense and potentially disastrous in the longer run'.[12]

The PCI has been realising this potential ever since. One study of the 1979 elections, in which the PCI lost 1.5 million votes nationally, observed that in the industrial cities of Bologna, Genoa and Verona: 'the PCI not only lost working-class votes, but it practically lost only working-class votes.'[13]

Wider surveys confirmed that it also lost votes in the south and among the young. Again Hellman accurately sums up the trends: 'The PCI's policy choices demobilised the working class and underclass, alienated young people, and discouraged the opinion voters of the more educated middle strata.'[14]

Hellman's latter point reveals another defect of the Eurocommunist strategy. In their quest for legitimacy in societies strongly influenced by anti-communist and reactionary Catholic prejudices, the communist parties went to great lengths to propitiate the establishment and the hierarchy and to display their own commitment to democratic principles and their respect for traditional moral values. As a result they often found themselves on issues of civil liberties and matters such as divorce and abortion, well to the right of an increasingly radical and secular public opinion. This was particularly striking in Italy where the PCI was nearly as shocked as the Vatican to discover in 1974 that 60 per cent of the population favoured divorce and in 1981 that 68 per cent supported a liberalisation of the abortion law.[15] Eurocommunism's determination to appear respectable meant that the communist parties were slow to respond to trends such as feminism and to the hostility of many young people towards the repressive state measures introduced in the guise of 'anti-terrorist' legislation.

Just as Labour's 'social contract' with the unions in Britain in 1974 led to the 'winter of discontent' in 1978–79, the austerity programmes of Eurocommunism provoked damaging conflict both within the unions and between the unions and the communist parties. In a period of rising unemployment and intensifying management attack, the influence of Eurocommunist moderation on the union leaderships provoked growing rank-and-file disillusionment. Union membership, particularly in traditional manufacturing where communist organisation was strongest, slumped. The defeat of the left in the 1978 elections in France led to a more aggressive government attack on the unions, at a time when the breakdown in the Union of the Left deepened divisions between the PCF-linked CGT and the PS-inclined CFDT. Both parties' attempts to use the unions to bolster their political strategies only exacerbated tensions: the formal cooperation between the major union federations that had prevailed through the 1970s broke down in the autumn of 1980. One survey summed up the outcome of the decade of Eurocommunism: 'From a position of growing strength and effectiveness in 1970, French unions had, by 1980 moved precipitously towards renewed weakness and divisive pluralism.'[16]

A similar trend was evident in Italy. When the PCI was on the verge of coalition power between 1976 and 1978, the CGIL preached restraint and austerity. One result was the riot that erupted when CGIL chief Lama, the leading advocate of austerity, came to address students at Rome University in March 1977, sparking off a wave of riots around the country. Another result was the massive metalworkers demonstration against the government and the PCI in Rome in December 1977. Mounting trade union unrest greatly reduced Berlinguer's room for manoeuvre in his 'historic compromise' negotiations with Christian Democratic leaders. When PSI leader Craxi subsequently became the key powerbroker, the CISL took the lead in calling for tighter official curbs on wage rises through the wage indexation system.

Though the PCI opposed PSI austerity measures, it maintained its moderate approach on wider trade union matters. The PCI's endorsement of the victimisation of 60 militants at the Fiat plant in Turin in 1979, which led directly to the major defeat for the unions at the plant in 1980, was a decisive setback for the party's prestige in the organised working class.[17] The 'march of the 40,000' – foremen, supervisors, technicians and white collar workers – organised in autonomous unions outside the traditional federations and protesting against the strike against job cuts by the bulk of the Fiat workforce, was an ominous sign of a trend that has become increasingly familiar in Western Europe in the 1980s. The growth of autonomous union organisation, particularly in the public sector, in some circumstances very militant, in others playing the role of scab unions, has contributed to the fragmentation of the unions. By 1984 the long-strained cooperation among the big three union federations in Italy was finally abandoned in a further round of conflict over the wage indexation system.

By the turn of the decade it was evident that the parties that had embraced Eurocommunism needed to reorient their strategy to avoid disaster. One result of the defeats of the late 1970s was the eruption of internal debate on an unprecedented scale inside the communist parties. Let's turn to look at how the major Eurocommunist parties responded to their loss of momentum and morale.

Survival strategies

The communist parties undoubtedly experienced a more difficult political climate in the 1980s. The capitalist classes in Western Europe entered the second phase of the recession with the balance of class forces tilted much more in their favour than it had been a decade earlier. Employers and governments now embarked on a more confrontational approach in their dealings with organised labour. Throughout Western Europe the working class was weakened by mass unemployment and increasingly disillusioned with its traditional organisations: union militancy and support for radical political change showed a general decline. While far left groups dwindled to insignificance and communist parties continued to decay, social democratic parties in southern Europe made headway by shifting to take advantage of the disarray of the right and occupying the centre. The revival of Cold War tensions after the Soviet invasion of Afghanistan in 1979, Ronald Reagan's election victory in 1980 and the Polish crisis in 1981 once again put the communist parties on the defensive over their historic allegiance to Moscow. A general shift of intellectual and middle class

opinion to the right, most notably in France, renewed the isolation of the communist movement from the mainstream
consensus.[18]

Three options have been widely canvassed in the communist
movement over the past decade. First, some have called for a return
to pro-Soviet orthodoxy and to the communist parties' proletarian
roots and traditions. It was, after all, the influence of the Russian
Revolution that launched the European communist parties in the
early 1920s and the prestige of the Soviet Union in alliance with
wartime resistance movements was crucial in their revival in the
1940s. Loyalty to Moscow remains strong among an older generation of working-class communists throughout Europe. However,
this is an ageing and declining section of society, and, even under
Gorbachev, the model of Soviet society holds no inspirational
appeal to the vast majority of the population of modern Europe.

Second, others have recommended that the communist parties
reach out to the 'new social movements' around issues of peace,
women's rights and the environment. Taking up these causes
could allow the communist parties to tap new layers of support
and absorb the impetus of radical movements which attract widespread and youthful support. The problem with this strategy is
that adopting fashionable policies might alienate traditional
supporters, who often espouse conservative and even hostile attitudes towards the new movements.

The third option has been the further pursuit of Eurocommunist
adaptations towards social democracy. In a period of growing
reaction, adopting more moderate policies appears to be the only
way to win wider popular approval, yet the tendency for established social democratic parties to gain at communist expense
creates grave tactical difficulties. The fact that all the communist
parties have at different times and to different degrees adopted all
three of these options explains the appearance of instability,
confusion and incoherence that is the most striking characteristic
of these parties in the 1980s. Let's look more closely at the cases of
France and Italy.

France

The French Communist Party has long had the reputation of being
the most pro-Soviet of the major Western communist parties so it
was inevitable that the failures of Eurocommunism would provoke
a vigorous backlash from the orthodox Stalinist camp. This was
already apparent at the 1979 congress, which, after a decade of

mounting criticism of Moscow, declared that the record of the Eastern bloc was 'on balance positive'.[19] The PCF was subsequently the only Eurocommunist party to back the Soviet Union over Afghanistan and it took a highly equivocal line over the suppression of Solidarity in Poland in December 1981. It maintained a broadly pro-Soviet, anti-American line on Third World conflicts and even refused to condemn the Soviet Union for shooting down a Korean airliner in September 1983.[20] However the PCF came into conflict with the Kremlin over its involvement in Mitterrand's coalition government at a time when it was supporting the installation of US missiles in Europe and even recommending a vote for the right in Germany over this issue.[21]

In 1988, with perestroika and glasnost in full swing, the Soviet press was openly critical of the PCF's 'sectarian' tactics in the presidential election; *L'Humanité* replied angrily with detailed criticisms of 'human rights violations' in the Soviet Union.[22] In any event it was apparent from the election results of the 1980s that a closer identification with the Soviet Union was not a vote winner. As Tiersky concluded in 1988, 'The time is past when radical changes in Soviet foreign policy could have decisive effects – even for the better, as Gorbachev's innovations once might have – on the political fortunes of French communism.'[23]

Though the PCF has long proclaimed itself a party of all the French people, its image has remained obstinately *ouvrierist*, reflecting its heavy reliance on the manual working class. The strongly conservative and chauvinist outlook long promoted by the PCF has rendered it particularly insensitive to wider developments in society. Hence radical trends have generally emerged outside, and often in a spirit of hostility towards, the PCF. This was true of the women's movement, which emerged around the radical upsurge of 1968 and the revival of interest in the writings of Simone de Beauvoir. It was also true of the greens who were encouraged in an aggressively anti-PCF direction under the influence of the former Stalinist Andre Gorz.[24] The virulent national chauvinism of the PCF meant that from 1977 onwards it supported the *force de frappe*, France's independent nuclear strike force. Hence when mass anti-nuclear missile demonstrations were taking place in the rest of Europe in the early 1980s, France remained quiescent. The PCF dismissed the peace movement as a manifestation of German irrationalism and anti-Soviet prejudice.[25] It was not surprising that later attempts by the PCF to climb on the anti-nuclear power bandwagon were greeted with some scepticism.

The PCF's anti-racist reputation was seriously discredited by the party's support for strict immigration controls and its record in local government. This was symbolised by two infamous incidents, one at Vitry in December 1980 when a mob including PCF members wrecked an immigrant hostel in a working-class suburb of Paris, and the second at Montigny in February 1981, when the PCF mayor led a demonstration outside the house of a Moroccan suspected of being a drug dealer.[26] The radical anti-racist movement '*SOS Racisme*' subsequently took off outside the influence of the PCF at a time when it was increasingly concerned about losing working-class support on issues of law and order, race and nation, to the far right *Front National*.

It was not until the mid-1980s that the PCF seriously set about trying to incorporate the new social movements. In 1984 it launched its new alliance strategy under the banner of the *Nouveau Rassemblement Populaire et Majoritaire*, which proclaimed the leading role of the PCF over a 'multiplicity of struggles'.[27] The new movement was characterised by the PCF's new-found modesty about propounding 'global' programmes for change and by an extreme flexibility. Given the record of the PCF and its inability to offer any distinctive direction to existing campaigns, their supporters remained sceptical of its capacity to play a leading role and the new movement has remained an empty shell. In 1987 the PCF's leading *renovateur*, Pierre Juquin, finally quit the party to run with the support of a number of radical factions on an independent 'Red/Green' platform in the 1988 presidential election, winning two per cent of the vote – half that of the official green candidate and nearly one-third of the vote for Andre Lajoinie, the PCF candidate.

Given the high risks of both the pro-Soviet and the new social movements options, the PCF leadership had good reason to stick cautiously with the Eurocommunist approach. As Marchais put it immediately after the 1978 election defeat, the party had 'no spare strategy'.[28] After a wide-ranging debate on the left's defeat in the 1978 election, the twenty-third congress of the PCF in 1979 opted to continue on the Eurocommunist course.[29] The congress opted to support autogestion, the combination of workers' control and workplace industrial democracy long promoted by the Socialist Party, but traditionally opposed by the PCF as a cover for class collaboration. The PCF also adopted a new constitution which formally ratified the abandonment of the dictatorship of the proletariat (first announced by Marchais on television back in 1976) and 'Marxism-Leninism'. It also repudiated 'democratic centralism' and loosened its conditions of membership, cell structure and restrictions on internal debate.

In programmatic terms the PCF showed its willingness throughout the 1980s to follow the PS in every policy adjustment towards the right. After Mitterrand's 1981 victory, the PCF offered its 'unreserved solidarity' for the socialist government and its ministers provided a left cover for austerity policies until trade union revolt in the spring of 1984 forced them to resign.[30] This did not mark any break in PCF approval for the main thrust of the PS programme of national economic rationalisation, nuclear and conventional militarism, and tougher policies on law and order and immigration. The problem, however, lay in devising an appropriate tactical approach towards the PS in a period in which it was steadily encroaching on the PCF's electoral base.

After the breakup of the Union of the Left and the 1978 debacle, the PCF attempted to strengthen its position against the PS by taking a more independent stand and by openly criticising the PS for its moderate and collaborationist policies. The anti-PS campaign ended abruptly with Mitterrand's victory in the first round of the 1981 presidential elections in which Marchais received a humiliating 15 per cent of the vote. It seems that the PCF had anticipated a victory for the right which would have crushed Mitterrand's pretensions and 'rebalanced the left' in favour of the PCF.[31] In the event the PCF dropped its condemnations of the PS overnight and recommended a vote for Mitterrand in the second ballot. From 1981 until 1984 the PCF's criticisms of the PS coalition were muted because of the presence of four PCF ministers in the government. The departure of the PCF ministers and the government's turn to more rigorous austerity policies under the regime of Laurent Fabius in 1984 allowed the PCF to take up a more oppositional role.

The PCF subsequently encouraged the CGT to take a more militant line in response to closures and mass redundancies, then devastating French manufacturing, leading to a number of confrontations between striking workers and riot police in 1984 and 1985. Yet the PCF leadership was wary of tarnishing its carefully nurtured democratic image with unpredictable outbreaks of industrial militancy, and after a decade of vacillation, most French workers were not enthusiastic about going into battle under the banners of the PCF. The 1986 elections to the National Assembly led to a victory for a right and further setbacks to the PCF; the outcome was 'cohabitation' between Chirac as the prime minister and Mitterrand as president. This result encouraged the PCF to adopt a more oppositional role in the hope of attracting the support of voters disillusioned with the whole period of socialist rule and its consequences in the run up to the presidential elections in 1988. Hence the PCF – and the CGT – played a more active role in a number of industrial disputes in 1987 and 1988 in the hope of attracting a protest vote.

However the PCF's new line appeared more successful only in deepening demoralisation in the unions and in further alienating middle-class voters than it was in consolidating working-class support. The 1988 presidential elections registered a further fall in PCF support as Marchais issued the now routine call on his supporters to support Mitterrand in the second round. In the run up to the March 1989 municipal elections, the PCF was forced to accept humiliating conditions as the price of securing the local alliances with the Socialist Party on which many of its remaining town hall seats depended – and it still lost ground to the socialists.[32] And in June 1989, the European elections confirmed the PCF's loss of electoral credibility. With only 8 per cent of the vote, they were beaten by both the *Front National* and the greens.[33]

Italy

Just as the PCF has always been the most pro-Soviet of the Eurocommunist parties, the Italian Communist Party has always taken the most independent line. Yet the Moscow link is still a crucial one for the PCI and it remained for some the best safeguard of the party's future after the apparent failures of Eurocommunism in the late 1970s. In November 1980, the month in which Berlinguer finally buried the 'historic compromise', party veteran Paulo Rubotti warned that if the PCI ever turned its back on the Soviet Union it would be 'swept away by the party base, unshakeably and for all eternity pro-Soviet'.[34] This was undoubtedly an exaggeration, but it contained an element of truth which no Stalinist party leadership could ignore. When the PCI leadership openly sided with Solidarity against the Stalinist regime in Poland in 1981, another PCI veteran Armando Cossutta spoke out on behalf of the party's pro-Soviet faction.[35] However, the orthodox Stalinist trend in the PCI did little more than warn the party leadership against going too far in an anti-Soviet direction. Few seriously believed that Moscow could provide any answers for the post-Eurocommunist malaise of the PCI.

Like the PCF, and for many of the same reasons, the PCI was slow to recognise the importance of the new social movements.

We have already noted how the PCI's deference to Catholicism and reaction rendered it aloof from secularising and radical trends in Italy. As a result it was outflanked at the polls by the radicals and the socialists. When it finally tried to connect with the new movements, by sponsoring independent feminist, gay and green candidates in the 1987 elections, its unfamiliarity with these issues was all too apparent. When PCI leader Alessandro Natta appeared to flirt with anti-abortionists, party officials had to rush in to rescue the party's feminist credentials.[36]

The PCI's approach was widely regarded as electoral opportunism – it also sponsored a Milanese banker and a friend of notorious land speculators in the south. As Hellman argues, the problems went deeper: the PCI revealed its 'rampant eclecticism, a pluralism devoid of central guiding principles'.[37] Not surprisingly, this strategy failed to win votes and the election registered further decline. However, for the new party leader, Achille Occhetto, who replaced Natta after the 1987 election setback, the PCI's future lies in promoting the party's green, feminist and pro-European policies – these were the main themes of the March 1989 congress.[38]

For the PCI, to an even greater extent than the PCF, there has been little real alternative put to pursue the adaptation towards social democracy that formed the core of the Eurocommunist strategy. Like the PCF, the PCI has proved willing to make any programmatic concession to the socialists, indeed to the demands of the Italian capitalist class. Yet even though the PCI started from a much more substantial social base in Italian society (around 30 per cent throughout the 1970s), and the PSI from a smaller base (around 10 per cent), the tactical problems of dealing with the socialists have proved a major headache for the PCI leadership.

For most of the 1970s the PCI dismissed the PSI as irrelevant as Berlinguer sought his 'historic compromise' with the DC. However, when the PSI advanced as the PCI declined, and Craxi began to act as key figure in Italian coalition-building – becoming prime minister himself in 1983 – the PCI was forced to take the socialists seriously. Craxi's party skilfully attacked the PCI from both the right (emphasising its Stalinist past and its questionable commitment to democracy) and from the left (denouncing its support for austerity, class collaboration and clerical reaction).[39]

In 1980 and 1981 the PCI attempted to redefine its policy towards alliances with Berlinguer's 'democratic alternative'. This proposed an alliance of various small parties and dissident DC factions under PCI leadership, but leaving out the PSI. It indicated the PCI's attempt to steer a course independent of the PSI which was proposing a 'left alternative' – an alliance between the PCI and the PSI. The PCI's independent stand infuriated not only Craxi but also the PCI's right wing headed by Giorgio Napolitano. When the PSI became part of the government coalition with the DC in 1983 relations between the two parties of the left deteriorated still further. However, the PCI's subsequent attempts to restore its relations with the working class through taking more militant anti-government positions – notably its defence of the wage indexation system in the 1985 referendum – backfired badly. The PCI lost heavily in the referendum, while the governmental status of the PSI was strengthened. The 1987 elections confirmed the steady rise in PSI support as the PCI decline continued; and in the June 1989 local elections, the socialists finally overtook the PCI vote.[40]

The PCI has cultivated relations with European social democratic parties, notably the German SPD, and has even suggested its desire to join the Socialist International. Yet the PSI remains the obstacle on the international as well as on the domestic level to the PCI's attempts to win full social democratic respectability.

Results

As we have seen, the communist parties' responses to the failures of Eurocommunism resulted in even worse disasters. The PCF's result in the 1988 presidential election was its worst since 1924. In 1987 the PCI was reduced to the position from which its take-off had started in the late 1960s, though it still retained the support of around one-quarter of the electorate. Elsewhere in Europe, with the exception of Greece, Cyprus, Portugal and Finland, communist parties are a marginal force.[41] In addition to losing voters, Communist Party membership has been decimated. Between 1976 and 1986 the PCI lost 12 per cent of its members, though it still claims 1.6 million. Between 1978 and 1984 the PCF lost 27 per cent, bringing it down to 380,000; in the same period the PCE lost 65 per cent of its members, reducing it to 60,000. In the smaller parties losses of the order of 30 to 60 per cent are commonplace. The official membership of the British party (CPGB), for example, declined from 29,000 in 1973 to 7000 in 1989, though active membership is scarcely 10 per cent of that figure.

The other legacy of Eurocommunism was internal strife and fragmentation. One of the most extreme cases is in Spain where there are now a handful of parties – a pro-Soviet party led by Civil War veterans Gallego and Lister, a grouping led by the former Eurocommunist party leader Carrillo, a majority faction led by new party leader Julio Anguita Gonzalez who succeeded former boss Gerardo Iglesias in 1988, and a few more.[42] In the PCF internal dissent erupted after the breakdown of the Union of the Left and the 1978 defeat. Prominent intellectuals such as Louis Althusser and Jean Ellenstein published extensive critiques of the party leadership in the mainstream press. For a period the leadership tolerated the debate and then in 1979 clamped down, forcing the resignation of Henri Fiszbin, secretary of the rebellious Paris federation and suppressing dissident publications.[43] However internal unrest continued, the self-styled *renovateurs* rallying around Pierre Juquin before his departure from the party in 1987. The events in Eastern Europe in 1989 unleashed another wave of discontent, focused on party leader Marchais, known for his consistent loyalty to the Romanian party and his holidays on the yacht of deposed head-of-state Nicolae Ceausescu. In the PCI, factional strife has long been institutionalised with a clearly defined right (Napolitano, Amendola), and radical (Ingrao), as well as orthodox Stalinist (Cossutta) wings. While tensions increased in the 1980s, the PCI avoided damaging splits.

In many of the smaller communist parties splits between orthodox pro-Soviet and resolute Eurocommunist factions accelerated the decline of the international communist movement. In the late 1980s there has been an apparently contradictory trend towards the reunification of formerly bitterly antagonistic Communist Party fragments. In both Spain and Greece, for example, orthodox Stalinist and Eurocommunist groupings have reformed common electoral platforms. But this indicates a clinging together out of a feeling of isolation and weakness, not a genuine rallying of forces with a positive sense of direction. In the 1989 national elections, both Greek and Spanish communist alliances picked up votes from their socialist rivals. But this indicates disenchantment with the increasingly crisis-prone socialist parties rather than a resurgence of interest in the communists. Their lack of political dynamism is likely to exacerbate tendencies towards disintegration than overcome them. On a wider international level no joint meeting of the European communist parties has taken place since 1976, (there has been no world conference since 1969). Indeed, many communist leaders echo Occhetto's view that: 'For us, the international communist movement does not exist.'[44] We turn finally to consider the future prospects of the European communist parties.

Can the communist parties recover?

It is useful to compare the position of the communist parties today with that of 20 years ago, when they emerged from the long Cold War years of isolation and stagnation. The communist parties were excluded from the political mainstream, but they retained strong regional bases of support among workers in the more traditional manufacturing industries. Their most important inheritance from the Stalinist tradition was its insistence on high standards of membership training, discipline and organisation. Hellman notes that the term 'professional revolutionary' was widely used in the PCI until the 1970s.[45]

The fact that the communist parties were cadre organisations enabled them to survive long periods of isolation, repression and even, in the cases of the Spanish, Portuguese and Greek parties, exile, when social democratic parties crumbled. For all their adaptations to social democracy, it was this organisational tradition that gave the communist parties their distinctively Stalinist character. It enabled the French and Italian communist parties to survive for decades with programmes that were obsolete (anticipating pauperisation at the height of the post-war boom), with strategies for leading non-existent mass struggles and with organisational structures which reinforced their remoteness from new social trends (the growth of white collar and female employment, urbanisation and secularisation).

The upsurge of working-class militancy and youth radicalism that shook Europe between 1968 and 1972 at first passed by the communist parties. In May 1968 in France the students revolted against the PCF as much as against the French establishment and workers came out on strike against the advice of the PCF and the CGT. In the 'hot autumn' of 1969 in Italy the initiative came from unskilled and unorganised workers, often newly arrived immigrants from the south, and beyond the influence of the PCI or CGIL. Yet the organisational strength of the communist parties enabled them to catch up with the radical upsurge and become its ultimate beneficiaries. Eurocommunism provided the vehicle through which the communist parties incorporated much of the energy of this period and turned it to short-lived electoral advantage.

Eurocommunism gave the communist parties a programme – state monopoly capitalism – that at least appeared modern. It also offered a strategy of advance through alliances with other social forces that appeared plausible and popular. Eurocommunism's emphasis on internal democracy and pluralism also helped to open the parties' formerly rigid structures to the influence of the new movements. Though the party leaders were slow to adopt the policies of the new movements, there is much evidence to suggest that at local level the communist parties were successful in attracting activists from diverse radical campaigns into their ranks during the 1970s. The very ferocity of internal debate in the PCF, the party with the most rigid and orthodox bureaucracy, is testimony to the extent to which it incorporated representatives of the new social movements into its ranks.

Hellman's fascinating study of Turin reveals two waves of recruitment to the PCI: the first, immediately after the 'hot autumn' appears to have been former party militants returning to the fold; the second took place between 1975 and 1977 as the new generation of 1968–69 found its way through other movements to the PCI.[46] It seems that the organisational strength of the PCI gave it a resilience during these turbulent years that was lacking in the groupings spontaneously thrown up in the course of struggles or spawned by various far left factions. When the spontaneous movements flagged, the PCI mopped up. As we have seen, the radical impetus of the early 1970s carried the Eurocommunist parties to their successes in the following years. Yet the 'generation of '68' turned out to be a Trojan horse inside the citadels of European Stalinism.

If we turn to look at the plight of the communist parties today, we find them again without a distinctive programme or strategy and isolated from the political mainstream. Indeed the most striking feature of the communist parties today is their programmatic exhaustion. Like Neil Kinnock with his 'Labour Listens' events in Britain, European communist leaders reveal their lack of any idea of the way forward with slogans such as the PCF's 'let the people set the pace' and 'let us discuss what you think', or the PCI's proposal to participate in a coalition government around a 'programmatic alternative' the content of which is entirely open to negotiation.[47] The new-found commitment of the communist parties to 'openness' and 'flexibility' is simply an admission of political bankruptcy. But what about the roots in the working-class movement and the traditions of cadre organisation that were so important in enabling the communist parties to rejuvenate themselves before?

Contrary to the impressions of many academic apologists for the electoral decline of the old labour movement parties, this cannot be attributed to the disappearance of the working class.[48] The working class is still there, with a more heterogenous character than 20 years ago, but it is now much more alienated from the communist parties. This is the result, not of changing styles of work or new patterns of consumption, but a response to the political failures of Eurocommunism. The Eurocommunist parties promised new ways of transforming capitalism into socialism but rapidly turned to persuading their supporters to pay the price for transforming crisis-stricken capitalist economies into more competitive national enterprises. The result was mass unemployment, poverty and repression – and mass disillusionment with the communist parties.

Over the past decade the communist parties have experimented with various means of winning back working-class support or attracting wider middle-class support, and have failed to achieve either. Indeed they have discovered that the old appeals for loyalty to Moscow or for more union militancy are simply ineffective in rallying the workers while they are quite effective in alienating the professional, administrative and technical strata. The communist parties retain a residual working-class base, but their capacity to reach beyond it now seems more circumscribed than ever.

Not only have the communist parties seriously destabilised their working class bases during the Eurocommunist period, they have also squandered their most precious asset – their tradition of cadre organisation. In all the major communist parties an older generation of activists, steeled in the Stalinist tradition, has been gradually replaced by a new layer of activists who have brought the characteristic features of petit-bourgeois organisation into the communist parties from the new social movements. These movements have made a virtue of indulging individualistic preoccupations, a lack of discipline and commitment and organisational sloppiness.

For example, George Ross has noted how in the decade from 1968 to 1978 there was a large influx of new members into the PCF, many from middle-class backgrounds, and how it cultivated a more open regime, and relaxed standards of recruitment and membership.[49] He (and Jane Jensen) also noted how declining standards of training and education led to a growing generation gap within the party.[50] Writing in 1978, Ross noted that 'the Eurocommunisation of the PCF has partially opened up the party's structures, in ways which, in certain circumstances, could make it extremely difficult for the leadership to control rank and file life.'[51] In the circumstances of mounting setbacks, such as the party experienced in the 1980s, the legacy of Eurocommunist principles of organisation was growing incoherence and fragmentation.

Hellman has noted a similar trend in the PCI in Turin. Whereas in the 1960s the PCI 'formed' its own activists, in the 1970s they came via other organisations, often organisations which had been opposed to the PCI.[52] By 1980 the 'generation of '68' was dominant in the party apparatus, but these activists were highly heterogenous and could not serve the same role as the generation of experienced and disciplined cadres they replaced, who had acted as a bridge between the party of the '50s and that of the '70s. The result was that during the '80s the PCI suffered organisational paralysis as well as its problems of programme and strategy. By the end of the decade, it was, as Hellman well summed it up, 'an organisation that [was] no longer in a position to set the political agenda, or even to catalyse dissent and carry forward a broad movement for change'.[53] One indication of its predicament was that the average age of party members was more than 50 and that of new recruits, 36; less than 10 per cent of party members were less than 30 years old and 30 per cent were pensioners.[54]

'Part of our identity is our rejection of any narrow, class-oriented vision of society', declared PCI leader Occhetto in an interview with *L'Unita* in September 1988, continuing that they 'must also address the problem of political consensus, the so-called conquest of the centre ... '.[55] This appears to indicate the ultimate social democratisation of Italian Stalinism, its repudiation of any affinity to the working class in its devotion to the nation. In fact it amounts to a liquidationist perspective, because the PCI's role in the Italian nation depends upon its capacity to represent the working class on the national stage. Occhetto's willingness to surrender what constitutes the essential identity of the PCI simply reflects the party's desperate instability and loss of direction.

The discussion around the March 1989 PCI congress about changing the party's name reflects the same anxieties. Right-wing party leader Napolitano told the press with evident approval that there had been several attempts to get rid of the name 'communist' since the 1960s.[56] Yet while Occhetto ruled out any immediate change, he seems as concerned to drop the word 'party' as 'communist' from the title. In his January 1990 interview with Eric Hobsbawm, Occhetto emphasised that 'we feel we need to reconsider the way of being political, the political party as an entity, the programmes of the left.' (*Guardian*, 26 January 1990) Some in the PCI now favour the party adopting the sort of 'light structure' appropriate for an organisation which seeks more to influence public opinion than to intervene in the class struggle.[57] The ultimate aim seems to be to transform the PCI into the metaphysical expression of a new Euro-left consensus. If the European communist parties continue down this road, their future appears bleak indeed.

The self-liquidation of European Stalinism will remove what has proved the most substantial barrier to the advance of the working-class movement in Europe since social democracy was fatally discredited during the First World War. Though in the short-term the forces of anti-communist reaction are likely to be strengthened, in the longer term the demise of Stalinism opens up unprecedented opportunities for building a genuine Marxist working-class movement in Western Europe.

Notes

1. Take the following example, published in 1979: 'It is hard to resist the optimistic feeling that this process [Eurocommunism] must culminate, sooner or later, in the "Westernisation" of the parties concerned and the end of the Leninist heresy.' A. Levi, 'Eurocommunism: myth or reality?', in P. Filo della Torre, E. Mortimer and J. Story (eds), *Eurocommunism: Myth or Reality?*, London: Pelican, 1979, p. 19.

2. See F. Richards, 'Revisionism, imperialism and the state: the method of Capital and the dogma of state monopoly capitalism', *Revolutionary Communist Papers*, No 4, February 1979.

3. See, for example, the special feature 'Eurocommunism: an obituary', *the next step*, April 1981.

4. See P. Lange, G. Ross and M. Vannicelli, *Unions, Change and Crisis: French and Italian Union Strategy and the Political Economy, 1945–1980*, London: Allen and Unwin, 1982, pp. 35–55.

5. 'Eurocommunism in Italy', by H. Machin (ed), *National Communism in Western Europe: A Third Way for Socialism?*, London/New York: Methuen, 1983, p. 136.

6. Martin Schain, *French Communism and Local Power: Urban Politics and Political Change*, New York: St Martin's Press, 1985.

7. Schain, *French Communism and Local Power*, p. 17.

8. Schain, *French Communism and Local Power*, pp. 44–5.

9. D.S. Bell and B. Criddle, 'Mortal allies: the French left in the eighties', *Parliamentary Affairs*, October 1986.

10. See J. Ruscoe, *The Italian Communist Party 1976–1981*, London/Basingstoke: Macmillan, 1982, pp. 193–6.

11. S. Hellman, *Italian Communism in Transition: The Rise and Fall of the Historic Compromise in Turin, 1975–1980*, New York/Oxford: Oxford University Press, 1988.

12. Hellman, *Italian Communism in Transition*, p. 82.

13. Corbetta quoted in Hellman, *Italian Communism in Transition*, note 48, p. 234.

14. Hellman, *Italian Communism in Transition*, p. 105.

15. For a fuller discussion on the PCI and the secularisation see T. Abse, 'Judging the PCI', *New Left Review*, 153, September/October 1985.

16. Lange, Ross and Vannicelli, *Unions, Change and Crisis*, p. 69.

17. The events at Fiat are discussed in M. Kreile, 'The crisis of Italian trade unions in the 1980s', *West European Politics*, January 1989, and in Abse and Hellman.

18. See G. Ross and J. Jensen, 'The tragedy of the French left', *New Left Review*, 171, September/October 1988.

19. M, Adereth, *The French Communist Party: A Critical History (1920–1984)*, Manchester: Manchester University Press, 1984, p. 244.

20. A. Antonian and I. Wall, 'The French communists under Francois Mitterand', *Politics Studies*, June 1985.

21. In April 1983 Jeannette Thorez-Versmeech, the staunchly pro-Soviet widow of the former Stalinist leader of the PCF, called on the party to leave the government and lead the peace movement. See Antonian and Wall. For further discussion of the PCF line on nuclear weapons see D. Johnson, 'The French left and the bomb', *New Left Review*, 146, July/August 1984.

22. R. Tiersky, 'The declining fortunes of the French Communist Party', *Problems of Communism*, September/October 1988.

23. Tiersky, p. 5.

24. See A. Hirsh, *The French Left: A History and Overview*, Montreal: Blackrose Books, 1982.

25. Johnson, 'The French left and the bomb'.

26. Adereth, *The French Communist Party*, p. 253–54.

27. See E. Dainov, 'Problems of French communism 1972-1976', *West European Politics*, July 1987.

28. Adereth, *The French Communist Party*, p. 221.

29. See Ross and Jensen, 'Conflicting currents in the French Communist Party', *Socialist Register*, 1979; and Adereth, pp. 247–55.

30. See Ross and Jensen, 'Pluralism and the decline of left hegemony: the French left in power', *Politics and Society*, 14, 2, 1985; and Antonian and Wall, p. 271–273.

31. See Dainov, p. 368–69.

32. *Financial Times*, 12 and 13 January 1989.

33. *Economist*, 24 June 1989.

34. Ruscoe, *The Italian Communist Party 1976–1981*, p. 56.

35. P. Daniels, 'The Italian Communist Party in the mid-eighties', *Journal of Communist Studies*, June 1985.

36. Hellman, 'Italian Communism in Crisis', *Socialist Register*, 1988, p. 280.

37. Hellman, 'Italian Communism in Crisis', p. 279.

38. See *Sunday Times*, 19 March 1989; and *Guardian*, 22 March 1989.

39. See Daniels.

40. *Guardian*, 31 May 1989.

41. For recent surveys see L. Marcou, 'The impossible ally: a survey of Western communism in the eighties', *Journal of Communist Studies*, September 1988.

42. For a blow-by-blow account see E. Mujal-Leon, 'The decline and fall of Spanish communism', *Problems of Communism*, March/April 1986.

43. See Ross and Jensen, 'Conflicting currents in the French Communist Party'.

44. *Time*, 17 July 1989.

45. Hellman, *Italian Communism in Transition*, p. 168.

46. Hellman, *Italian Communism in Transition*, pp. 58–64.

47. Hellman, *Italian Communism in Transition*, p. 220; and Dainov.

48. For a discussion of this debate in the context of the decline of the British Labour Party see M. Freeman, 'The decline and fall of British Labourism', *Confrontation*, No 4, Summer 1988.

49. 'Crisis of Eurocommunism – the French case', *Socialist Register*, 1978, pp. 185–7.

50. 'The uncharted waters of destalinisation: the uneven evolution of the French Communist Party', *Politics and Society*, 9, 3, 1980.

51. 'Crisis in Eurocommunism', p. 187.

52. Hellman, *Italian Communism in Transition*, pp. 172–76.

53. Hellman, *Italian Communism in Transition*, p. 214.
54. Hellman, 'Italian Communism in Crisis', p. 260.
55. Republished in *The Italian Communist*, No 3, July/September 1988.
56. *Sunday Times*, 19 March 1989.
57. See Hellman, 'Italian Communism in Crisis', p. 264. For a British example of a similar trend, see S. Benton, 'The party is over', *Marxism Today*, March 1989. Benton, once a prominent Eurocommunist, is now political editor of the Kinnockite *New Statesman and Society*.

8 Marxism Before and After Stalinism

> Marxism ... cannot stand aside from what has happened in Eastern Europe. Marx was no more responsible for the Gulag than Nietzsche was for Auschwitz. But it is the case that the legitimacy claimed by Lenin and Stalin was that bequeathed by Marx, and the sad fact is that after all allowance has been made for 'backwardness' and 'underdevelopment', the one social and political alternative to capitalism constructed on the basis of Marx's ideas, though arguably more egalitarian, has also proved itself to be more authoritarian, less efficient and less desirable than the system it was supposed to replace.[1]

The familiar image of overlapping profiles of Marx and Engels, Lenin, Stalin, headed by Mao Zedong, Fidel Castro or some other national figure, cast in stone or bronze or painted on banners or badges, has long symbolised the reliance of Stalinist regimes around the world on the legitimacy conferred by the Marxist tradition. For many years too the enemies of Marxism have used this sequence in reverse, seeking to discredit the project of proletarian revolution by identifying a direct logical link between the stagnant and repressive regimes of twentieth-century Stalinism and the theories of Marxism and Leninism. The most striking consequence of the disintegration of Stalinism in the late 1980s is that this connection is now recognised by those, like the historian Gareth Stedman Jones, who at least until recently considered themselves to be Marxists, as well as by traditional apologists for the capitalist order.

There can be no doubt that there is a relationship of sorts between Marxism and Stalinism. But it is vulgar idealism to suggest that they are identical or that one leads to the other through a simple linear evolution of theory and practice. The relationship between Marxism and Stalinism can only be understood in the specific historical context in which it developed and in the

171

interaction among social and political forces which shaped this process. In his response to those who equated Stalinism and Bolshevism in the 1930s, Trotsky forcefully challenged the idealistic approach: 'Certainly Stalinism "grew out" of Bolshevism, not logically, however, but dialectically; not as a revolutionary affirmation but as a Thermidorian negation. It is by no means the same.'[2]

The origins of today's disintegration of Stalinist regimes and movements around the world can be traced to the emergence of the Stalinist perspective of building 'socialism in one country' as the negation of the Marxist commitment to international working-class revolution. To clarify this process it is necessary to go back to Marx's analysis of capitalism as a world system that could only be transcended at a global level. We can then trace the development of the fateful dialectic of nationalism and internationalism in the working-class movement in the half century after the death of Marx.

The material basis of proletarian internationalism

Marx and Engels located the possibility and necessity of socialism in the contradictory nature of capitalist production. For Marx, capital's relentless drive to expand and to develop the productive powers of society on a global scale provided the basis for the development of a new and higher form of society – socialism:

> There appears here the universalising tendency of capital, which distinguishes it from all previous stages of production. Although limited by its very nature, it strives towards the universal development of the forces of production, and thus becomes the presupposition of a new mode of production.[3]

From its foundations in different nation states, capitalism expanded into a global system with the enhanced productive capacity provided by an international division of labour. The level of productivity encouraged by the world market provided the starting point for a new social order.

Yet, as Marx's analysis continued, in the very process of raising productivity the capitalist system encountered the limitations on further expansion resulting from the subordination of economic activity to the cause of making profit for the private owners of the means of production:

Beyond a certain point, the development of the powers of production becomes a barrier for capital; hence the capital relation is a barrier for the development of the productive powers of labour ... The growing incompatibility between the productive development of society and its hitherto existing relations of production expresses itself in bitter contradictions, crises, spasms. The violent destruction of capital, not by relations external to it, but rather as a condition for its self-preservation, is the most striking form in which advice is given to it to be gone to give room to a higher state of social production.[4]

For Marx, communism was a 'higher state of social production' because it allowed the further 'development of the productive powers of labour'.

Capitalism not only provided the material basis for socialism, but its development into a world system revealed elements of the new society inside the old. The marked tendency of late nineteenth century capitalism to transcend its national origins to establish greater interdependence and cooperation among national capitals signalled the potential for going beyond the old order:

In the case of the world market, the connection of the individual with all, but at the same time also the independence of this connection from the individual, have developed to such a high level that the formation of the world market already at the same time contains the conditions for going beyond it.[5]

The consequences of this analysis were clear: socialism could only be built through further developing the international division of labour, not by retreating to the nation state.

From their earliest writings Marx and Engels emphasised that if the working class was to succeed in developing the world economy beyond the limitations imposed by the capitalist system, its struggles had to have an international character. In a key passage in the *Communist Manifesto* they emphasised that the struggle of the working class was national in form, but not in content: 'Though not in substance, yet in form, the struggle of the proletariat with the bourgeoisie is at first a national struggle. The proletariat of each country must, of course, first settle scores with its own bourgeoisie.'[6]

In form the working-class struggle was directed against the ruling class of its own country. In content, however, this struggle had to be informed and guided by the worldwide goals of the international working-class movement.

Engels later emphasised the relationship between the international character of the capitalist economy and the international content of proletarian struggle:

> By creating the world market, big industry has already brought all the peoples of the earth, and especially the civilised peoples, into such close relations with one another that none is independent of what happens to the others. Further, it has coordinated the social development of the civilised countries to such an extent that in all of them the bourgeoisie and proletariat have become the decisive classes and the struggle between them the great struggle of the day. It follows that the communist revolution will not merely be a national phenomenon but must take place simultaneously in all civilised countries, that is to say, at least in England, America, France and Germany.[7]

Engels' view that 'the communist revolution will not merely be a national phenomenon' was not a dogmatic formula, but simply a theoretical generalisation based on his recognition of the centrality of the global division of labour in the project of communist revolution. After the Russian Revolution revisionists alleged that reality had refuted Engels' predictions and some later claimed that Stalin's collectivisation had proved the possibility of building socialism in one country that Engels had excluded. In fact, as we shall see, history confirmed Engels' view that, to be successful, communist revolution had to take place in the more advanced capitalist countries.

Marx and Engels never envisaged that revolution would follow some rigidly prescribed schema, erupting at the same moment in all the advanced capitalist countries. This is why they emphasised the national form which the class struggle would take in every capitalist country. However, they also emphasised that the project of building a new form of society depended on taking advantage of the global scale and development of the capitalist system. Thus, to be successful, communist revolution had to take place internationally. Furthermore, they insisted that the only guarantee of the international character of the struggle of the working class lay in its ideological and political independence.

For Marx and Engels proletarian internationalism was not the abstract and pious sentiment that it later became among social democratic and Stalinist politicians. They sought to advance an internationalist perspective on all the practical questions facing the working-class movement. It was with this objective that Marx personally played an active role in the First International, based in London between 1864 and 1870.[8] Both Marx and Engels constantly emphasised the role of internationalism in forging the ideological independence of the working class at a time when bourgeois propagandists were promoting nationalist and chauvinist prejudices as a means of blurring and containing class conflict. This was the content of their repeated exhortations to the British labour movement to oppose British rule over Ireland and their practical initiatives on this issue.[9]

Marx sharply criticised the draft programme of the German Social Democratic Party (SPD) for its narrow national perspective: 'not a word, therefore, about the international functions of the German working class'.[10] Marx and Engels had no time for the platitudes about 'international brotherhood' contained in this and many similar labour movement programmes. For them internationalism was a concrete question directly related to the programme for seizing state power. 'Proletarian internationalism' could not be formulated as a set of general principles abstracted from the day-to-day struggles of the working class; internationalism was the heart of working class independence.

The rise of social chauvinism

The emergence in the three decades after Marx's death of a powerful international working-class movement proclaiming its allegiance to Marxism, revealed the potential for making the world revolution anticipated in his life work. In the case of the strongest section of what became known as the Second International, that of Germany, there were close personal ties to both Marx and Engels which conferred considerable legitimacy on their successors. However, by the outbreak of the First World War the internationalist potential of the working-class movement had been destroyed by the influence of what Lenin characterised as 'social chauvinism' – 'socialism in words, chauvinism in deeds' – over the leadership of the social democratic parties in each European country.[11] The shameful slide of social democracy in 1914 into national chauvinism was the result of the ascendancy of revisionism in the sphere of theory and reformism in politics, a process which had slowly gathered momentum since the 1880s.

The whole of the Second International, and German social democracy in particular, formally upheld the Marxist principle of proletarian internationalism. In its programme drawn up at Erfurt in 1891, the German SPD appeared to take to heart Marx's criticisms of the Gotha programme and proclaimed an internationalist outlook fully in the spirit of the Communist Manifesto:

> The interests of the working class are the same in all countries with a capitalist mode of production. With the extension of world trade and production for the world market, the position of the workers of every country is becoming ever more dependent on the position of workers in other countries. The emancipation of the working class is therefore the task in which the workers of all developed countries participate equally. Recognising this, the Social Democratic Party feels and declares itself one with the class conscious workers of all other countries.[12]

Yet even at this early stage the SPD's commitment to internationalism was more of a gesture to the past than a practical policy platform. The influence of trends in a national reformist direction was apparent when Georg von Vollmar, the SPD leader in the more backward and conservative southern region, rallied some support for his call for the removal of the statement of Marxist principles in the Erfurt programme.[13]

Over the next decade important developments in German society encouraged the conservative wing of the SPD. The economy expanded rapidly, if unevenly, and living standards steadily improved for the majority of German people. After decades of repression the regime repealed its law banning socialist political organisations and encouraged the SPD to play a prominent role in parliament. The state embarked on a major programme of welfare reforms, providing sickness and unemployment benefits and various pensions. The effect of all these changes was, as Lenin later summed it up, 'to foster opportunism, firstly as a mood, then as a trend, until finally it formed a group or stratum among the labour bureaucracy and the petit-bourgeois travellers'.[14]

The apparent prosperity and stability of German society provoked a growing questioning of some of the basic elements of Marxist theory among intellectuals in and around the SPD. These doubts were systematically expressed in a series of articles by Eduard Bernstein in the late 1890s, which were published together as *Evolutionary Socialism* in 1899.[15] In this founding text of revisionism, Bernstein sought to revise Marx's theory of capitalist crisis and his strategy of proletarian revolution as the means to establishing socialism. Bernstein argued that the capitalist system could evolve harmoniously towards capitalism under the pressure of the working-class movement, organised in trade unions and in parliamentary parties, and working in collaboration with the middle classes.

At the same time that Bernstein's revisionist theories were gaining influence in the SPD, the strategy of relying on the state to achieve reforms also became increasingly popular among SPD leaders. While the economy was expanding and the German state appeared more responsive to working-class pressure through parliament, the view that the state was a neutral and potentially beneficent force in society attracted growing support. The notion that capitalism could be gradually reformed into socialism led to the elevation of parliamentary activity into the dominating principle of SPD politics. Once the ascendancy of parliament was accepted, it also became acceptable to enter a coalition with a bourgeois party (as the SPD did in 1912) or even to enter bourgeois coalitions (as it did in 1914). The separation of trade unionism from political activity, of day-to-day struggles from the struggle for socialism, all followed from the notion of state neutrality.

Despite its slow drift towards policies of class collaboration and national reformism, the SPD, in common with the Second International as a whole, retained its formal internationalism right up to the eve of the First World War. International social democratic conferences echoed to resounding declarations of international solidarity, and resolutions agreeing to a general strike in the event of imperialist war were supported to the end. However, signs of chauvinist prejudice in the ranks of social democracy were evident long before August 1914. The intensification of rivalries among the major imperialist powers in the first decade of the twentieth century strengthened nationalism and unleashed major propaganda campaigns designed to win the labour movements over to the national flag. In these circumstances the opportunist trends evident in documents like the Erfurt programme soon came to the fore.

In most of the major Western powers there were signs that chauvinist campaigns – such as that around the Boer War in Britain – achieved some resonance in the labour movement. In Germany the 1907 elections, in which colonial policy in Africa became a major issue, were a significant test for the SPD, which did badly as a result of the impact of right-wing nationalist agitation.[16] The SPD responded by adapting to German nationalism and major figures like Vollmar and Noske argued that the party should take up a position in support of 'the defence of the fatherland'. As the drive towards the First World War gathered momentum over the next seven years the voices of social chauvinism in the SPD grew louder.

With the exception of the Bolsheviks in Russia, the left in the Second International proved ineffectual in combating the combined influences of revisionism and reformism. Though Rosa Luxemburg issued a powerful polemical rejoinder to Bernstein, she proved unable to develop Marx's theory of capitalist crisis in response to the rise of imperialism.[17] She was even less successful in the sphere of political strategy, where she one-sidedly emphasised 'revolutionary' tactics such as the mass strike against the 'reformist' methods of social democracy, a mistake common to much of the Second International left. The left was certainly subjectively more militant than the SPD leadership, but it could not advance a revolutionary strategy based on a materialist analysis of objective conditions. Hence the left could neither defeat revisionism nor arrest the reformist drift of the party leaders. The result was that in all the important debates of the pre-war years – on the relationship between the unions and the party, on parliamentarianism, on the national question, on militarism – the left was defeated by the right.

In August 1914 the SPD and the other major parties of the Second International were faced with a stark choice when their ruling classes declared war. As is well known they abandoned proletarian internationalism in favour of social chauvinism and, with varying degrees of enthusiasm and equivocation, joined the war effort of their national bourgeoisies. As the workers of one nation slaughtered those of another on a scale unprecedented in history, the cause of proletarian unity and independence suffered a historic setback.

The Bolsheviks: the revival of internationalism

Both in the years leading up to the Russian Revolution and in the immediate post-revolutionary period Lenin and other leading Bolsheviks made a major contribution to the principles and practice of proletarian internationalism. In the pre-1917 period, Lenin polemicised against Kautsky and the other 'renegade' social democratic leaders who had led their labour movements into the imperialist war.[18] In response to the betrayal of August 1914, Lenin campaigned relentlessly against the social democrats, constantly emphasising the urgency of building a new International. In the months leading up to the Russian Revolution in October 1917 he returned again and again to the theme of international organisation. Number 10 of the famous 'April Theses' produced by Lenin on his dramatic return to Petrograd in April 1917 is headed 'a new International': 'We must take the initiative in creating a revolutionary International, an International against the social-chauvinists and against the "Centre".'[19]

As soon as the Russian Revolution had been achieved, the new regime set about organising the new, Third or Communist, International. Its first congress was held in Moscow in March 1919. Through its statutes and conditions for admission (adopted in 1920), the Communist International (Comintern) outlined the Bolshevik approach:

> Proletarian internationalism ... demands
> 1) the subordination of the interests of the proletarian struggle in one country to the interests of the struggle on a world scale;
> 2) that the nation which achieves victory over the bourgeoisie shall display the capacity and readiness to make the greatest national sacrifices in order to overthrow international capitalism.[20]

The revolutionary approach of the Comintern stimulated the formation of communist parties throughout the world. For the first time in history, proletarian internationalism had acquired a coherent political and organisational form.

The Bolshevik victory in Russia provided the Comintern with a base for international activity. For the Bolsheviks, the defence of the Russian Revolution was not a matter for the Soviet Union alone, but an issue for the international working class. Lenin constantly emphasised the importance of other working-class movements following the Bolshevik example:

> Things have turned out differently from what Marx and Engels expected and we, the Russian working and exploited classes have the honour of being the vanguard of the international socialist revolution; we can now see clearly how far the development of the revolution will go. The Russians began it – the German, the Frenchman and the Englishman will finish it, and socialism will be victorious.[21]

Again in November 1920 Lenin insisted on the dependence of the Soviet state on the world revolution: 'Until the revolution takes place in all lands, including the richest and most highly civilised ones, our victory will be only a half victory, perhaps still less.'[22]

For Lenin the fate of the Soviet Union was tied to the progress of the communist movement abroad in two ways. First, in basic military terms, the Bolsheviks relied on the international working class movement to thwart imperialist attempts to invade the Soviet Union and restore capitalism. Second, in a more fundamental social sense, the attempt to build socialism could not succeed within the confines of an isolated and relatively backward country. The Bolsheviks knew that they could make a start towards socialism in the Soviet Union, but they also knew that they could not finish this task without the support of revolutions in the advanced capitalist countries. In 1922, the fourth congress of the Comintern reiterated the importance of world revolution: 'The proletarian revolution can never triumph completely within a single country; rather it must triumph internationally as world revolution.'[23]

The objective link between the Russian Revolution and the struggle for socialism internationally provided the foundations for the revolutionary political practice of the Comintern in its early years. The newly formed and largely inexperienced communist parties made many mistakes, but during the first four congresses of the Comintern, they implemented the principles of proletarian internationalism on a scale that has yet to be surpassed.

Stalin and 'socialism in one country'

In the early 1920s the Soviet state was in a highly precarious position. It had survived revolution, civil war and imperialist intervention, but at a tremendous cost. Its economy was devastated, its industry was in ruins and the agricultural sector overwhelmingly backward; the working class was decimated and vastly outnumbered by the peasantry. In 1921 Lenin reflected in a keynote speech on the two conditions on which the success of the revolution depended:

First on the condition of its support at the right moment by a socialist revolution in one or several leading countries. As you know we have very much compared with what was done before to bring about this condition, but far from enough to make it a

reality. The other condition is a compromise between the proletariat, which puts dictatorship into practice or holds state power
in its hands, and the majority of the population.[24]

Though the Comintern continued its efforts, the prospects of
achieving the first condition in the short term appeared slight.
Thus the Bolshevik government was obliged to pursue a compromise with the peasantry in the form of the New Economic Policy
which allowed some scope for private enterprise in agriculture.

Within a few years it became apparent that, though the prospects of revolution in the West had receded further still, the NEP
had been fairly successful in encouraging a revival of economic
activity in the countryside. During the same period the defeat of
the proletarian forces in the Soviet Union resulted in a steady
bureaucratisation of the Bolshevik party. The success of the NEP
and other compromise measures encouraged the gradual merger of
party and state functionaries into a bureaucratic layer that increasingly dominated life in Soviet society. The emerging bureaucracy
responded pragmatically to events by elevating the tasks of
domestic reconstruction more and more over the project of world
revolution, which had always been regarded as the first precondition for building socialism. The temporary expedient of the NEP
soon turned into a long-term national development strategy.

Stalin, who personified the bureaucratic trend, generalised from
the experience of the NEP at a time when the Soviet Union was
forced to try to develop in isolation from the world economy,
arguing the proposition that it was possible to create 'socialism in
one country'. The combination of internal demoralisation and
external isolation ensured that there was a positive response to
Stalin's national reformist strategy, especially among the
burgeoning bureaucracy. The tactical compromise of the NEP
became a socialist principle; the necessity enforced by the
weakness and backwardness of the Soviet regime became a virtue.

Stalin attempted to reconcile his theory of 'socialism in one
country' with Marxism by resorting to the familiar argument of
the revisionists that changing circumstances since the death of
Marx and Engels necessitated a new theory of socialist transformation. Whereas the notion of world revolution was appropriate in
the nineteenth century, the subsequent rise of imperialism justified a national approach:

In the new period, the period of the development of imperialism, when the unevenness of development of the capitalist

countries has become the decisive factor in imperialist development, when inevitable conflicts and wars among the
imperialists weaken the imperialist front and make it possible
for it to be breached in individual countries ... in these conditions the old formula of Engels becomes incorrect and must
inevitably be replaced by another formula, one that affirms the
possibility of the victory of socialism in one country.[25]

Stalin presented the 'law of uneven development', which he
claimed was 'discovered by Lenin', as the basis of 'socialism in one
country'. But 'uneven development' is simply a description of
reality, it cannot be 'the decisive factor' in anything.

Stalin refuted Marxism with the absurd proposition that revolution is simply the result of inter-imperialist rivalries. His argument
amounts to little more than the identification of some link
between the First World War and the Russian Revolution, viewing
both events in narrowly military and political terms. Marx, by
contrast, sought to explain inter-imperialist rivalries through his
analysis of the competitive tensions resulting from capital accumulation on a world scale. The Marxist perspective never ruled out
the possibility of revolution taking place in a single capitalist
country. Indeed, as we have seen, Marx and Engels recognised that
the struggle of the working class had to take a national form. What
Marxism emphatically denied was the possibility of proletarian
revolution establishing socialism in a single country isolated from
the world economy. Stalin never seriously engaged this argument,
but simply asserted the opposite. It was a measure of the degeneration of the Marxist tradition in the Soviet Union and abroad by
the mid-1920s that such a travesty of Marxist theory could be
taken seriously.

When it came to the question of building socialism in the Soviet
Union, Stalin abandoned the 'law of uneven development' and
produced a new formula, identifying two sets of contradictions:

One group consists of the internal contradictions that exist
between the proletariat and the peasantry. The other group
consists of the external contradictions that exist between our
country, as the land of socialism, and all other countries, as
lands of capitalism.[26]

Stalin considered that the internal problems of the Soviet Union
could be overcome. On the other hand he conceded that the
efforts of the Soviet Union itself could not defend the land of

socialism against imperialist intervention. Hence he acknowledged that 'the final victory of socialism is only possible on an international scale.'[27] Yet by mechanically separating the internal fate of the Soviet Union from the project of world revolution, Stalin destroyed the whole purpose of the Comintern and restored a national outlook to pride of place over internationalism.

Though the danger of imperialist intervention was a real consideration for the Soviet state, the military threat was not the only, or even the most important, of its problems. As we have seen, for Marx and Engels, and for Lenin, the project of building socialism had to begin from the global level of development of productive forces already achieved under capitalism. Just before his death Lenin had acknowledged that socialism could not be built in the Soviet Union in isolation.[28] Though the political prerequisites (the proletarian dictatorship) had been established, the material conditions for socialism did not exist in the backward and ravaged Soviet economy. The early Soviet state had been forced to impose a state monopoly on foreign trade to protect its feeble economy from the competitive pressures of the more productive capitalist world. On his deathbed Lenin urged Trotsky to take up the struggle against Stalin and his collaborators who were in favour of relaxing this monopoly.[29] For Lenin, who understood that the economic weakness of the Soviet state was the major threat to its survival, it was 'impossible to yield on this question'. Stalin, who understood the threat of imperialism only in narrow military terms, failed to appreciate the importance of the state's trade monopoly.

Stalin's preoccupation with military intervention as the main threat to building socialism in the Soviet Union led to the replacement of Lenin's tactical approach to alliances with Western powers with the strategic goal of peaceful coexistence. For the Bolsheviks compromises with the imperialist powers, such as the treaty agreed with Germany at Brest-Litovsk in 1918, were necessary to create a breathing space for the fragile Soviet regime. Lenin recognised, however, that in the long term it would be impossible for the Soviet state to live in harmony with its neighbours:

> We cannot for a moment believe in lasting trade relations with the imperialist powers: the respite will be temporary ... The existence of the Soviet republic alongside of capitalist countries – a Soviet republic surrounded by capitalist countries – is so impossible to the capitalists that they will seize any opportunity to resume the war.[30]

Whereas for Lenin treaties with imperialists simply provided a temporary respite for the Bolshevik regime, for Stalin the object of diplomacy was to establish 'a certain minimum of international conditions which are necessary in order that we may exist and develop socialism'.[31]

Abstracting the Soviet Union from the capitalist world economy, Stalin focused on the military policies of the great powers towards the Soviet Union. From this perspective, the imperialist countries could be distinguished as 'peaceful' or 'aggressive' according to their policy towards Moscow. If, through diplomacy, a policy of armed intervention could be neutralised, then Stalin believed that there would be no further obstacle to the 'final victory' of socialism in the Soviet Union. By 1944 Stalin could claim that the wartime alliance between the Soviet Union, Britain and the US was 'founded not on casual, transitory considerations, but on vital and lasting interests'.[32] Whereas Lenin deduced the threat of military intervention from the fundamental contradiction between the social relations of the Soviet state and those of the capitalist world, Stalin reduced the problem of building socialism to a technical matter of keeping imperialist troops out. He ended up arguing that collaboration with the most rapacious imperialist powers in history could make a lasting contribution to building socialism in the Soviet Union. The durability of this alliance was revealed when the Western allies launched the Cold War three years later.

Stalin's national perspective separated the project of building 'socialism in one country' from that of achieving the 'final victory' of socialism worldwide. This was a new formulation of Bernstein's dictum that for him the movement meant everything and the final aim of socialism nothing. Like Bernstein, Stalin separated the struggle for what was possible under capitalism from the struggle for socialism, and subordinated the struggle for socialism to what was possible under capitalism. Not only did Stalin's approach reinforce the isolation of the fragile workers' state and make it even more difficult to advance towards socialism in the Soviet Union, but through the Comintern it subordinated the international class struggle to the pragmatic diplomacy of the Kremlin.

The theory of 'socialism in one country' had two consequences for the international communist movement, as Trotsky pointed out in 1928. The first priority of the communist parties was no longer to fight for the conquest of power in their own countries, but to take whatever position was consistent with the defence of the Soviet Union: 'The task of the parties of the Comintern assumes therefore an auxiliary character; their mission is to protect the Soviet Union from intervention and not to fight for the conquest of power.'[33]

The subordination of the parties of the Comintern to Stalin's policy turned them into local agents of his diplomacy.

The theory of 'socialism in one country' also had the effect of encouraging the communist parties to pursue 'national' roads to socialism at home. This approach inevitably brought them closer and closer to social democratic parties that had long accepted the framework imposed by the capitalist nation state:

> If it is at all possible to realise socialism in one country, then one can believe in that theory not only after but also before the conquest of power. If socialism can be realised within the national boundaries of backward Russia, then there is all the more reason to believe that it can be realised in advanced Germany. Tomorrow the leaders of the communist party of Germany will undertake to propound this theory ... The day after tomorrow the French party will have its turn. It will be the beginning of the disintegration of the Comintern along the lines of social patriotism.[34]

Trotsky concluded that the result would be that the Comintern would 'not differ in any substantial manner from the evolutionary social democracy which ... stumbled decisively on 4 August 1914 over this very same question'.[35]

Trotsky's parallel between the disintegration of the Comintern along the lines of social patriotism and the collapse of the Second International in 1914 was percipient. But, just as it took some years for the embryonic nationalism that was already evident in the debate around the Erfurt programme in 1891 to develop into the destructive chauvinism of 1914, so the centrifugal consequences of the theory of 'socialism in one country' only gradually became apparent. Indeed we can see the current fragmentation of the official communist movement as the ultimate result of this process.

The slow disintegration of Stalinism

The remarkable feature of the disintegration of the Stalinist world that is taking place today is that it has taken so long to occur. To understand the slow evolution of the centrifugal trends within the official communist movement it is useful to begin by contrasting the Third and Second Internationals.

The loose federal structure of the Second International reflected its highly heterogenous character. It included the stolid and respectable British Labour Party as well as militant anarcho-syndicalist socialists from France, Spain and Italy. Individual parties, such as the German SPD, included moderate parliamentarians and trade union officials as well as revolutionary militants like Luxemburg and Liebknecht. Reformism emerged as a Europe-wide phenomenon, but it assumed different forms in different national conditions. The fact that the roots of social democracy lay in different nation states meant that the 'international cooperation' fostered by the International always came second to local considerations. The fact that each social democratic movement regarded its nation state as the agency of socialist transformation ensured growing antagonisms among the member parties of the International as inter-imperialist rivalries increased in the first decade of the twentieth century.

The collapse of the International in 1914 revealed that there was no real basis for reformist internationalism.

The tight, centralised organisational structure of the Comintern, by contrast, reflected its organic link to the proletarian dictatorship in the Soviet Union and its commitment to proletarian internationalism. In its early years the Comintern was not merely the sum of its national parts, but an important political force in the worldwide struggle for communism. It was a democratic centralist body that played a major role in encouraging its member movements to achieve ideological clarity and to pursue a coherent revolutionary strategy. The fact that the Comintern leadership had to intervene in most member parties in the early 1920s to clarify basic questions of revolutionary politics revealed the strength of the legitimacy conferred by the Russian Revolution and the relative immaturity of most of these organisations. Unfortunately, this same political immaturity subsequently enabled Stalin to take advantage of the centralised structure of the Comintern to impose his opportunist policies on the whole of the international communist movement.

Though, as we have seen, Stalin's revision of Marxism had much in common with earlier reformist theories, his political strategy had a significantly different starting point from that of the leaders of the Second International. Stalin's policy priority of building 'socialism in one country' presupposed the Russian Revolution, the overthrow of the capitalist state by the working class. Thus his policy did not begin from an evolutionary theory of socialism, but acknowledged the need for class struggle, for working-class unity and revolution. Hence the nationalist aspect of Stalin's outlook was not immediately apparent and it did not immediately provoke conflicts among the member parties of the Comintern.

There was certainly a logical link between the theory of 'socialism in one country' and the strategy of a peaceful, national road to socialism. But in a period of major upheavals in Europe, when social democratic parties were on the defensive against powerful communist movements inspired by the example of October 1917, the reformist tendencies in the Comintern generally remained submerged. During the 1920s the communist parties, for the most part, retained a subjectively revolutionary outlook. Their lack of political independence was expressed more in relation to Moscow than in their attitude to their ruling classes at home. Hence the official communist movement could continue to project a militant anti-capitalist image and maintain its stand to the left of social democracy, despite the ascendancy of Stalinism over the Comintern.

It is important to recall that the international Stalinist movement emerged under the firm control of the Soviet bureaucracy at a time when the tendency of communist parties to move towards a national reformist position had yet to materialise. Thus the contradiction between the subordination of the communist parties to Moscow and their national reformism was not yet apparent. Indeed to most observers the defining feature of Comintern membership was the way its members slavishly followed the dictates of the Kremlin in matters of foreign affairs.

The extent to which the communist parties had become tools of Soviet foreign policy appeared to be forcefully confirmed in the period between 1928 and 1934 when the Comintern leadership instructed member parties to pursue ultra-left policies. In anticipation of the imminent collapse of capitalism and the advent of fascist dictatorship, communist parties virulently denounced social democrats and prepared for insurrections. But it is important to understand this twist in Comintern policy in its historical context. At a time of unprecedented worldwide capitalist crisis, Stalin was concerned at the deterioration of relations with the West and the mounting danger of intervention. The left turn of the Comintern was designed to put pressure on the imperialist powers at home. However, Comintern instructions to communist parties to pursue policies that were unrelated to local circumstances provoked growing tensions. The destruction of the German Communist Party in 1933 as a result of its pursuit of inappropriate policies reinforced pressures for a shift away from the ultra-left line, both in Moscow and in the member parties of the Comintern. Indeed, certain parties, such as the Italian Communist Party, never implemented this line in the first place. By 1934 pressures for a national reformist policy had begun to emerge in the Comintern in response to the most intense period of dogmatic Moscow domination.

In his writings on France, Trotsky later argued against those who regarded Stalinism one-sidedly as the subordination of sections of the Comintern to Moscow's diktat:

> I cannot agree that the policy of the International was only a materialisation of demands from Moscow. It is necessary to see the policy as a whole, from the internal and the international points of view, from all sides ...
>
> Also, you cannot think of the Comintern as being merely the instrument of Stalin's foreign policy. In France in 1934 the CP had declined from 80,000 to 30,000. It was necessary to have a new policy ... At the same time, Stalin was seeking to have a new foreign policy. From one side and the other we have these tendencies which go to make the new turn. They are different sides of the same process ... The French CP is not only an agency of Moscow, but a national organisation with members of parliament, etc.[36]

The dependence of the communist parties on the Soviet bureaucracy was not a rigidly fixed relationship, but one which interacted with the influence of domestic political forces.

Given the lack of political independence of the communist parties, they tended to adapt to ruling-class pressures on the working-class movement. While at certain moments, such as the period from 1928 to 1934, Moscow prescribed a militant class struggle policy, at others, such as during the popular front period from 1935 to 1939, it encouraged communists to collaborate with bourgeois political forces and suspend the class struggle. This policy reached its climax in the Second World War when the communist parties in the Allied powers supported the war policies of their national bourgeoisies – the very position that had precipitated the collapse of the Second International in 1914.

The fact that it was the Soviet bureaucracy that reinforced the nationalist outlook of the communist parties tended to obscure the potential conflict that it created between these parties and the Kremlin. Trotsky perceptively drew attention to this potential conflict in 1938:

The growth of the communist parties in recent years, their infil-tration into the ranks of the petit-bourgeoisie, their installation in the state machinery, and trade unions, parliaments, munici-palities, etc, have strengthened in the extreme their dependence on national imperialism at the expense of their traditional dependence on the Kremlin ...

The growth of imperialist antagonisms, the obvious proximity of war danger, and the equally obvious isolation of the Soviet Union must unavoidably strengthen the centrifugal national tendencies within the Comintern ... Henceforth the communo-chauvinists will have to worry about their own hides, whose interests by no means always coincide with the 'defence of the Soviet Union'.[37]

The potential for conflict noted by Trotsky was not realised until the emergence of the 'polycentric' international communist movement after Second World War. The slow process of disinte-gration began with the secession of Yugoslavia from the Moscow camp in 1948, and it continued with the rift with China in 1960 and the rise of Eurocommunism in the 1970s. In 1979–80 open warfare between China and Vietnam, and the Vietnamese occupa-tion of Cambodia, revealed the utter collapse of any notion of solidarity within the official communist movement. The advent of perestroika in the Soviet Union in 1985 and its impact on the Eastern bloc and further afield in the late 1980s marked the final abandonment by the Stalinist bureaucracy itself of the project launched by the October Revolution and the foundation of the Comintern. It is important, however, not to confuse the results of the process of Stalinist disintegration with the starting point – the theory of socialism in one country and the abandonment of Marxism that it represents.

Marxism after Stalinism

'Marxism ... cannot stand aside from what has now happened in Eastern Europe', proclaims Stedman Jones in the passage with which we started this chapter. But Marxism has no need to stand aside from the consequences of the degeneration of Stalinism. We simply acknowledge that because the Soviet Union was unable to take advantage of the global division of labour and development of productivity achieved under capitalism, it ended up with an economy more backward than the system it was designed to replace. The responsibility for this historic failure lies not with

Marxism, but with the imperialist encirclement of the early Soviet state and the futile Stalinist strategy of 'socialism in one country'.

It is ironic that the last service of the Stalinist bureaucrats to the apologists for capitalism is to add their authority to the view that the decay of the Soviet system is a direct consequence of Marxism itself. It is only to be expected that Western fellow-travellers with Stalinism on the New Left, such as Stedman Jones, should add their voices to this chorus of reaction. Throughout the West, representatives of the establishment draw comfort from Stalinist confessions that legitimise the capitalist way of life. Stalinist self-criticism is presented as a positive endorsement of the market, capitalist exploitation and parliamentary democracy. Hence in the short term the crisis of Stalinism can only help to consolidate reaction. In the Soviet Union and Eastern Europe the working class will inevitably opt for political movements that are explicitly anti-communist, or even anti-socialist. In the West, the authorities will find a ready popular resonance for the view that any attempt to challenge the established order risks repeating the Soviet experience.

In the long run, however, Marxism will emerge stronger from the collapse of Stalinism and the parallel crisis of the capitalist world order. During the long years in which Stalinism appeared to be a dynamic and positive alternative to capitalism, it was difficult to popularise genuine Marxism. The fact that Stalinism was universally accepted as the legitimate inheritor of the Marxist tradition enabled the Soviet bureaucracy to retain its influence over key sections of the international working class. At the same time the very existence of the Stalinist states became the most powerful practical argument against Marxism and Leninism in the rest of the world.

The decay of Stalinism now offers the potential to revive Marxism as a living force in the world. The disintegration of the Eastern bloc is already exacerbating tensions within the Western alliance, most prominently over the reunification of Germany. The Soviet Union has been fully exposed as a historical dead end and the decks have been cleared for a fresh start at a time of unprecedented flux in the international balance of forces. Once the Gorbachev phenomenon has achieved its full impact in the Soviet Union, Eastern Europe and beyond, it will no longer be possible to blame Marx and Lenin for the failures of the Stalinist bureaucracy. Nor will the rulers of the West be able any longer to point to the Soviet Union as the inevitable outcome of any attempt to devise an alternative to capitalism. Instead the devastating consequences of the restoration of the market in the

East will provide a powerful argument for a system of planned production and workers' democracy, organised on a global scale. Whatever the short-term cost of capitalist restoration in the Stalinist world, the destruction of Stalinism will remove a historic barrier to the self-emancipation of the international working class.

Notes

1. Gareth Stedman Jones, 'Marx after Marxism', *Marxism Today*, February 1990.
2. Leon Trotsky, 'Stalinism and Bolshevism', *Living Marxism*, April 1990.
3. K. Marx, *Grundrisse*, Harmondsworth: Pelican, in association with *New Left Review*, 1973, p. 540.
4. Marx, *Grundrisse*, p. 749–50.
5. Marx, *Grundrisse*, p. 161.
6. 'Though not in substance, yet in form, the struggle of the proletariat with the bourgeoisie is at first a national struggle. The proletariat of each country must, of course, first of all settle matters with its own bourgeoisie.' Karl Marx and Frederick Engels, *Manifesto of the Communist Party*, Moscow: Progress Publishers, 1986, p. 44.
7. F. Engels, *The Principles of Communism*, London: Pluto Press, 1972, p. 15.
8. Marx, *The First International and After*, ed. by David Fernbach, Harmondsworth: Pelican, 1974.
9. Marx and Engels, *On Ireland*, London: Lawrence and Wishart, 1971, p. 294.
10. Marx, 'Critique of the Gotha programme', in *The First International and After*, p. 323.
11. Vladimir Ilyich Lenin, 'The war and Russian social democracy', in *Collected Works*, Volume 21, Moscow: Progress Publishers, 1964.
12. K. Marx, 'The Erfurt Programme', in *Proletarian*, No 3, p. 19.
13. See C.E. Schorske, *German Social Democracy 1905–17: The Development of the Great Schism*, Cambridge, Massachusetts: Harvard University Press 1972.
14. Lenin, 'Opportunism and the collapse of the Second International' in *Collected Works*, Volume 22, Moscow: Progress Publishers, 1964, p. 111.
15. Eduard Bernstein, *Evolutionary Socialism: the Classical Statement of Democratic Socialism*, New York: Schocken, 1961. See also 'Bernstein and the Marxism of the Second

International' in Lucio Colletti, *From Rousseau to Lenin*, London: 1972; and Peter Gay, *The Crisis of Democratic Socialism*, New York: Columbia, 1952.

16. See Schorske, *German Social Democracy 1905–17*, Chapter 3.
17. Rosa Luxemburg, *Social Reform or Revolution*, London: Merlin Press, no date. For a critique of Luxemburg's flawed analysis of capitalist crisis, see Henryk Grossman, *The Law of Accumulation and Breakdown of the Capitalist System: being also a Theory of Crisis*, London: Pluto, 1991.
18. See Lenin, *Imperialism, the Highest Stage of Capitalism*, Moscow: Progress, 1986, first edn. 1916.
19. Lenin, 'The tasks of the proletariat in the present revolution', in *Selected Works*, Volume 2, revised edn., Moscow: Progress, 1977, pp. 31 and 32.
20. 'Theses on the national and colonial questions adopted by the second Comintern congress', 28 July 1920, in J. Degras, *The Communist International 1914–43*, Documents Vol 1, Oxford: Oxford University Press, 1956, p. 143.
21. Lenin, 'Report on the activities of the council of people's comissars', 11 January 1918, in *Collected Works*, Volume 26, Moscow: Progress, p. 472.
22. Lenin, *Collected Works*, Volume 31, p. 393.
23. 'Extracts from the resolution of the fourth Comintern congress on "five years of the the Russian Revolution"', 5 December 1922, in Degras, p. 144.
24. Cited in E.H. Carr, *The Bolshevik Revolution 1917–1923*, Volume 2, Penguin, 1974, p. 277.
25. Josef V. Stalin, 'The social democratic deviation in our party', report delivered at the fifteenth all union conference of the CPSU(B)', 1 November 1926, in *On the Opposition*, Peking: Foreign Language Press, 1974, p. 395.
26. Stalin, 'The results of the work of the fourteenth conference of the RCP(B)', 9 May 1925 in *On the Opposition*, p. 207.
27. Stalin, 'Results', *On the Opposition*, p. 215.
28. Lenin, 'Better fewer, but better', in *Collected Works*, Volume 33, p. 501.
29. Leon Trotsky, *The Stalinist School of Falsification*, New York: Pathfinder, 1971, p. 60.
30. Lenin, *Collected Works*, Volume 31, p. 472.
31. Stalin, 'Once more', in *On the Opposition*, p. 539.
32. Stalin, *War Speeches, Orders of the Day and Answers to Foreign Press Correspondents during the Great Patriotic War 3 July 1941 – 22 June 1945*, London: Hutchinson, 1946, p. 112.

33. Trotsky, *The Third International after Lenin*, New York: Pathfinder, 1970, p. 61.
34. Trotsky, *The Third International after Lenin*, p. 61.
35. Trotsky, *The Third International after Lenin*, p. 61.
36. Trotsky, 'On the history of the left opposition' in *Writings 1938–39*, New York: Pathfinder, 1974, pp. 263 and 265.
37. Trotsky, 'A fresh lesson – after the imperialist "peace" in Munich', in *Writings*, p. 71.

Suggested Reading

Chapter 1 The failure of perestroika

Abel Aganbegyan, *Moving the Mountain*, (London: Bantam Press, 1989).

Anders Aslund, *Gorbachev's Struggle for Economic Reform*, (London: Frances Pinter, 1989).

Jon Bloomfield ed., *The Soviet Revolution*, (London: Lawrence and Wishart, 1989).

Christopher Donnelly, *Gorbachev's Revolution*, (Jane's, 1989).

Frank Furedi, *The Soviet Union Demystified*, (London: Junius, 1986).

Marshall Goldman, *Gorbachev's Challenge*, (London and New York: W.W. Norton, 1987).

R.J. Hall and J.A. Dallenbrandt, *Gorbachev and Perestroika*, (Edward Elgar, 1989).

Joyce, Ticktin and White, eds., *Gorbachev and Gorbachevism* (Cass, 1990).

Tatyana Zaslavskaya, *The Second Socialist Revolution: An Alternative Soviet Strategy*, (London: I.B. Taurus, 1990).

Chapter 2 The stirrings of the Soviet working class

Bob Arnot, *Controlling Soviet Labour: Experimental Change from Gorbachev to Brezhnev*, (London: Macmillan Press, 1988).

Donald Filtzer, *Soviet Workers and Stalinist Industrialisation*, (London: Pluto Press, 1986).

David Lane, ed., *Labour and Employment in the USSR*, (Surrey: Wheatsheaf Books, 1986).

David Lane, *Soviet Labour and the Ethics of Communism: Full Employment and the Labour Process in the Soviet Union*, (Surrey: Wheatsheaf Books, 1986).

Michal Reiman, *The Birth of Stalinism: the USSR on the eve of the 'Second Revolution'*, (London: I.B. Taurus, 1987).

Blair A. Ruble, *Soviet Trade Unions: Their Development in the 1970s*, (Cambridge: Cambridge University Press, 1981).

Elizabeth Teague, *Solidarity and the Soviet Worker*, (London: Croom Helm, 1988).

Chapter 3 The upsurge in the national republics

J. Armstrong, *Ukrainian Nationalism*, (Colorado: Ukrainian Academic Press, 1980).

E. Bacon, *Central Asians under Russian Rule*, (New York: Cornell University Press, 1966).

Y. Bilinsky, *The Second Soviet Republic: the Ukraine after World War II*, (New Jersey: Rutgers University Press, 1964).

T. Dragadze, *Rural Families in Soviet Georgia*, (London: Routledge, 1988).

F. Kazemzadeh, *The Struggle for Soviet Transcaucasia*, (Oxford: George Ronald, 1951).

I.S. Koropechyj, *Location Problems in Soviet Industry before World War II: the case of the Ukraine*, (Chapel Hill: University of North Carolina Press, 1971).

F.J. Misunias and R. Taagepera, *The Baltic States – Years of Dependence 1940–1980*, (London: C. Hurst and Co., 1983).

A. Nassibian, *Britain and the Armenian Question 1915–1923*, (London: Croom Helm, 1984).

R.G. Suny, *The Making of the Georgian Nation*, (Indiana: Indiana University Press, 1984).

A. Taheri, *Crescent in a Red Sky: the Future of Islam in the Soviet Union*, (London: Hutchinson, 1989).

Chapter 4 Eastern Europe in ferment

Fernando Claudin, *The Communist Movement, from Comintern to Cominform*, (Harmondsworth: Penguin Books, 1975).

Karen Dawisha, *The Great Challenge: Eastern Europe, Gorbachev and Reform*, (Cambridge: Cambridge University Press, 1988).

Francois Fejto, *A History of the People's Democracies*, (Harmondsworth: Penguin Books, 1974).

Mike Freeman, ed., *Confrontation 5*, (London: Junius, 1989).

Frank Furedi, *The Soviet Union Demystified*, (London: Junius, 1986).

Gabriel Kolko, *The Politics of War, The World and United States Foreign Policy 1943–1945*, (New York: Vintage, 1970).

Olga Narkiewicz, *Eastern Europe 1968–1984*, (London: Croom Helm, 1984).

Chapter 5 China: the road to Tiananmen Square

J.P. Burns and S. Rosen, eds., *Policy conflicts in post-Mao China: a documentary survey with analysis*, (London: M.E. Sharpe, 1986).

M. Chossudovsky, *Towards capitalist restoration? Chinese socialism after Mao*, (London: Macmillan Educational, 1986).

S. Feuch Fwang, A. Hussain, T. Pairault, eds., *Transforming China's economy in the eighties, Volume 1: The rural sector, welfare and employment: Volume 2: Management, industry and the urban sector*, (London: Zed, 1988).

D. Goodman and G. Segal, eds., *China at forty: mid-life crisis*, (Oxford: Clarendon Press, 1989).

D.M. Lampton, *Policy implementation in Post-Mao China*, (Berkeley: University of California Press, 1987).

F. Leeming, *Rural China Today*, (London: Longman, 1985).

V. Nee and D. Stark, eds., *Remaking the economic institutions of socialism: China and Eastern Europe*, (California: Stanford University Press, 1989).

E.J. Perry and C. Wong, eds., *Political economy of reform in Post-Mao China*, (Cambridge, Massachusetts: Council on East Asian Studies, Harvard, 1985).

C.R. Riskin, *China's political economy: the quest for development since 1949*, (Oxford: Oxford University Press, 1987).

M. Selden, *The political economy of Chinese socialism*, (London: M.E. Sharpe, 1988).

Chapter 6 Revolutions betrayed: the Soviet Union in the third world

G.W. Breslauer, *Soviet Strategy in the Middle East*, (Boston: Unwin Hyman, 1990).

K.M. Campbell and S. Neil MacFarlane, eds., *Gorbachev's Third World Dilemmas*, (London: Routledge, 1989).

P.J.S. Duncan, *The Soviet Union and India*, (London: Routledge/RIIA, 1989).

E.J. Feuchtwanger and P. Nailor, eds., *The Soviet Union and the Third World*, (London: Macmillan, 1981).

F. Fukuyama, *Moscow's post-Brezhnev reassessment of the Third World*, (Santa Monica: Rand, 1986).

M. Gorbachev, *Perestroika*, updated edn., (London: Fontana, 1988).

E. Karsh, *The Soviet Union and Syria*, (London: Routledge/RIIA, 1988).

A. Korbonski and F. Fukuyama eds., *The Soviet Union and the Third World*, (New York: Cornell University Press, 1987).

V. Kubalkova and A. Cruikshank, *Marxism and International Relations*, paperback edn., (Oxford: Oxford University Press, 1989).

A.Z. Rubinstein, *Moscow's Third World Strategy*, (Princeton: Princeton University Press, 1988).

J. Steele, *The Limits of Soviet Power*, revised edn., (Harmondsworth: Penguin, 1985).

Chapter 7 Farewell to Eurocommunism

M. Adereth, *The French Communist Party: a critical history 1920–1984*, (Manchester: Manchester University Press, 1984).

Grant Amyot, *The Italian Communist Party: the crisis of the popular front strategy*, (New York: St Martin's Press, 1981).

Paolo Filo della Torre, Edward Mortimer and Jonathan Storey, eds., *Eurocommunism: myth or reality?*, (London: Pelican, 1979).

Stephen Hellman, *Italian communism in transition: the rise and fall of the historic compromise in Turin 1975–1980*, (Oxford: Oxford University Press, 1988).

Arthur Hirsch, *The French left: a history and overview*, (Montreal: Blackrose Books, 1982).

R.W. Johnson, *The long march of the French left*, (London: Macmillan, 1981).

P. Lange, G. Ross and M. Vannicelli, eds., *Unions, change and crisis: French and Italian union strategy and political economy: 1945–1980*, pub. 1982.

Howard Machin, ed., *National communism in Western Europe: a third way for socialism?*, (London and New York: Methuen, 1983).

Eusebio Mujal-Leon, *Communism and political change in Spain*, (Bloomington: Indiana University Press, 1983).

——, 'The decline and fall of Spanish communism', *Problems of Communism*, March/April 1986.

George Ross, *Workers and communists in France: from Popular Front to Eurocommunism*, (Berkeley: University of California Press, 1982).

James Ruscoe, *The Italian Communist Party 1976–1981: on the threshold of government*, (London and Basingstoke: Macmillan, 1982).

Martin A. Schain, *French communism and local power: urban politics and political change*, (London: Frances Pinter, 1985).

Chapter 8 Marxism before and after Stalinism

E.H. Carr, *The Bolshevik Revolution 1917–23*, (Harmondsworth: Penguin, 1974).

Lucio Colletti, 'Bernstein and the Marxism of the Second International' in *From Rousseau to Lenin*, (London: New Left Books 1972).

J. Degras, *The Communist International 1914–43*, (Oxford: Oxford University Press, 1956).

Peter Gay, *The Crisis of Democratic Socialism*, (New York: Columbia University Press, 1952).

Rosa Luxemburg, *Social Reform or Revolution* (New York: Pathfinder, no date).

C.E. Schorske, *German Social Democracy 1905–17: The Development of the Great Schism*, (Cambridge, Massachusetts: Harvard University Press, 1972).

Leon Trotsky, 'Stalinism and Bolshevism', in *Living Marxism*, April 1990.

——, *The Third International after Lenin*, (New York: Pathfinder, 1970).

——, *Writings 1938–39*, (New York: Pathfinder, 1974).

Index

Abalkin, L., 9, 38, 43
Abkhazia, 64, 67
Afghanistan, 127, 130, 133, 147, 153, 155
Africa, 127, 128, 131, 132, 135–7, 139, 140, 144, 177
Aganbegyan, A., 13, 42
Algeria, 137
Althusser, L., 161
Amendola, G., 161
ANC (African National Congress), 135, 136, 140
Andropov, Y., 31, 32, 130
Angola, 130, 131, 135
Anti-Semitism, 45, 47, 60, 80, 82
Arabs, 132–5
Argentina, 136
Armenia, 53, 54, 64, 65, 67, 68
Assad, H., 134
Asia, 103, 112, 128, 131, 137
Asoyan, B., 135
Azerbaijan, 53, 54, 64–8

Bakhradze, A., 66
Baku, 53, 66, 67
Balkanisation, 54, 69
Baltics, 46, 53–61, 64, 65, 69, 70
Barre plan, 149
Beijing, 5, 93, 104, 109, 111
Berlin Wall, 71, 73, 74, 86
Berlinguer, E., 149, 152, 158, 159
Bernstein, E., 176, 178, 184
Bhutto, A., 139
Bhutto, B., 139
Bohemia, 77
Boldyrev, Y., 43
Botha, Pik, 136
Bovin, A., 126
Brazil, 36, 136
Brest-Litovsk, 183
Brezhnev, L., 1, 14, 32, 37, 66, 76, 125, 126, 130–2, 142

Brezhnev doctrine, 77, 85, 91
Britain, 2, 15, 68, 70, 74, 111, 126, 133, 152, 174, 175, 177, 184
  CPGB (Communist Party of Great Britain), 145, 146, 160
Budapest, 75, 83, 84
Bulgaria, 71, 73, 75, 76, 80–2, 86
Bush, G., 88, 110, 111
Byelorussia, 54

Cambodia, 131, 139, 189
Caribbean, 137
Carrillo, S., 147, 148, 160
Castro, F., 139, 171
Catholic Church, 63, 70, 71, 150, 151, 158
Ceausescu, N., 71, 76, 161
Central Asian Republics, 39, 40, 64, 68
CFDT (Confédération Française Démocratique du Travail), 152
CGIL (Confederazione Generale Italiana di Lavoratori), 152, 162
CGT (Confédération Générale du Travail), 149, 152, 157, 158, 162
Chernobyl, 42
Chernyak, V., 62
China, 3, 5, 7, 18, 27, 93–100, 102–5, 108–17, 129, 139, 189
  CCP (Chinese Communist Party), 94, 95, 97–9, 101, 103, 106, 107, 109, 114–6
Chirac, J., 157
Churchill, W., 55, 78
CIA (Central Intelligence Agency), 127
CISL (Confederazione Italiana di Sindicati Liberi), 152
Comecon, 73, 76, 86
Cominform, 79, 82

Comintern, 2, 79, 179–81, 183–9
Cossutta, A., 158, 161
Craxi, B., 152, 159, 160
Crocker, C., 135
Cuba, 3, 135, 139
Cyprus, 160
Czechoslovakia, 7, 71, 73, 75–7, 81–6, 91, 133, 147

Dalian, 103
De Beauvoir, S., 155
Dementev, V., 15
Deng Xiaoping, 98, 104, 108, 110, 111, 113, 114
Dobrynin, A., 142
Doi moi, 139
Donbas, 62, 63
Donetsk, 43, 44
Dubcek, A., 76, 84

East Germany, 7, 71, 73, 75, 76, 83, 86
Efimov, V., 68
Egypt, 133, 134
Ellenstein, J., 161
El Salvador, 140
Engels, F., 121, 171–5, 179, 181–3
Erfurt programme, 176, 177, 185
Estonia, 5, 46, 53, 55–9
    Estonisation, 58
Ethiopia, 130, 132

Famine, 17, 21, 60, 96, 102, 132, 138
Finland, 5, 85, 86, 160
    Finlandisation, 85
Fiszbin, H., 161
FMLN (Farabundo Marti Liberation Front), 140
FAO (Food and Agricultural Organisation), 103
France, 68, 133, 174, 186
    PCF (French Communist Party), 146–50, 152, 154–64, 185, 188
    PS (French Socialist Party), 147–50, 152, 157
Franco, F., 147
Fujian, 103
Fukuyama, F., 130

Gallego, I., 160
Gandhi, R., 126
GATT (General Agreements on Tariffs and Trade), 103
Georgia, 27, 54, 64–7
Gerasimov, G., 85

Germany (West), 5, 68, 102, 155, 174, 175, 183
    Berlin Wall, 71, 73, 74, 86
    East Germany, 7, 71, 73, 75, 76, 83, 86
    German Communist Party, 185, 187
    Nazis, 3, 55, 60, 79–81
    reunification, 6, 88, 190
    SPD (German Socialist Party), 160, 176–8, 186
Glasnost, 23, 24, 36, 42, 43, 61, 67, 86, 87, 125, 155
Goldman, M., 10
Gonzalez, F., 148
Gonzalez, J.A., 161
Gorbachev, M., 4–6, 9–11, 15, 16, 18–21, 23–6, 30, 31, 35–7, 39, 45, 47, 54, 69, 86, 89, 91, 190
    and Eastern Europe, 77, 85, 87, 88, 91
    and foreign policy, 73, 76, 86, 89, 91, 125–30, 134, 136–9
    and the national republics, 53, 55, 57, 59–63, 67, 68
    and the working class, 29, 32–4, 42
Gorz, A., 155
Gotha programme, 176
Greece, 146, 147, 160, 161
Greens, 75, 155, 156, 158, 159
Gromyko, A., 142
Grosz, K., 91
Guangdong, 103, 104, 108, 109, 112, 113
Guinea Bissau, 138
Guomindang, 111

Hainan, 103, 104, 107
Harare, 136
Havel, V., 71
Hebei, 113
Hellman, S., 151, 159, 162, 163, 165
Hitler, A., 3, 55
    Hitler-Stalin pact, 59
Hobsbawm, E., 145, 165
Holland, 146
Honecker, E., 73, 76
Hong Kong, 102–4, 110–13
Hu Yaobang, 109, 114
Hungary, 7, 71, 73–5, 77, 78, 80–3, 86, 91
    HSWP (Hungarian Socialist Workers Party), 74, 92
Hurd, D., 111

Iglesias, G., 161
IMF (International Monetary Fund),
    103, 129
India, 126, 128, 136
Ingrao, P., 161
Interfront movement, 46, 58
Iran, 65, 131, 133, 134
    Iran/Iraq war, 134
    Shah of Iran, 131
Iraq, 133, 134
Ireland, 175
Israel, 133, 134, 140, 143
Italy, 154, 186
    DC (Italian Christian Democrats),
        148, 159, 160
    PCI (Italian Communist Party),
        145, 146, 148–53, 158–63, 165,
        166, 188
    PSI (Italian Socialist Party), 152,
        153, 159, 160
Ivashko, V., 62

Jacques, M., 145, 146
Jakes, M., 76
Jamaica, 139
Japan, 68, 78, 102, 103, 109, 112,
    113, 122, 123
Jaruzelski, W., 72, 75, 90
Jensen, J., 164
Jews, 47, 134
Jiang Zemin, 115
Jiangsu, 109, 113
Jones, G.S. 171, 189, 190
Juquin, P., 156, 161

Kautsky, K., 178
Kazakhstan, 35, 36, 40, 43
Kennan, G., 78
Kenya, 137
KGB (Komitet Gosudarstvennoy
    Bezopasnosti), 127
Khrushchev, N., 1, 10, 14, 15, 17, 23,
    77, 83, 84, 128
Kiev, 44, 60–3
Kinnock, N., 163
Klerk, F.W., 136
Kolosovsky, A., 127, 128
Korea, 155
    Korean war, 94
    North, 113, 139
    South, 102, 112, 113, 137
Korniyenko, G., 142
Kostov, T., 82
Kozyrev, A., 129

Kravchuk, L., 62
Kryuchkov, V., 127
Kurasvilli, B., 33
Kuwait, 133, 134

Lajoinie, A., 156
Lama, L., 149, 152
Laos, 131
Latvia, 46, 53, 55, 56, 58
Latin America, 136, 137
Lebanon, 134, 137
Left, 2, 6, 7, 26, 146, 147, 149, 152,
    153, 156, 157, 159–61, 163,
    165, 178, 187, 190
Leipzig, 88
Lenin, V.I., 1, 55, 79, 126, 128, 139,
    171, 175, 176, 178–80, 182–4,
    190
    Leninism, 55, 145, 171, 190
Li Peng, 106, 108
Liu Guogang, 119
Libya, 134
Liebknecht, K., 186
Ligachev, Y., 22, 41
Lister, E., 160
Lithuania, 53, 55, 56, 58–60
Luxemburg, R., 178, 186, 192
Lvov, 63

Macao, 103, 104
Malaya, 136, 137
Mandel, E., 10, 26, 27, 49
Mandela, N., 136, 140
Manley, M., 139
Mao Zedong, 93–8, 101, 107, 110,
    113–16, 171
    Maoism, 95, 100, 105, 107, 114,
        116
Marchais, G., 148, 156–8, 161
Marx, K., 121, 171–6, 178, 179, 181–
    3, 190
Marxism, 2, 6, 7, 116, 145, 171, 175,
    181, 182, 186, 189, 190
    Marxism-Leninism, 1, 147
    Marxists, 7, 11, 12, 125–7, 166,
        171, 172, 175, 176, 182, 190
Mazowiecki, T., 72, 74, 90
Mexico, 36, 136
Michnik, A., 63
Mill, J.S. 10
Mitterrand, F., 148, 149, 155, 157,
    158
Moldavia, 19, 46
Moncloa pact, 149

Moro, A., 148
Morocco, 156
Mozambique, 131, 135
Muslim fundamentalism, 68

Nagorno-Karabakh, 53, 67, 68
Namibia, 135, 139, 140
Napolitano, G., 160, 161, 165
Nasser, G.A., 133
Nato (North Atlantic Treaty
    Organisation), 82, 88
Natta, A., 159
NEP (New Economic Policy), 181
    nepmen, 35
Nicaragua, 6, 130, 131
Nics (newly industrialised countries),
    137, 138
Nietzsche, F., 171
Nixon, R.M., 110
Nkomati accord, 135
Noske, G., 178

Occhetto, A., 145, 159, 161, 165
Oman, 134
Ossetians, 64

Pacific, 78, 111, 137
Pakistan, 133, 139
Palestinians, 133, 134
    PLO (Palestine Liberation
        Organisation), 140
Pan-Slavism, 54, 64
Perestroika, 4, 9, 13, 15, 23, 24, 26,
    29–31, 33, 37–9, 42, 43, 46, 47,
    54, 57, 61, 62, 64, 76, 86, 125,
    127, 139, 155, 189
Philippines, 137
Piadyshev, B., 131
Poland, 7, 32, 60, 72, 74, 75, 80, 81,
    83, 86, 90, 153
    CWPP (Communist Workers Party
        of Poland), 79
Solidarity, 49, 63, 71, 72, 74, 75, 77,
    85, 155, 158
Ponomarev, B., 142
Pope John Paul II, 63
Portugal, 103, 131, 147, 160, 162
Potsdam conference, 78
Pozsgay, I., 73, 75
Primakov, Y., 126–8

Rajk, L., 82
Reagan, R., 153
Renovateurs, 156, 161

Riskin, C., 100
Romania, 71, 73, 75–7, 80, 81, 85, 86,
    161
Rome, 63, 64, 126, 129, 149, 152
Roosevelt, F.D., 78
Ross, G., 164
Rubotti, P., 158
Ruch, 62, 63
Russia, 2, 9, 46, 64, 65, 69, 70, 184,
Ryzhkov, N., 19, 21

Sadat, A., 133
Sajudis, 60
Sandinistas, 131
São Paulo, 36
Saudi Arabia, 133
Scandinavia, 5, 25, 56
Schain, M. 150
SEZ (Special Economic Zone), 103,
    104, 108, 112, 113, 121
Shah of Iran, 131
Shandong, 113
Shanghai, 102, 104, 116
Shangkun, 114
Shantou, 103
Shanxi, 101
Shatalin, S., 38
Shcherbitsky, V., 61, 62
Shenzen, 103, 108, 112
Shevardnadze, E., 65, 132, 135
Shmelyev, N., 13
Siberia, 10, 29, 30, 36, 40, 43, 45, 46,
    62, 137, 193
Silesia, 77
'Sinatra' doctrine, 85
Singapore, 103, 110, 112, 136
Slansky, R., 82
Sling, O., 82
Slovo, J., 136
Smith, A., 15
    Adam Smith Institute, 74, 90
Solidarity, 49, 63, 71, 72, 74, 75, 77,
    85, 155, 158
Somoza, A., 131
South Africa, 6, 131, 132, 135, 136,
    139
    ANC, 135, 136, 140
    SACP (South African Communist
        Party), 135, 136
Spain, 146–9, 160–2, 186
    PCE (Spanish Communists), 148,
        160
    PSOE (Spanish Socialists), 148
Sri Lanka, 136